VINEYARD
CONFIDENTIAL

VINEYARD
CONFIDENTIAL

350 Years of
Scandals, Eccentrics,
and
Strange Occurrences

HOLLY NADLER

DOWN EAST BOOKS

ISBN: 0-89272-687-3 13-digit: 978-0-89272-687-5
LCCN: 2006928627

Cover art by Jim Sollers
Book design by Janet L. Patterson
Printed at Versa Press, E. Peoria, Ill.

2   4   5   3   1

Down East Books
A division of Down East Enterprise, Inc.
Publisher of *Down East,* the Magazine of Maine

Book orders: 1-800-685-7962
www.downeastbooks.com

To Trina Mascott,
Mom, best buddy,
favorite source of inspiration

Martha's Vineyard

I own an island in the sea

I do not own it actually

I claim it only by right of need

Defying those who hold the deed

Perhaps a truer phrase would be

There is an island which owns me.

—Louise Aldridge Bugbee

Contents

How I Came To Be a Tell-All Living on Martha's Vineyard

Two CONDITIONS COMMINGLED to get this book written: I live on an absolutely nutty island full of wacky people, past and present, and I have a big mouth. Heaven only knows what makes some of us discreet, zipped-up individuals like Greta Garbo and Supreme Court Justice John Roberts, and what makes others of us like Joan Rivers and Rona Barrett, crazed to regale all and sundry with a good story. Clearly, I'm on the Rivers/Barrett side of the spectrum.

I'm not proud of the fact that when I hear of a scandal most dire or a juicy piece of gossip or a tale of human folly, you'd have to tackle me and seal my mouth with duct tape to keep me from blabbing. These days I can somewhat be trusted with a secret, for the sake of avoiding friends' and family's wrath, but I need to be warned on no uncertain terms that to talk is to die.

Frankly, I believe most writers possess this loose-lips gene, which comes with a three-part operating system: The first is a libido for the goods, the story. We hear it at someone's dinner table and thirty-seven years later we remember it down to what Party A was wearing and what Party B was smoking. The second is the overwhelming urge to pass the tasty treat along, either verbally or on paper or both. The third is the need to run away to Rio for fear someone will slap us silly for disclosing what should have been locked in a bombproof vault.

But why else would we bestir ourselves to write, if not for the sheer bliss of passing along some splendid piece of information?

So from the time I moved to Martha's Vineyard, I've had an accordion file in my head that over the years has bristled with oddball anecdotes, unmentionable footnotes of history, crackpots I've known and loved, celebrities' quirks, data unbelievable, and "say what?" tales. It's time to spill the beans.

There's a reason this island has become scarily famous. Oh, part of it is the scenic beauty. But there are heaps of scenically beautiful places around the world. None of them, however, have preppie senators driving mini-skirted interns off bridges or princesses and presidents rocketing down in August or movie sharks yanking naked girls down into midnight waters or young political scions plunging single-engine planes into the wine-dark sea only miles from their glamorous, reclusive mothers' 375-acre estates.

So how did the Vineyard get to be America's favorite resort soap opera?

It beats me. Maybe in a similar fashion to the way boats and planes disappear in the Bermuda Triangle, folks in our environs are cosmically scheduled for an extra injection of drama in their lives—or, if not drama, then tragicomedy, or outright comedy, or outright tragedy.

I've been coming here since the spring of 1976. Up until then I had spent most of my years in Los Angeles. Okay, cards on the table—I'm a Valley Girl, and that in and of itself may explain my love of good dish. In any event, my future ex-husband, Marty, and I bought a summer home here in 1981, had our son, Charlie, on the island in '84, and moved here year-round in '91, just after Hurricane Bob cleared the brush out from the wetlands surrounding our little beach cottage.

Meanwhile, not a single colorful story has escaped my all-too-curious gaze. I know where the bodies are buried—metaphorically and even physically. And while, after this book is published and circulated, no one will ever confide in me again, it nonetheless gives me great pleasure to share with readers glimpses into the Vineyard as I've come to know and love it— wild, iconoclastic, unpredictable, and for all its insanity, everlastingly lovable.

Not all history writing needs to be as irreverent as my romp through the highlights and lowlifes of the Vineyard. A serious historian might consider statistics about, say, cod fishing or tax collection in the 1800s every bit as wild and wooly and fun fun fun as I do murder,

mayhem, and high frivolity. To that end, you'll find at the back of this book a fairly extensive bibliography, not so much to prove that I've done my research—although I have—but to demonstrate how much information has been published over the years about our little island.

My own culling of true-life stories, then and now, involved the same process as picking only the red M&Ms from a five-pound bag. That's not to say that all the other flavors and colors can't also be enjoyed. So I do urge one and all to read further, but be forewarned: any and all applied studies of Martha's Vineyard, like chocolate, are addictive.

Divas, Inc.

From Long-Ago Temptresses to Princess Di: Nine Drama Queens—
Including Two Midgets—Who Left Their Stamp on the Island

The Woman in Red

N O ONE COULD BELIEVE that any chit of a girl could be so brazen. In the summer of 1890, she strolled the public beach of Cottage City (now Oak Bluffs) clad in outrageously little for the time—a baggy, knee-hugging red woolen bathing gown fortified by thick red woolen stockings. Too shocking! The green-eyed, porcelain-skinned, Botticelli-style beauty's vivid red hair fell in a sensuous tumble to her waist.

Who was she, this Venus on a half-shell assuming a living, breathing form? No one knew anything about her, but her sudden appearance on these shores caused a stir from the gilded lounges of the Sea View Hotel to the honky-tonkiest of billiard parlors on Circuit Avenue. Every noontime as bathers backstroked to rhythms of the Foxboro Brass Band tootling from the pavilion, young men in straw boaters lined the bluffs waiting for a glimpse of their unknown goddess. Her devotees trailed behind her, a Pied Piper brigade on a libidinous mission.

This woman of such mystery and allure was actually an unassuming young miss named Nellie Sands, daughter of a New York pharmacist who housed his family above his Madison Avenue storefront. But, lusterless origins aside, Nellie's looks and choice of swimsuit attire thrust her into circumstances of ever-increasing notoriety.

By the end of August, Nellie was discovered by the island's premier bachelor, one Captain Joseph de la Mar (no this is not a Harlequin romance; that was the man's actual name). A prospector who hit the proverbial mother lode of gold ore in Idaho, Captain de la Mar returned to the island where once he'd been known as a down-at-the-heels marine wrecker. Although Joseph de la Mar and Nellie Sands may have honestly fallen in love, we can safely assume that he beheld her beauty, and she took full stock of his fifteen million dollars, and they thought of one mind, "It's a match!"

After Nellie and Joseph married, they bought a mansion in Newport with hopes of finding favor with the Astors and Vanderbilts who disported there. But the local elite shunned the newly rich upstarts. After all, this same elite had become newly rich only a generation or two before; why stir up inconvenient memories? Nellie lacked the requisite cleverness and Joseph was raw from too many years on ships and in mining camps to be acceptable in Newport society. Much was made of the fact that he picked his teeth with a pocket-knife—*quel horreur*! And he seemed to make no distinction between the off-color jokes appropriate in the barbershop, and those suitable for the drawing rooms of high society. Try as they might, the de la Mars flopped in Rhode Island.

Europe proved to be a different matter. In their grand apartment overlooking the Bois de Boulogne, the American pair attracted the entire Proustian crowd of aristocrats and literati, who delighted in Nellie and Joseph's fresh and unpretentious ways. (This scenario was borrowed in an old movie starring Debbie Reynolds and Harve Parnell: *The Unsinkable Molly Brown.*) Fashionable portrait painters vied to immortalize the unsinkable Nellie on canvas, and by the end of the century, whenever newspapers published features on the most beautiful women of the age, the list ran as follows: The Czarina of Russia, Vera Boardman, Princess Pless, and Nellie Sands de la Mar—

sun-kissed and nourished by the soft sea breezes of Cottage City.

Only one fly stuck in the Sands/de la Mar marital ointment: For all of Nellie's charms, her husband still harbored undying love for another stellar Vineyard damsel, Miss Lillian Norton, a.k.a. the great opera soprano/coloratura Madame Nordica.

The Lily of the North

LILLIAN NORTON'S ANCESTORS left Martha's Vineyard in the early 1800s to settle in Farmington, Maine. The future songbird, youngest of six, was born in her family's picturesque cottage on December 12, 1857. Showmanship ran through her gene pool in the person of her grandfather, John Allen, the most famous Maine revivalist of that time who spewed such fiery rhetoric as, "Come down out of that [skepticism], you ill-begotten, slab-sided, God-forsaken stackpole of Hell! Come down and give your soul to God!" (This and other quotations by way of Ira Glackens's biography *Yankee Diva: Lillian Norton and the Golden Days of Opera,* 1963.)

When Lillian was in her teens, her mother divorced Lillian's father and relocated her brood to the Vineyard. Lillian attended school in West Tisbury. Her summers were given over to local delights—clambakes, hay rides, barn dances. The diva-to-be worked part-time sorting mail in Vineyard Haven. Two themes revolved around Lillian's young life: her musical talent and the family's relative poverty. From the age of six the girl could sing. In her teens she thrilled local audiences with solos at the Union Chapel. But even the most naturally exquisite voice needs training if the bearer of that voice wishes to sing professionally. Without instruction, Lillian Norton was destined to croon for local functions, marry, have children, and in

her middle years take up directorship of the church choir.

Enter Captain Joseph de la Mar to transform the young songster's destiny.

In 1871, the nineteen-year-old Lillian met the dashing marine wrecker, fourteen years her senior. They walked the beaches and enjoyed buggy rides down country lanes as Joseph impressed Lillian with tales of derring-do on the high seas. For her part she confided her deep yearnings to study at the Boston Conservatory of Music. The young captain fell madly in love with the talented and earnest young country lass with her soulful, pale face, mass of black hair, and enormous, glittering dark eyes. Did Lillian love Joseph? More than likely she was flattered by his attentions and piqued by the unfamiliar titillations of puppy love, but above all, was loyal to her gift and to the sense of destiny that gift instilled in her.

One day at the end of summer, Captain de la Mar showed up at the Norton home and made an amazing request of Lillian's mother. He offered to become the girl's benefactor; he would pay for her studies at the Boston Conservatory. Mrs. Norton was scandalized; it was possible she knew nothing of the attentions this rough-and-tumble seaman had paid to her daughter. The same ruffian qualities in Joseph that in future years would dismay the crème-de-la-crème of Newport dampened the staid Mrs. Norton as well. For all the family's lack of money, they were descended from one of the

Vineyard's premier families and, before that, the best of English Anglo Saxon stock. This Dutchman with callused hands, clumsy grammar, and questionable livelihood held no appeal for Lillian's mother.

She responded with an equally outrageous proposal. The Nortons would accept de la Mar's money for Lillian's musical training if he in turn promised to stay away from the girl for an indefinite period of time. The besotted young man eagerly agreed, and went off to amass the necessary fortune.

Joseph acquired a wrecking lighter named *The Screamer*, hired a crew, and sailed to Bermuda to remove marble from a sunken barque. The marble was recovered and sold for a good price. In the rashness of young love, Joseph stiffed his crew of their pay, leaving a slew of lawsuits in his wake. He returned to the island to lay the entire proceeds of the Bermuda expedition at the feet of Lillian's mother. The stricture against visiting her daughter was still in force, however, and Lillian left for Boston to pursue her musical education. Joseph decided he needed still more money to win over the supercilious Norton matriarch, so he traveled out west in search of a gold mine to call his very own.

Joseph and Lillian would not meet again for twenty years.

After Lillian's years at the Boston Conservatory, acclaim from her teachers won her an invitation from a renowned opera instructor, San Giovanni of Milan, to continue her studies under his mentorship. As Lillian's singing flourished, the enraptured teacher dubbed his sublimely gifted student La Giglia Nordica, Lily of the North. In April 1879, La Giglia debuted in *La Traviata* at Brescia, Italy. She received nine curtain calls. Cadres of fans followed her back to her hotel, where their cries of devotion summoned her out to her balcony, an homage offered to only the rarest of opera stars. Overnight the lovely young Vineyard girl became a diva nonpareil.

During the next three decades, Lillian Norton, a.k.a. La Giglia Nordica, a.k.a. Madame Nordica, toured continuously at the most glittery pinnacles of the opera circuit. Of her many accomplishments, she was the first singer to be heard in the new Trocadero in Paris. She was the first American woman to sing at the Bayreuth Festival at which the great composer Wagner declared her the most accomplished female vocalist ever to sing his scores. La Nordica made repeated appearances at St. Petersburg, the Paris Grand Opera, the Paris Academy of Music, Symphony Hall in London, and at the Met in New York. At the opening of the Boston Opera

From Farm Girl to Goddess

Lillian Norton, of Tisbury, became the full-throated Madame Nordica, international opera star. However, her musical training was underwritten by a somewhat shady source.

MARTHA'S VINEYARD HISTORICAL SOCIETY COLLECTIONS (env. 756)

House she starred in *La Gioconda*. Before the royal family at Windsor Castle she sang two acts of *Lohengrin* after which Queen Victoria presented her with a diamond brooch. Music critics extolled the singer's "liquid purity," "exceptional range," and "magnificent power."

In the early 1890s Lillian paid a rare visit to Martha's Vineyard. And so, coincidentally—or maybe not so coincidentally—did Captain Joseph de la Mar.

The former marine scavenger by this time had stumbled across his mother lode of gold in Idaho (interestingly, he extracted the precious metal with the same hooks and pulleys and assorted gear he'd used in the marine salvaging business). He now possessed money enough to satisfy the financial requirements of any New England WASP. But whereas Lillian's vast travels had exposed her to the very best of European culture, polishing her speech, comportment, and personality to a fine finish, Joseph's adventures had kept him in the rough camps of the mining trade. Nothing had been done to improve his manners; he continued to pick his teeth with a pocketknife.

It was clear to everyone that Lillian bore a great affection for the old boyfriend who'd endowed her youth with romance, and whose insane generosity had made her career possible. But now he was even less suitable as husband material than he'd been in the idyll of their long-ago summer. Moreover, Lillian's entourage included a handsome, cultivated actor named Zoltan Dome, many years her junior, also in hot pursuit of her. Throwing her lot to the more cultivated of her two suitors, she sailed away from the island under cover of darkness. Joseph took after the fleeing diva in his own sumptuous yacht, but once he caught up with her she spurned him one last time.

Brokenhearted, Joseph returned to the Vineyard to meet the gorgeous Woman in Red. If the one he wanted was out of reach, he would settle for the most beautiful woman in America.

Those closest to Lillian later reflected that after this final rebuff of Joseph de la Mar, life began to fall apart for her—it was as if Fate had decreed that she marry her first love. Immediately after Lillian's escape from the island—and from Joseph—her jewels were stolen. She married the effete Zoltan to have him gamble away her savings on misguided Wall Street investments. Her years of stretching her voice up and down the octaves of the soprano and coloratura ranges began to wreak havoc on her vocal chords. Consequently, her performances were far less bravura than they'd once been.

At last, in the spring of 1914, she booked herself on a tour of the South Pacific for what was called in one of her obituaries "a last sad pilgrimage of song." In Batavia, Java, she caught cold which turned rapidly to pneumonia. As she lay dying in her hotel room, she murmured a wish to her few hangers-on to hear music. A violinist was hired to play in her room.

Her last words were a whisper of deepest pleasure: "Isn't it beautiful?"

And what became of the marriage of Joseph de la Mar and Nellie Sands, this union born of heartbreak for the one and social climbing for the other? Not surprisingly, the couple divorced after five years. The liaison had yielded one daughter, Alice de la Mar, who died in 1983, cited in her own obituary as the heir of "The Idaho Monte Cristo." During Nellie and Joseph's divorce proceedings, one of Mrs. Sands de la Mar's points of contention was her husband's "expensive gifts [more than fifty thousand dollars] made to Madame Nordica."

Little Big Women

At Nab's Corner in Chilmark, in the early 1860s, into a family with four normal-sized children, two exquisite midgets were born—Lucy Palmer Adams in 1861 and Sarah Butler Adams in 1863. Their father was a sea captain, Moses Adams, and their mother, Susan, was his second wife. Lucy and Sarah were normal-sized babies at birth but they grew so imperceptibly as to be recognized as midgets almost from the start. Later in life Lucy griped that the most commonly asked question of her and her sister was "Were you always small?" Did these people think she and Sarah had been downsized by aboriginal headshrinkers? Lucy would answer with a slight sneer, "Oh no, indeed, we used to be large." (Quotes gathered from the August 1979 issue of the *Duke's County Intelligencer*, the Martha's Vineyard Historical Society's quarterly journal.)

They enjoyed an idyllic childhood on their family homestead built by ancestor Edliashib (not a name likely to make a comeback) Adams in 1728. At the one-room Chilmark School, the little girls were passed around as precious playthings, all the other girls vying to carry and cuddle them for games of Mommy and Baby. Their dad fashioned shoes for his wee daughters—at the age of four, Sarah's feet were only two inches long.

A key factor in their upbringing was the strict Methodism that had most of the Vineyard in its thrall in the second half of the nineteenth century. Thus the two midgets destined to be nationally known showgirls started out singing and dancing at church benefits. Their own small congregation on Middle Road incubated their talents, but soon other religious centers all over the island clamored for their gospel beat, including the sailors at Seaman's Bethel and Marine Hospital in Vineyard Haven. News of two bewitching little girls traveled off Island. They were invited to take part in an operetta inspired by Little Red Riding Hood with a professional group in Plymouth. Lucy won the lead role.

The keys to the kingdom came in the form of Mrs. Tom Thumb, who traveled from Middleboro to Martha's Vineyard to woo the talented tiny teens. She proposed to sign the both of them to a contract with the General Tom Thumb Company, a traveling group of performing midgets. Lucy and Sarah's father had died a few years previously, so the decision was up to their mother. Mrs. Susan Adams deplored the idea of her two teeny darlings touring the country with a show business outfit, no matter how diminutive. The little Mrs. Thumb persisted, however, and at last the Adams matriarch gave in, provided her daughters were never

Guess Who's the Eleven-Year-Old

Singing and dancing stars, Lucy and Sarah Adams, midget sisters raised in Chilmark, pose with an unknown Island grade schooler.
MARTHA'S VINEYARD HISTORICAL SOCIETY COLLECTIONS (env. 711)

obliged to perform on Sundays. For the whole of their long theatrical careers, Lucy and Sarah never violated the sanctity of the Sabbath.

The little ladies debuted in New York in 1880. Lucy, nineteen, stood forty-nine inches tall and weighed sixty-five pounds; Sarah, seventeen, always the smaller of the two, stood forty-four inches tall and weighed fifty-one pounds. From the very start they yearned for their talents to outshine what they feared would be their freak appeal. To that end they threw themselves with a vengeance into their training for singing, dancing, and acting, even developing skits for themselves with such names as Little Annie Rooney and Thumbalinissima. Their popularity soared seemingly overnight: Songwriters begged them to showcase new numbers. A new vessel in New York harbor was christened the *Lucy and Sarah Adams*. As they toured with the General Tom Thumb Company, "The Adams Sisters" lit up marquees all over America.

"Does it promote clean, pure thoughts to sit beside a person with very little clothing on?"

The girls also performed with the Barnum and Bailey Circus and the Lilliputian Opera Company, though their primary loyalty remained with the Tom Thumb group, with whom they toured for twenty years. After the turn of the twentieth century, Lucy and Sarah booked their own engagements. Their religious roots were pulling them away from the froufrou and greasepaint of the theater; for the second half of their performing careers they limited themselves to appearances at church societies and schools. No more taffeta and bangles; the Adams Sisters were now gospel singers—their talent had become a ministry.

They traveled in the fall and winter, but spring and summer they spent at Nab's Corner in Chilmark, converting the family homestead into a tearoom, At the Sign of the Spinning Wheel. Along with tea, chocolates, and caramels, guests were treated to a medley of songs from the sisters stationed at the family organ.

On tour in 1930, Sarah fell from a moving vehicle when the car door swung open. She landed on asphalt, bursting a hip artery. The sisters tried to perform another four or five times, but it was no use; Sarah was too disabled to travel any longer.

The previous year they'd inherited from a cousin a Victorian cottage in the Methodist Campground in Oak Bluffs. Often called "dollhouses," these gingerbread homes marked the perfect venue for the two living dolls. They sold the Chilmark farm and moved for year-round living in the Campground.

Sarah died in December 1938 at the age of seventy-five. Lucy worked off her bereavement by plunging into ever more indefatigable church work. Known to be a small but fiery person, she dealt tongue-lashings to whichever pastor was intemperate enough to veer from Lucy's sense of Methodist orthodoxy. At the age of ninety-two, she wrote scrappy letters to the paper supporting another letter writer who'd complained about summer visitors clad in scanty apparel. Lucy chimed in, "Does it promote pure, clean thoughts to sit beside a person with very little clothing on?"

Coming from a former showgirl, this was heady stuff.

She'd been more daring in her younger days. In a newspaper interview she said that Sarah was the quiet, sedate sister, whereas "I would chat with anyone who wanted to spend the time." Lucy was fond of light reading while Sarah pored over the essays of Ralph Waldo Emerson. When they traveled with the Lilliputian Opera Company, Lucy was the only girl who engaged in winter sports with the boys— all of them, of course, miniature in size. Sarah used to scold her sister, saying that, if it weren't for her influence, Lucy would "go to the dogs."

Once a male midget who happened to be a European count or baron invited both sisters to lunch. Sarah thought she sniffed alcohol on the little man's breath and ejected him from their parlor. It turned out to be a whiff of cleaning fluid used earlier to tidy his jacket.

In Lucy's final years, she attributed her long, healthy life to natural advantages: "I live all alone. Lots of people get to be ninety but not many are as well and as smart as I am." Her sense of a healthy diet sounds foreign to today's ears: "I don't touch vegetables. I eat meat and potato with plenty of gravy." She also drank three or four glasses of milk every day (we can only surmise that this habit survived her Victorian childhood, when milk must have been pushed on the midgets as a sure way of helping them to grow).

In December 1954 Lucy Adams died two weeks short of her ninety-fourth birthday.

The Victorian cottage that must have seemed like a palace to the little sisters still stands at Fourth and Rock Avenue in the Campground.

From Harlem Renaissance to Oak Bluffs Pastorale

For several decades she sat on the book that would make her famous.

Dorothy West was born in Boston in 1907. Her father, Isaac West, ran a wholesale fruit company in Haymarket Square. An ex-slave from Virginia, his later success in business earned him the nickname "the Banana King of Boston."

Dorothy began writing at the age of seven, and won literary awards long before she was old enough to vote. At the age of fourteen she sent a short story to *Mademoiselle* magazine. The editor rejected it, but opined in passing that the young author possessed the maturity of a forty-year-old. In what Ms. West called her "exuberant youth," she moved to New York, and in the 1920s joined the black literary royalty known as the Harlem Renaissance—in the company of such writers as Zora Neale Hurston, Langston Hughes, Countee Cullen, and Clark McKay.

Ms. West also acted in her Harlem days, and a role in a play called "Porgy" brought her to London. Shortly thereafter she traveled to Russia to participate in a film about American blacks. She stayed for more than a year, writing, teaching, and working with other filmmakers.

In the 1930s back in the States, Ms. West launched a literary magazine called *Challenge*. She entered the field of social work in Harlem before joining the Federal Writers Project under the banner of the WPA, all the while writing countless articles for the *New York Daily News*.

But all of the glamour and travel and professional success was a dress rehearsal for what she would come to consider her real and true life on Martha's Vineyard.

Starting in the summer of 1908, when baby Dorothy was one year old, the Wests began summering in Oak Bluffs. They arrived in the wake of the original handful of prosperous black families who began buying property on the island. In the 1940s Ms. West gave in to her heart's desire and moved to the Vineyard full time. She published *The Living Is Easy*, a semi-autographical novel about her parents' marriage, in 1948. This book secured her literary reputation for all time.

The writer's larger dream was to settle into the daily rhythms of nature and community on the Vineyard, from the vantage point of her grey-shingled house on Myrtle Avenue (her section of road has since been renamed in her honor). She began writing for the *Vineyard Gazette*, and in time her byline crystallized into the Oak Bluffs Column, which over the decades tracked the comings and goings of friends and acquaintances, celebrities, and local notables, anyone who caught the lens of Ms. West's interest and insight.

She also recorded in her columns the seasonal arrivals of backyard avian life, granting a visiting eagle, cardinal, and purple finch their own fifteen minutes of fame. The passing of dogs—her own and others'—attracted particular comment. One August afternoon in 1985 she described the perfect death of blind pianist David Crohan's golden retriever, Skipper. Long released from service, Skipper had enjoyed the run of the neighborhood, "stopping at this house for a word or two and a biscuit, stopping at another to climb the porch steps and sit awhile with an elder in need of his company."

Jackie O learned that Dorothy W had over the decades been nursing a second novel.

Over the course of his last summer, Skipper had been slowing down. One August afternoon, he slowed still more, until at last he lay on the grass, and slipped serenely into a coma. David's two kids, with three others in tow, made a garland of flowers and placed it on Skipper's head. Meanwhile David's wife, Kate, also blind, brought out a tray of fresh-baked blueberry muffins for the children because, as the columnist observed, "The routine of life is often an anchor."

At the scent of muffins, Skipper's eyes boinked open. The oldest Crohan child, Stephan, offered the dog his own muffin. Skipper chomped it down. The other children gave over their muffins. The dying golden retriever was for the space of several minutes enfeebled no longer as he glumphed down the treats. Again he closed his eyes, slipping back into a final snooze and full-bellied death.

In the mid-1980s another literate islander, one Jackie Onassis, contacted Dorothy West to enthuse about her weekly column. Jackie O learned that Dorothy W had over the decades been nursing a second novel. As the most famous editor at Doubleday, Ms. Onassis was in a position to reintroduce the elderly author to the larger world.

With some trepidation, Ms. West handed over a long-dormant manuscript. Although she had finished it in the early 1960s, she was aware at the time that the flourishing Black Panther movement, and other annals of African-American militancy, gave her novel an old-fashioned ring. She decided to bide her time until the day might come—and she knew it might never come—when American life settled down enough to welcome *The Wedding*.

Set in the 1950s on Martha's Vineyard, *The Wedding* was published in 1995 to great acclaim. The eighty-eight-year-old author wrote in her dedication: "To the memory of my editor, Jacqueline Kennedy Onassis. Though there was never such a mismatched pair in appearance, we were perfect partners."

Ms. West's final Oak Bluffs column appeared in the August 13, 1993, issue of the *Vineyard Gazette*. She wrote in one of her last missives to her community: "I have lived in various places, but the Island is my yearning place. All my life, whenever I have been abroad, New York, Boston, anywhere, whenever I yearned for home, I yearned for the Island . . . the home of my heart."

Katharine Cornell, Mistress of Chip Chop

During the 1930s, '40s, and '50s, Katharine Cornell was hailed as the greatest actress of American theater. For those rare hours when she happened not to be treading the boards of Broadway, she lodged in her townhouse on Beekman Place or escaped to her country manse at Sneden's Landing, New York, with its eighteenth-century French and English antiques, or to her eighteen-acre estate on Martha's Vineyard, a densely wooded peninsula breasting into Vineyard Sound. There she'd built a rustic main house, two guest cottages, a pool, and a cabana. She named her blessed retreat Chip Chop.

Her low-key style of blending in won the hearts of the islanders. When Vineyarders traveled to see her in a play in Boston or New York, they would find warm welcome backstage in her dressing room. She fed them cookies and caught up on island gossip. At home on Chip Chop, she wore faded blue slacks and an old blue do-rag bandanna. Every day she paddled a canoe into town, docking at Owen Park. She would come ashore, collect her mail, and sit on the curbstone to read it. Next she'd do her marketing and, back at home, much of her own cooking and washing up. At her feet was a constant pack of dachshunds.

But if all this sounds a mite too plain for a celebrity of Ms. Cornell's stature, the weekends at Chip Chop were livelier and significantly more glamorous. The guest list over the years was almost unbearably illustrious: The Lunts, Helen Keller, Rex Harrison, Noel Coward, Sir Lawrence Olivier, and Vivien Leigh. But wait! There's more: James Cagney, Pearl Buck, Somerset Maugham, and James Thurber, and so on and so forth. Each illuminato was handed a marking pen and told to scribble something witty on the walls of Ms. Cornell's guest bathroom. In one of those misguided efforts at remodeling, future owners of Chip Chop gutted the bathroom, along with the rest of the house, without considering that those four walls of famous graffiti would have been well worth preserving—perhaps for the lobby of the Vineyard Playhouse. Ah well . . . .

Many of Ms. Cornell's weekend guests loved to skinny-dip in her pool. To enhance their privacy, the actress had had the windows removed from the kitchen to keep the staff from stealing a peek at Mr. Maugham's and Sir Lawrence's bare buttocks.

One anecdote from Chip Chop days: On a weekend that Lawrence Olivier and Vivien Leigh came to stay, the actress who gave us Scarlet O'Hara found herself in the grip of a crippling depression. Ms. Cornell suggested that she and Ms. Leigh closet themselves in the study to perform the mad scene from "Hamlet." We can only presume Ms. Leigh played Ophelia and Ms. Cornell, with her greater theatrical range, the prince of Denmark; it's difficult to picture it the other way around. Afterward, the actresses informed the other guests that they'd turned in the performances of their lifetimes. They had taken the trouble to record the event, but the tape has gone missing these many years. It's something to look out for at garage sales, along with the lost four walls from the Chip Chop guest bath.

The Meanest Woman on Martha's Vineyard

Lillian Hellman was the celebrated author of the plays *Little Foxes* and *The Children's Hour* and the best-selling books *Pentimento* and *Scoundrel Time,* about her travails, and those of her companion, mystery writer Dashiell Hammett, at the hands of Senator Joe McCarthy and the House Un-American Activities Committee. The most famous line she delivered to the Committee was "I cannot and will not cut my conscience to fit this year's fashions."

In 1955 she and Mr. Hammett bought the Mill House in West Chop, the long-ago dwelling of Molly Merry, daughter of Captain Timothy Chase, who fought in the Revolution. Legend had it that Ms. Merry lent money, charging high interest, and hid her loot in pudding bags under the stairs. The mill portion of the house was built in 1812, and was later moved to Edgartown, then back to Tisbury, once along Spring Street, and on to Manter Hill, after which, in 1883, a General Carrey bought it and moved it once again to attach it to the original Merry house.

When Ms. Hellman and Mr. Hammett first bought the property, it had three wings and four staircases. Newly arrived guests got lost in the maze of rooms, and their hosts would joke that a search party must be organized. It was called a cheerful house for a writer of cheerless plays. Much of the furniture came from Ms. Hellman's theatrical sets. After Mr. Hammett died in 1961, she sold the Mill House and moved to a smaller, beautiful white house with green trim down below on the beach.

To know Lillian Hellman was to find oneself confronted with an incurable crabapple. In the last years of her life, a roster of physical ailments left her in a great deal of pain, which only exacerbated her tendency to inflict pain herself. Vineyarders passing the author on the sidewalk saw her shuffling along behind a walker, a cigarette dangling from the corner of her mouth as she barked orders at whatever poor nurse tagged along at her side. The director of a nursing agency once told me Ms. Hellman churned through two or three helpers a week, all of whom quit in disgust.

Once at the long-ago Helio's Restaurant on State Road in Vineyard Haven, Ms. Hellman stopped in to have lunch. The waitress assigned to her table was pulled aside by another more knowledgeable waitress (who later confided the tale to me):

"You have a celebrity in your section—that's Lillian Hellman!"

"Really?" cried the waitress before dashing off to gush to her customer, "Miss Hellman, I just love your mayonnaise!"

The writer shot the girl a withering glare.

I had my own brush with the cantankerous lady: In the spring of 1982 my then-husband Marty bought from Red Barn Antiques two of Lillian Hellman's canary yellow wing chairs, priced at five hundred dollars apiece. Proprietors Bruce and Brandy, delightful fellows keen on having everyone socialize and be happy, told us about a subsequent conversation they had with Ms. Hellman when they suggested that

Lillian Hellman in a (for Her) Good Mood

The Vineyard's first lady of letters, while famous internationally for her writing, was best known locally for her peevishness.
ALISON SHAW

she might enjoy meeting the man who'd bought her chairs.

"He lives right across the Chop from you, Lillian." They brought her out to her sunroom to stare over the water. "He's a writer, too."

Suspicious, she asked, "What has he written?"

Bruce and Brandy rattled off Marty's television credentials: *The Odd Couple, Happy Days, Laverne and Shirley, Chico and the Man*.

She turned her beady stare to the two antiques dealers. "If he wants to meet me, he can meet me." She added with a sneer, "But it's going to cost him another thou."

At her funeral, novelist William Styron said he and Lillian fought all the time, and not about politics or philosophy, but over such details as whether a Smithfield ham should be served hot or cold. And speaking of her last rites, one of the men from the undertaker's later told us that when they set to work in the cemetery at Chilmark digging Ms. Hellman's grave, his equipment clanged against a boulder-sized rock, and he muttered, "Just like her!"

Jacqueline (Rhymes with Queen) Kennedy Onassis

FOR ALL OF US who've shared Vineyard soil, if only for a few seconds, with our most ridiculously famous summer resident of all time, three essential elements come to mind: Her gorgeous face with the chiseled cheeks and jaw and wide-set hazel eyes, her massive 375-acre estate in Aquinnah (which, as we'll see, was never quite enough for her), and her ferocious need for privacy.

About her face, there is nothing new to add. Unless we were born in the past few years and do not as yet even know who the Beatles were, all of us have seen that puss—in magazines, newspapers, and books—perhaps ten thousand times more than was necessary to imprint us with her features.

For Vineyarders, Jackie O's face—rarely glimpsed, but now and again viewed on town streets as she went about her business in her favorite island gear of jeans, tee shirt, and blue and white do-rag—meant only one thing: Pretend you don't see her. We were so protective of her privacy that even today, years after her death in May 1994, you cannot torture information out of the people who serviced her summer needs: Did she order anything interesting from the Chilmark Store or did she send her maid to the less expensive up-island Cronig's? How often did she obtain pedicures and what was her favorite color of polish? Did she ever rent videos? Which ones? Even posthumously no one's talking (well, one person revealed a few juicy tidbits, and we'll get to that in short order).

In her will she requested that all her benefactees, especially her two grown children, John Jr. and Caroline, continue to respect her privacy.

So what was she protecting? I think we can all rest assured that the former first lady had no shady habits other than the thoroughly untitillating gossip that her septuagenarian boyfriend, businessman Maurice Templesman, while he had an adjoining bedroom of his own in Mrs. Onassis's big house on the island, also occasionally shared the bed of his hostess. No Pamela Anderson/Tommy Lee–style pornographic video has ever surfaced to document this fact, and if such footage existed it's doubtful that many people would be keen to view it. But still, leaked information from a member of her staff long ago assured us that JFK's widow had a perfectly normal love life.

Somehow we intrinsically knew that Jackie's yen for privacy was a natural reaction shared by all but the most extroverted among us. You take a retiring personality and make her unimaginably famous to the point where people trail her into restrooms, sneak on to her property day and night, foist upon her inane chatter anytime she appears in public, and try to catch her bikini-clad in the crosshairs of a telescopic lens, and almost any of us would head for the hills in similar fashion.

And she had those hills—all 375 acres of them. You would think that a tract of oceanside land large enough to contain the capital of a small Balkan country would provide enough breathing space for a single one-hundred-ten-pound woman.

Nope.

In the early 1980s, shortly after Jackie O acquired the property, a television director and his wife found a three-acre parcel of land in the eastern reaches of Chilmark. When they returned to the real estate office to sign the purchase and sales agreement, their agent picked up the phone to find Mrs. Onassis's attorney on the line. The chain of events had happened faster than the Hollywood couple could sign on the dotted line: Jackie's caretaker, Albert Fisher, had noticed the broker and the couple patrolling their coveted parcel, and he relayed the news immediately to his employer. His sighting of them proved they in turn might enjoy all too much visual access to her. Mrs. O promptly phoned her lawyer and authorized him to enact the following two-part transaction:

(1) Buy the couple land with a home already on it, paid in full, in any other location.

(2) Purchase the adjoining Aquinnah parcel for Herself ASAP.

Another time that Mrs. Onassis's privacy seemed to her to be in jeopardy occurred when she realized her nearly four hundred acres engulfed an acre and a half of beachfront property that for years had belonged to an extended Wampanoag family. For centuries—make that millennia—tribal members had wandered down from the hills to swim, fish, and stroll on the beaches without stopping for a minute to concern themselves with access rights and legal trails. This particular Wampanoag family had never been barred from tromping across someone else's land to arrive on their own deeded beach. Now Jackie O, having settled into her newly built house with its commanding view of the Atlantic Ocean, was horrified to realize that at any given time locals would be picking their way helter-skelter—without even taking the time to establish a specific path—across her property. Once again she flew into action. She authorized her lawyer to offer the tribal unit a lump sum to purchase another beach somewhere else.

This time the privacy spoilers could not be bought off. The family sued to retain their own land, and the dust up was covered extensively in the newspapers. Sympathy clearly lay with the Indians. After a couple years of messy public wrangling, the matter was settled when Mrs. Onassis upped her offer and the family bought another sandy cove down the shore.

My own theory about Jackie O's beyond-the-limits desire for privacy is that the woman wanted no one to realize how truly little she needed to conceal. In other words, no one must know how insanely vapid were her days and nights on Martha's Vineyard. Although none disputed that Jackie O was bright, superbly educated, and spoke an awesome enough French to discover Egyptian author Naguib Mahfouz in that language, it seems to me when examining her on-island lifestyle that—during the summer at least—the stiff up-island breezes would have no trouble whistling through the vacant spaces in the lady's head.

Jackie O's typical summer day, according to her former maid, Marian Ronan, who spilled the beans to the *National Enquirer* after her employer's death, presented a picture of the lady's nutrition and exercise that suggest what you get when you blend a triathlete with a Tibetan monk. She would glide out of bed at seven a.m. and tuck into a breakfast of bran, skim milk, and either a banana, a peach or two plums. The morning warm-up included a two-hour swim in one of Ms. O's conveniently located ponds, followed by lunch on her porch, a towel wrapped around her damp swimsuit, as she nibbled cottage cheese with cut-up veggies, a slice of unbuttered toast, and two glasses of iced herbal tea. Afternoon encompassed a pecs 'n' hamstrings workout: one or two hours of bicycling followed by two or three hours of canoeing or kayaking. Dinner consisted of broiled or baked fish or chicken, and broiled potatoes and vegetables. No red meat and no sweets, ever, though she permitted herself an occasional glass of white wine.

(By the way, Jackie's death via cancer at the age of sixty-four should prove once and for all that so rigorously healthy a lifestyle is downright dangerous.)

Within the context of all that wholesome eating and physical exertion, it's hard to imagine that Jackie O was still reading Naguib Mahfouz in French.

The maid, Ms. Ronan, spoke lovingly of her employer's kindness, generosity, and her fondness for sitting around the kitchen table, chatting up the staff, Herself barefoot, with hair in curlers. She did, however, expect the help to call her "Madam."

Jackie O's house rules were otherwise lax, though she exhibited a degree of scrupulosity regarding her bedroom, an inner sanctum that had to be kept as spotless as a polished conch shell. The king-size bed was made up daily with military precision, although it's hard to imagine Mrs. Onassis—given rich people's aversion to actual cash and coinage—actually bouncing quarters off the bedspread. The Irish linen sheets were changed daily and sent out to a local laundress to be hand washed and ironed. A freshly laundered nightgown was placed nightly on the bed. Her comb and hairbrush had to be meticulously clean at all times—a single hair found on either implement would be a source of deep displeasure. And a final odd feature of Jackie's bedroom: Every morning the butler would light a fire in the fireplace, even in ninety-degree, humidity-in-the-beserk-range weather.

The tattling Ms. Ronan also had this to report about John Jr.'s wild parties: Whenever Mama O was away, the scion would play. The big house was surprisingly plain, with only the most basic of furniture and an almost total lack of ornamentation; nonetheless a great deal of mess could still be made when the young playboy consumed barrels of wine and beer with thirty or more friends. John Jr. had his own quarters, a dwelling called the Barn, replete with a silo where, up a spiral staircase, he vacationed with his famous sweetie, Daryl Hannah. According to Ms. Ronan, whenever his mother left him to his own devices, he charged into the main house and took it over with all the ferocity of an invading army. One weekend in the late 1980s he wrecked the ancestral manor once too often. The cleaning crew discovered wet towels on the floor, empty champagne bottles strewn about, food smeared on furniture, discarded on carpets, and even smushed into the walls. The head maid, Marta, reported the travesty to Madam. From that point forward, John Jr. was banished to the barn.

Every morning the butler would light a fire in the fireplace, even in ninety-degree weather.

Getting back to our original thesis: To Mrs. Onassis, privacy was as essential a middle name as was Bouvier or Kennedy. And we on the island, with the exception of Marian Ronan (and now me), honored this need with a gallantry unknown in modern times. But what did the divine Ms. O give back to the Vineyard? "Jacqueline Kennedy Onassis Leaves Island Legacy of Grace" read an editorial by Amy Callahan in the *Vineyard Gazette* of May 27, 1994. And "grace" might have been the long and the short of what JKO bequeathed to us. It's perfectly normal for rich people to make anonymous donations, and Jackie O's executors may have been writing checks like crazy to such worthy Vineyard nonprofits as hospice or the food pantry or the animal shelter or the playhouse, but if the lady's eleemosynary impulses did extend to the island, this fact has gelled into a better kept secret than whether she preferred jam made from Aquinnah-grown beach plums or rose hips.

And money aplenty she had to dispense. So obsessively discreet a public figure,would have writhed to see the details of her will aired in news publications around the world, right down to the gratuities of twenty-five thousand apiece left to her maids and butler. Larry Neumeister, writing for the Associated Press on June 2, 1994, reported that the will did "not specifiy the exact value of her estate except to say it is more than $500,000" (duh!). Mr. Neumeister went on to say that Mr. Templesman handled his famous friend's finances and was thought to have at least quadrupled the twenty-six million she secured from the estate of her second husband, Aristotle Onassis.

So hats off to you, Lovely Lady, if you remembered the island folk who cosseted you all those years and yet managed to leave no trace of your largesse, like checks writ on water. Maybe someday we'll learn about it, and you will have astonished us all the more.

We all say it, but we have difficulty truly believing it: Money brings no lasting happiness. When you examine the life of Jacqueline (she pronounced it Jackaleen—rhymes with queen) Kennedy Onassis, once again the old chestnut proves itself to be true.

Here she was, luxuriously fortressed on her four hundred acres, a woman in her prime enjoying life on her own terms, with an apartment on Fifth Avenue in Manhattan and an estate in New Jersey where she continued to ride to hounds, with money from the Kennedy fortune reinforced by a settlement from the Onassis pile, and yet she once confided to a friend, who in turn slipped it to the *New York Times*, "I have come to the conclusion that we must not expect too much from life."

So put that in your pipe and smoke it the next time you think that winning the lottery will make you any happier than you are at this exact perfect moment.

Princess Diana Making Our Island Even *More* Fab

SHE SPENT A MERE ten days on the Vineyard, back in August 1994, but that one supersecretive touchdown—the press had a better chance of finding Elvis the week that Princess Di was here—linked her name to ours for all time. Cast your eye over any Martha's Vineyard website or travel guide and you're certain to see the late royal's name emblazoned as one of the island's prime visitors.

So why did she choose the Vineyard? The newly announced intention to divorce her husband—the future king of England—had been picked up by the press internationally and beamed into every household equipped to receive the news, even via the most primitive of battery-run radios. Look at it from Her Royal Majesty's point of view: How would you like it if your divorce or misdeed with the IRS or worst embarrassment in high school were discussed over everyone's breakfast cereal?

And yet Princess Di came here, of all places. Vineyard journalist Tom Dunlop editorialized in the *Gazette* during the week of the royal's stay, "After Chappaquiddick, *Jaws,* the advent of Jacqueline Onassis and the Clintons, it seemed that the Vineyard had become a place of many spotlights and few shadows, the last piece of land on which the most photographed woman on the planet ought to hide."

But hide she did. Beautifully. And whoever had any truck with her kept her secret.

At the heart of the undercover mission was Diana's close friend, Lucia Flecha de Lima, wife of the Brazilian ambassador to the U.S. The de Limas had vacationed before on the island, and knew that this place, for all its glamour and cachet, was also an ideal locale in which to disappear. Mrs. de Lima's plea to the community was printed in our local papers, and the message boiled down to: This poor princess is unable to enjoy a vacation in her own country. Please allow her some time to relax and heal on the island.

So covert was the princess's arrival that, supposedly, Mrs. de Lima declined to give her husband any specific info about Diana's ETA, and the policeman dispatched to convey the princess from the airport to the de Lima summerhouse was sworn to secrecy. Even Diana's sons, the princes William and Harry, were out of the loop, stashed far away, in Greece on vacation with their dad.

The ambassador's wife rented a perfect retreat for concealing a princess. On the shores of isolated Lake Tashmoo, the antique farmhouse sat on land as remote as Thoreau's cabin on Walden Pond once was, surrounded by meadows and woods of conservation land.

Another factor aided and abetted the princess's privacy. She was placed in the custody of the Conover family of Edgartown, who performed a dandy job of royally—pun intended—entertaining the princess without calling attention to her or themselves. Timothy Conover organized the daily top-secret excursions. He arranged for Diana to jet ski in private coves. They beach-combed, hiked, and picnicked, and they reeled over squelchy wet beaches astride four-wheel drive vehicles. On at least one grand occasion, the princess cruised the harbor in the Conover family's gleamingly restored *Miss Asia*, a 1923 motorboat.

Meanwhile, paparazzi lurked everywhere.

A single photograph was worth the weight of the princess herself in gold. Reporters could churn out all the verbiage they could muster about Diana eating ice cream or skinny-dipping in a secluded cove (the news folk should be so lucky), but written blurbs were nothing against the force of a single picture of the royal doing anything—bicycling, nibbling a hot dog, adjusting her bra strap. It's amazing when you realize that one ordinary anything caught on film could achieve such onerous alchemy on front pages all over the world.

And so helicopters scoped the terrain from above. Airplanes disgorged legions of journalists and photographers. News vans bumped over twisty back roads in search of a princess petting a pony or scratching a poison ivy itch on her ankle.

To my knowledge, only two photographs emerged from those pivotal ten days. One is a blurry shot of Diana's back in a summer shift outside the de Lima farmhouse. (A trio of Scotland Yard agents had immediately grabbed the paparazzo and whisked him from the premises.) The other photo, published in the *Boston Herald*, is actually a beautifully composed portrait, captured by a steady hand behind a telephoto lens, of Princess Di under *Miss Asia's* striped canopy, her head bent in tête-à-tête with gentleman seaman Leo Conover, Timothy's dad.

The princess's Scotland Yard boys took great pains to ensure her privacy. Diana's desire to enjoy a normal vacation was often nixed by her own security detail. One evening Lucia de Lima had determined that she and her family and the princess would have a merry old time at Oak Bluff's trendiest restaurant, The Oyster Bar. The Yardies checked it out and gave it the thumbs-down: Too wild, they decreed. (And indeed it was, although the noise level of the eatery could have easily drowned out any hysteria created by the presence of a princess supping on oysters and dirty martinis.)

Throughout this astonishing ten days, a

brilliant decoy lay in the Vineyard Haven harbor, although no one was ever able to establish whether or not this red herring was planned or merely, triumphantly, coincidental. Day after day, a gorgeous 130-foot yacht named *The Opal* caught the sunlight and gleamed like the jewel for which it was named. The Australian flag flew from the highest deck. The equipage included a helicopter pad, a revolving dining room, and a Jacuzzi in the master stateroom. A bit of checking disclosed to the press that the yacht was worth an estimated twelve million dollars, and it rented for a cool sixty-five thousand a week.

News vans bumped over twisty back roads in search of a princess petting a pony or scratching a poison ivy itch on her ankle.

Did the princess reside on *The Opal*? Did the crew smuggle her to the island hidden under the canvas sheets of a dory? As Diana's stay unfolded, more and more spectators clustered at the edge of the harbor, eyes trained on the swan-like boat, to catch sight of the planet's most famous royal.

As news of Diana's vacation traveled to every part of the island, it became increasingly difficult for the lady to sample our pleasures incognito. One day she and her de Lima hostess attempted a shopping excursion in Vineyard Haven. There the ambassador's wife, accompanied by Diana dressed in black jeans, a white tee shirt, and Audrey Hepburn-sized sunglasses, went to Murray's, where Ms. Lucia exchanged a garment purchased the day before. The sales ladies later reported that the princess kept very much to herself, speaking to no one, thus creating a barrier over which it would be mortifying to attempt to address her. But the buzz had hit the streets, and when Diana emerged from the shop, a crowd of tourists pushed and shouted to get close to her.

Daisy Kimberly, owner of the chic clothing store Alley Cat, witnessed the rude throngs and the security detail that whisked the princess into a van. "I think people chased her right out of town. Whoever she's staying with never should have advised her to come into town on a cloudy August day."

Awareness of the royal's presence had apparently increased exponentially each successive day. It became clear to the de Limas and their guest that a quick getaway might buy Diana a few more days of incommunicado bliss. Accordingly they steamed to Nantucket on a sleek beige yacht with a matching beige helicopter. Once on Nantucket, Di was observed licking an ice cream cone at Odie's. She wore a periwinkle blue sweatshirt and a baseball cap. One Nantucket teen approached her and remarked, "That color is marvelous on you."

Diana replied with apparent sincerity, "Oh, thank you so very much."

Those were the only words captured in print to commemorate the princess's holiday.

Which feeds into my personal theory about Her Royal Majesty's overblown mystique: When you combine an obscenely exalted role with one sweet, introverted girl who has nothing of interest to say, the public's desire to know her, really know her, goes continuously unsatisfied and, thereby, further heightens her allure. (The same syndrome pertained to Jackie Onassis.)

All celebrities are imposed upon by the press, but if they're lucky enough to be witty, like Jon Stewart or Whoopi Goldberg, or principled, like Jane Fonda or Bruce Springsteen, or contagiously kind, like the Dalai Lama or the late Mother Teresa, they can satisfy the press—and by extension their fan base—simply by uttering a choice comment before going on their merry way. There is no disputing the value of Princess Di's commitment to such noble causes as land mine victims, the environment, and AIDS patients, but her famous photo shoots in support of these crusades mostly involved other people sermonizing while Diana lent only her face and her lank body swathed in some forty-five-thousand-dollar ensemble.

Even those with intimate contact with her—such as her butler, Paul Burrell, whose book, *A Royal Duty,* gave us a daily look at Princess Diana up close and personal—had little to add to what is already known: She was warm and gracious, adored her children, and possessed a good sense of humor, but was not clever enough to leave us with more than one morsel of wit in the seventeenth edition of *Bartlett's Familiar Quotations:* "There were three of us in the marriage, so it was a bit crowded." Period. Following the princess's visit to the Vineyard, the Conover family offered the same general—ultimately unfulfilling—comments about their royal charge.

Katherine Graham, the grande dame of the American press, and another of the Vineyard's august residents, supplied a telling glimpse into the black hole of Princess Di's personality. The Princess of Wales was on several occasions the luncheon guest of Ms. Graham, then owner of the *Washington Post,* at her splendid estate on the north shore of the island. During the course of the princess's stay, the two women had time for at least one heart-to-heart. According to a friend of Mrs. Graham's who wishes to remain unnamed, the wise and accomplished self-made older woman could discern that the princess was floundering at this point in her life: Diana was morose, insecure, lost. Ms. Graham's advice to her royal guest: "Go back to school, your Highness, and get yourself a college education."

This was an echo of an earlier caustic remark of Prince Charles's, that Diana's father could have done his daughter—and the nation—a service if he'd packed her off to university.

Could reading Shakespeare and learning calculus and immersing herself in sociology have helped Princess Di to a better life? Would she have sped around Paris with Dodi if she could, to borrow from Gilbert and Sullivan, "Know the kings of England and quote the fights historical, from Marathon to Waterloo in order categorical?"

It couldn't have hurt.

VIPs

Very Idolized Persons, Male, and One Shark That We've
Come to Think of as Practically Human

The Ivy League Indian

WHEN THE FIRST white settlers—only twenty—established roots on the Vineyard in the 1630s, two to three thousand Native Americans whose ancestors had been residing on these shores for, oh, roughly five thousand years were firmly in place. Woefully outnumbered, the newcomers were inclined to be fair to their predecessors.

That didn't stop the itch to convert the "savages" to Christianity, however. Matthew Mayhew, grandson of Thomas Mayhew who bought the Vineyard in 1642 from a couple of English grandees, devoted his life to saving Native souls. His first task was to disabuse the Indians of their devotion to their favorite deity, a giant named Moshup who lived in a cave below the cliffs of Aquinnah, tossed boulders about, and whenever he blew his stack, transformed his relatives into dolphins. Jesus, yes, Moshup, no: Such was the Reverend Mayhew's policy on worship.

Mayhew's most notable protégée was the brilliant Caleb Cheeshahteamuck who learned to read and write so quickly and so well that he was sent to the newly founded Harvard University. In 1665, at the age of twenty-five Mr. Cheeshahteamuck graduated from a class of seven, with honors in Greek and Latin. Sadly, in 1667 the Wampanoag whiz kid sailed with the Reverend Mayhew to England. Their ship was lost at sea, a tragic deficit for both the white and Native populations of Martha's Vineyard.

Dr. Feel Good

IN THE LAST DECADES of the nineteenth century, Dr. Harrison Tucker held the key to Oak Bluffs Society. The season was considered officially open when Dr. Tucker arrived on island in early summer, and officially kaput when he departed in the fall for any one of his houses in Brooklyn, Providence, Boston, and Foxboro.

A monument bearing Dr. Tucker's name still remains in the southwest quadrant of Ocean Park in Oak Bluffs. If you stand on the grass with your back to the sound and swivel your head to the right you will see the big, pale yellow house with dark green trim, jagged balconies, gingerbread doo-dads, and a rooftop pavilion—the manor house that looks as if it were designed by a Swiss architect on LSD. Built in 1873, that's the Tucker House.

Dr. Tucker made his fortune by patenting a tonic called Diaphoretic Compound #59. This was touted to treat nervous and compulsive disorders, rheumatism, lameness, backache, headache, toothache, three kinds of cholera, dysentery, summer complaints, diseases of the liver, stomach, and bowels; pretty much anything that ailed you. We know today that many of these nineteenth-century remedies, all of them obtainable over the counter, contained loads of opium. Clearly, no matter what condition plagued the patient, even all three kinds of cholera combined, he or she was bound to feel much better, at least for a couple of hours, after ingesting a tablespoonful of Dr. Tucker's kickapoo joy juice.

This merchandizing genius conceivably partook of regular doses himself, accounting for his incessantly convivial personality. He was the Mrs. Astor of Vineyard social life, the man all other hosts and hostesses consulted when planning their parties to make sure they weren't overlapping with any bash thrown by him, Dr. Big. Every July the New York Yacht Club fleet sailed into the harbor and the doc was on hand to launch the summer's galas at the sumptuous Oak Bluffs Club located down the beach-hugging lane from the Tucker house. During August 1874 he saved the day when President Ulysses S. Grant was ignominiously ejected from the Campground.

The visiting prez had been the guest of a Methodist bishop in the Wesleyan Grove. Asked to speechify from his host's balcony, Grant, in full view of the strictest church group in all of New England, without a second thought, yanked a flask from his pocket and swigged mightily. Later he claimed his throat had been dry, and the flask held nothing but water.

He had already alienated the Wesleyans by falling asleep during a sermon, which dashed any grand hope that the hero of the Union Army and the sitting president would rush down to the pulpit to be saved. When the flask fiasco occurred, the Campground trustees refused to give their commander-in-chief the benefit of the doubt and booted him. Rules are rules, after all.

Ever hospitable, Dr. Tucker offered the disgraced Ulysses asylum under his own ornate roof. Days later, the two men watched a display of fireworks in Ocean Park from the vantage point of the Tucker balcony. The jazzy rooftop

pavilion we see today hadn't yet been erected, but apparently Dr. Tucker later added this feature in hopes of a presidential rematch, which never materialized. Despite the booze flowing in the larger Oak Bluffs area, Grant may have chafed from the memory of how damn hard it was to hoist a drink in the heart of the village.

The house still stands, even though the Diaphoretic Compound #59 that financed it has gone the way of other snake oils. Perhaps forgotten bottles of it can still be found in island attics. For anyone who comes in contact with said item, be sure to check the expiration date.

Show Me the Way to the Next Whisky Bar

President Ulysses S. Grant (seated on the far right), spent his 1874 visit to the Methodist Campground feeling sorely thirsty. Eventually he was asked to leave after knocking back a swig from his pocket flask in full view of hundreds of congregants.

MARTHA'S VINEYARD HISTORICAL SOCIETY COLLECTIONS (env. 250a)

Solo Sailor

THE VINEYARD HAS ALWAYS claimed Captain Joshua Slocum as its own because of his farm in Chilmark, the only land he ever owned, and on which he spent any time whatsoever. *Terra firma*, however, never became the captain's favorite stomping ground. Like so many hardy Yankees before and after him, his greatest joy in life was to skim along a fair sea with the wind at his back.

Born in Nova Scotia, he ran off to sea at the age of fourteen, winning a job as cook on a New Bedford schooner. It took only one meal for the sailors to mutiny over the boy's lack of culinary experience. Though he was thrown off that boat, he soon found another maritime posting. His passion for sailing earned him rapid boosts up the nautical ladder, and by the age of twenty-five he'd made it to captain. The ships kept getting bigger and more prestigious as he circumnavigated the world many times. At one point when he touched down in Australia, he married in a maritime minute, and took his bride with him on his travels (see "The Captain's Wife" in the "Love, Vineyard Style" chapter).

Fortunes ebb and flow, and Captain Slocum's began to ebb until, in his forties, he found himself up a creek without a literal paddle, in other words, stranded on land. However, an encounter with an old pal of a sea captain turned his life around.

"I have a boat in Fairhaven," the friend told the downwardly mobile master mariner. "It needs some repairs, but it's yours for the taking."

Slocum's spirits must have sagged when he first beheld the *Spray*, a thirty-seven-foot sloop more than a hundred years old, propped up by boards and actively rotting in a farmer's field in Fairhaven. Never daunted for long, the sea captain began rebuilding the boat to his own precise specs—in addition to his years of captaining boats, he was also a brilliant architect of anything that moved on water. By the time he had finished the *Spray*, few of its original materials remained.

At the age of fifty-one, in April 1895, he sailed alone, east out of Fairhaven, north to Gloucester, then across the open Atlantic, reaching Gibraltar by August. His route took him back across the ocean to the coast of Brazil, around the Horn, and through the Straits of Magellan *twice* (the first attempt spit him out to sea in a southward-driving gale). Next he traversed the un-pacific Pacific by way of Samoa to Australia, and crossed the Indian Ocean to South Africa. He rounded the treacherous Cape Hope, and finally glided north to the Caribbean, and home to New England. The trip took a drop longer than three years.

No one had ever circumnavigated the globe alone before. In fact, no one believed it was possible to sail across the Chesapeake Bay without at least one extra hand. The sheer impossibility of Joshua Slocum's feat produced a number of skeptics. Then in 1898 he published a fascinating account of the adventure, *Sailing Alone Around the World*, and little doubt remained. The details in his account were too rich, the dangers too harrowing, and the nautical skills too apparent for him to have fabricated this.

Even during the voyage itself, Slocum engendered his own publicity by contacting newspapers at South American ports of call to blow his own (ship's) horn. The story ran ahead of him, so by the time he rounded Cape Horn and made it safely through the Straits of Magellan on his second pass, every port into which he sailed had a band and a welcoming committee on hand to extend free anchorage. Heads of state were keen to wine and dine him, educational groups invited the captain to give lectures about his life at sea, and rich patrons bought him new rigging, sails, and provisions.

Other sailors continued to wonder how he had managed a global circuit alone in a small sloop across mighty oceans. Clearly, this was a job for three guys, minimum. To all who were interested—and their numbers were legion—Captain Slocum detailed how, once the helm was lashed in place and sails were set for wind draught, he'd descend to the cabin for a good night's sleep, or in daylight sprawl on the deck to give himself up to his second favorite passion—reading. He had taken great pains to craft a boat capable of running on this brand of autopilot. He had also been lucky that on the nights the *Spray* was left to its own devices, no hapless vessels ever rammed him, even though he suffered other close calls—murderous savages in Tierra del Fuego, numerous gales, one worse than the next, rogue waves, and a goat that ate the captain's chart, leaving him exposed to dangerous shoals and rocks.

With enough hair-raising adventures to stock the story files of ten authors, Captain Slocum was himself a deft writer, on top of all his other abilities. Consequently, *Sailing Alone Around the World* continues to be in print.

Captain Slocum kept on sailing, although periodically he'd stay home on his farm with his second wife (the first having died at sea) and roster of children. In the fishing village of Menemsha, the mariner puttered with the sloop as famous as he was, and on November 14, 1909, at the age of sixty-five, with crowds thronging the dock to see him off, another tributary band tooling away, Captain Joshua Slocum set his jib and glided north by northwest out of the harbor, off on another far-flung adventure.

Joshua and his beloved *Spray* were never seen again.

Though it probably wouldn't have mattered, did I mention that the man had never learned to swim?

The Owen in Owen Park

ONE OF THE PRETTIEST of the island's captains' houses sits on William Street in Vineyard Haven, on the southwest corner of Colonial Avenue. It was purchased in the 1900s by a fellow named William Barry Owen, who invented the Victrola, otherwise known as the Victor talking machine. Even the youngest among us might have seen copies of the quaint ads for the original record player: A fox terrier, head cocked, listens to the trumpet curving up from a clunky wooden box. This famous pooch, as a point of historical trivia, is buried inside the high stone walls encircling the garden of Mr. Owen's former house (now owned, FYI, by film producer Victor—another Victor in this house!—Pisano and Judy Belushi, widow of comedian/movie star John Belushi).

William, son of Arctic whaling Captain Leander Owen, made a pile of money with his talking machine. He lived in England for five years, but sent his laundry back home weekly to the Vineyard (an unsubtle PR drive to remind islanders how well he was doing). Always

a show-off, he returned to the Vineyard with a long white automobile, a chauffeur, two fine horses, a coachman, a gardener, an under-gardener, and a butler named Ruffles (complete with an upper-crust English accent). The Victrola king renovated his William Street house and also bought up several acres on the Vineyard Haven harbor.

His plan had been to build a mansion on this superb property. To this end, he hired men to haul away the three aged houses sitting there; for the whole of that winter, Main Street remained cluttered with all the equipment and horses needed to remove the dwellings. Unhappily, the mogul's money leaked away, and his seaside mansion became nothing more than a fleeting dream. After he died in his fifties, his bequest of the property to the town proved to be of lasting value. Today, this acreage, decked with a white gazebo, is known as Owen Park.

Mr. Menemsha Sunsets

STARTING IN 1937, the Menemsha Inn housed a distinguished guest who rented the same bungalow year after year for the whole of August—Alfred Eisenstaedt of *Life* magazine. Known to fans and friends alike as "Eisie," he has long been hailed the father of American photojournalism, and his photographs have graced any number of museum exhibitions. His most acclaimed shot features a sailor in Times Square on V-J day as he swoops up a young nurse in white dress, heels, and white stockings, and treats her to a kiss such as we see on the covers of bodice-rippers. Did they know one another? Had they just met and, having kissed with such passion, proceeded to coffee and wedding bells before the weekend was over? All of Eisie's photographs tell a riveting tale. In fact, he told Mark Lovewell in a 1992 interview for the *Vineyard Gazette*, referring to his MO with a camera, "Put me in an empty room and I'll give you a story."

The changing light over sea and fields brought Eisie back to the Menemsha Inn for every August of his life, including the final August of 1995 when he died at the age of ninety-six at Martha's Vineyard Hospital.

An Eisie-in-Menemsha story related by the master himself in 1994 at one of his many receptions at the Granary Gallery in West Tisbury: Once on a summer afternoon in the mid-1980s, the photographer strolled along the Gay Head cliffs. A young couple called out to him, asking if he'd take their picture with the ocean at their backs. When he agreed, they handed him their Instamatic. The man who'd photographed Winston Churchill, Mussolini, Somerset Maugham, FDR, and Sophia Loren, to name but a few, and who'd won a slew of awards for photojournalistic achievements, snapped the picture, smiled, and without a word returned the camera. Then, unable to resist, he quipped, "That'll be fifteen hundred dollars."

A bit of celebrity gossip concerning Alfred Eisenstaedt: After his beloved wife, Kathy, died in 1972, the great photographer shortly found comfort in the company of his sister-in-law, Lucille "Lulu" Kaye, who remained his boon companion for the rest of his life. In true Vineyard fashion, no one on the island—from Menemsha Inn staff to his famous island friends, such as Walter Cronkite and Katharine Graham, to the reporters who came to interview him over the years—ever raised a brow at his late wife's unorthodox replacement.

A Shark Named Bruce

FOUR EVENTS IN the twentieth century kicked up the Vineyard's fame a major notch. The first occurred in 1968 when Ted Kennedy and Mary Jo Kopechne crashed off the bridge on Chappaquiddick. This put Martha's Vineyard on the map ("Where the heck is that?" was a standard response when the story was broadcast over the evening news). The second Big Thing was the 1974 filming of *Jaws*, which positioned the Vineyard as one of the top summer resorts, along with Key West, the Hamptons, and Bar Harbor. The third milestone spanned the early 1990s when President Bill Clinton, with much fanfare, spent August holidays on these shores, thus raising the Vineyard glitz factor to an almost intolerable level. And number four, the all-time topper to date—Princess Di spent ten notorious days here.

It was only a caprice of nature that caused *Jaws* to be filmed on Martha's Vineyard instead of Nantucket. Peter Benchley, author of the best-selling book about the fish from hell, had encouraged the movie's production designer, Joe Alves, to check out Nantucket, Benchley's ancestral summer home. When a storm shut down the ferry to the farther island, Mr. Alves decided to kill time by scouting Martha's Vineyard. Once he saw Edgartown, the fictional town of Amity came to life for him; it was quaint, quiet, and quintessentially New England. The beaches, he determined, were idyllic, the tides on the placid side, and the sandy bottoms near shore measured an average twenty-six feet—perfect for the shark-killing ketch *Orca.*

So why did it take six months to shoot what should have been a three-month production? Why in WW II did the Allies require a full year to defeat Germany after the invasion of Normandy? *Merde* happens. And buckets of it got dumped on the film crew on Martha's Vineyard.

On the plus side for islanders, fortunes were made and family farms were saved overnight. In particular, businessman Bob Carroll—whose hotel, the Kelley House, and boatyard in Edgartown were rumored to be ready for seizure by evil bankers—made a deal to house the *Jaws* crew starting at a time of year when a couple of lights glowing in a couple of the guest rooms would have constituted success. The half year of Kelley House occupancy, boatyard fees, and pricey house rentals transacted by Carroll and Vincent Real Estate, all of it paid for by Universal Studios, more than pulled Mr. Carroll's chestnuts from the fire. He went on to shore up the grand Harborview Hotel and a good chunk of the island of Anguilla.

All over this island people of every age, gender, and trade were mobilized to service the movie. Local kitchen hands helped L.A. movie caterer Rolly Harper provide daily lunches for more than sixty people, many of whom were served on the rough-hewn tables of a work barge dubbed *Garage Sale.* Hundreds of islanders were hired as extras at twenty dollars a day. Boatmen, for the piloting and use of their crafts, received ninety dollars *per diem.* Andrea Morton, a young waitress at the Kelley House, was tapped to supply the dead arm of the young midnight bather, Christy, who is munched by

the shark in the opening sequence. When, a couple of scenes later, Christy's remains are discovered on the beach, we cut to a bluish-gray arm on the sand, coated with seaweed and overrun with feed-frenzied sand crabs. That was the arm of the sportin' Ms. Morton.

A funny story about the arm: Joe Alves and his clever production staff dutifully applied crabs to the deceased's appendage (with the very live waitress/extra at the other end of it trying desperately not to shiver in the nippy May air), but the tiny beach critters hunkered down, unmoving. Perhaps they understood better than the humans on the set that it was too early in the year for filming beach scenes. One of the production crew had the bright idea of tossing hot coffee at the crabs. Man, did they scramble, and you can see the results when you watch the movie. You can also further appreciate the intrepid Ms. Morton for not allowing her arm to spasm.

Other more pivotal casting choices were made according to island affiliations. Jeffrey Kramer, who played the deputy sheriff (you may recall him, with method actor punctilio, puking in the sand alongside young Christy's remains), was only secondarily a handsome, winsome, bushy-tailed (and bushy-haired in those days!) young actor. What placed him ahead of other bushy-haired young actors was his family connection to the Vineyard, going back to his grandfather, Henry Cronig, who dealt in island real estate throughout the better part of the twentieth century. In addition to Jeffrey, two adorable island boys were hired to play Chief Brody's sons: ten-year-old Chris Rebello and toddler Jay Mello. Lee Fiero, active in island community theater, was cast in the emotive role of Mrs. Kintner, whose nine-year-old son is pulled from his rubber raft by the maws of the monster. I later interviewed her about the experience.

When Ms. Fierro was first summoned to audition for the part, Mr. Spielberg asked her to improvise a scene—the one where she refuses to let her son go back in the water because his hands are "pruning up." With casting director Sherry Rhodes gamely playing the child, Ms. Fierro held firm that her son must remain on shore. Finally Mr. Spielberg cried out, "Lee, you've got to let him go back in the water or we have no movie!"

Local doctor Robert Nevin had a speaking part as the Amity coroner. His wife, Barbara Nevin, smart, efficient, and plugged in to Edgartown society and politics, was hired as production secretary. From director Steven Spielberg on down to the most junior of the teamsters, Barbara was hailed as indispensable to the daily operations. In tribute to her take-charge character they called her "Sarge."

Islanders felt they could dispense with movie idols Roy Scheider, Robert Shaw, and Richard Dreyfuss. For them, the real star of the picture was island legend Craig Kingsbury. Crusty, curmudgeonly, and—when it suited him—surprisingly literate, Mr. Kingsbury rambled barefoot for the better part of each year until his feet were as coarse as an armadillo's. Back in the day, he'd been arrested for driving a team of oxen, himself drunk, down Circuit Avenue in Oak Bluffs. A fisherman, a farmer, and a ranter at town meetings, he also bore the dubious distinction—for long years thought to be apocryphal—of introducing skunks to the island. It was on Craig Kingsbury's persona that the Royal Shakespeare Company actor Robert Shaw based his character, the gruff and demented shark hunter Quint.

Mr. Shaw studied tapes of Mr. Kingsbury's speech patterns. Daughter Trina Kingsbury recalls that in particular the English actor learned how to swear Yankee style, with her dad freely supplying the lingo: "Sonsabitches, whores of Babylon, fish gut s—t heads!" Mr. Shaw hung out with the local crackpot and probably learned more than he'd ever needed to know about livestock, whisky, and scalloping in the teeth of bitter nor'easters. What you see on the screen in Mr. Shaw's performance is Craig Kingsbury himself, who died in 2002 just shy of his ninetieth birthday.

Mr. Kingsbury enjoyed his own few minutes of cinematic fame in *Jaws*. He played Ben Gardner, one of the many fishermen who, inspired by a three thousand dollar reward, take up the hunt for the killer shark. It is he who provides the first big audience squeal when his decapitated head pops out of a sunken fishing vessel. A cast of Mr. Kingsbury's features had been molded into a rictus of death and fear with a good helping of fake gook and sea corrosion slapped on for a maximum "eeewww!" effect. When Mrs. Kingsbury saw the likeness, she phoned her daughter in California to warn her that the freak-out object in the movie was not in fact her dad's actual head.

Trina Kingsbury recalls that the movie crew drove her mother mad with their daily requests. One morning a man from Wardrobe said they needed to retrieve the shirt Mr. Kingsbury had worn at the previous day's shoot, "You know, ma'am, the blue shirt with the seagull s—t on it?" Indignantly Mrs. Kingsbury replied, "If my husband comes home with seagull s—t on his shirt, it goes right into the washing machine!"

Their time on the island became painful for the stars as the schedule fell apart. Three months over deadline and three and a half million dollars over budget (a much less digestible sum in those days) was the fault of a problematical mechanical shark (in actuality three sharks, all christened Bruce), frequent bad weather, a gridlock of sailboats on what was supposed to be a lonely sea, and Mr. Spielberg's perfectionism, which I'm told amounted to twenty takes on any given scene.

Robert Shaw had his own time constraints, and they involved taxes. Any extra time he spent in the States reportedly meant he'd get nicked by the IRS for monies owed on *The Taking of Pelham, One, Two, Three* and *The Sting*. Consequently whenever the shooting schedule could cope without him, he fled to Canada to log fewer days in this country. Another ailment for him was seasickness.

Knowing this, it gives us an insider's chuckle to watch him onboard the *Orca*, looking for the world like the toughest of old sea salts; somewhere under all the brilliant acting, though, his gills were deeply green.

Roy Scheider missed his home life, and tended toward testiness—a trait that showed up in his character where it was perfectly appropriate to the action. He often succumbed to seasickness, exacerbated by all the scenes when he was obliged to toss over-ripe chum into the waters to attract *El Monstro*. According to screenwriter Carl Gottlieb, who documented the filming in his book, *The* Jaws *Log*, Mr. Scheider in these moments used all his willpower to keep from vomiting on camera. Of course the agony paid off in his delivery of perhaps the greatest line in the history of adventure movies: After two-thirds of the action provides only intimations of the shark—the *da-dum-da-dum* soundtrack, the monster's point of view of rippling bodies through gorgeous blue waters, boats suddenly battered by an unseen force—at last Chief Brody tosses a shovelful of squid over his shoulder, and Mr. Great White rears up with chompers big as a Buick. Dazed, Brody backs into the cabin and deadpans to Quint, "We're going to need a bigger boat."

Richard Dreyfuss, then twenty-six (the same age as Steven Spielberg), was fresh from the success of the Canadian film *The Apprenticeship of Duddy Kravitz*. The outrageously smart young actor acclimated best to the island. He kept the troops entertained during the filming and hit the social circuit at night, his cachet as a new movie star proving a boon to his romantic life. Since that time he has spent many summers vacationing on the island; generally he rents a house in Vineyard Haven, where other movie stars have been known to congregate.

Character actor Murray Hamilton played the self-serving mayor. Carl Gottlieb's book recounts how, like so many others in the cast and crew, Hamilton began to fall apart as the schedule threatened to push its way into the next decade. One night at the end of August, Mr. Hamilton is said to have overindulged in an Oak Bluffs bar and set out to walk—or perhaps lurch would be a more accurate verb—to his motel. On the way, he stopped to pet a cute doggie sniffing at the underside of a dumpster. The black "doggie" with the white stripe down its back turned and sprayed Mr. Hamilton with a full payload of stink juice.

The story goes that the actor was too far gone to realize the extent of his problem, and he staggered to the motel for a good night's sleep in preparation for a five a.m. wake-up call. Back in his room, he was jolted awake again and again by a foul smell. Each time he careened upright to open another window. Back to sleep. Up again. "What's that stench?" He grumbled to himself. Finally, to escape the odor, which he presumed originated in his room rather than from himself, he groped his way to the empty lobby and flopped down on the couch. At last sleep overtook him until, in the morning, a grossed-out motel clerk shook him awake and advised him to burn his clothes.

Cut to a bluish-gray arm on the sand, coated with seaweed and overrun with feed-frenzied sand crabs.

At the end of September the final pieces of second unit filming were "in the can" and the last members of the crew had left the island. It was all worth it, of course. Box office receipts proved *Jaws* to be the most successful movie of its time, and stellar careers evolved for the lead actors and the director, as well as the shark itself (i.e., all three Bruces), which starred in three successful sequels. Watching *Jaws* on TV or DVD today, Vineyarders are always struck by how many friends, neighbors, and acquaintances they recognize—how young they were, how many of them are no longer with us. In addition to movie stars Roy Scheider, Robert

Shaw, and Murray Hamilton, Dr. Robert Nevin, Barbara Nevin, Craig Kingsbury, and Chris Rebello are gone.

It's particularly poignant to see little Chris, ten years old and small for his age, with huge brown eyes and curly dark hair, an adorable island tot with skin burnished by summer rays. He died of a heart attack in 2002 at the age of thirty-seven, having deepened his Vineyard roots as both a landscaper and coach of the high school football team. In the immortal *Jaws* he remains forever young.

Where the Sidewalk Ends at Shel's House

He looked like a bag man lumbering up and down the streets of Oak Bluffs in sandals, scruffy jeans, and baggy gray sweatshirt, his bald head in pale contrast to his huge and furry black eyebrows and black beard. A glower on his face warned the uninvited to stay well away.

Not that author, playwright, songwriter, and cartoonist Shel Silverstein was a mean man. On the contrary, stories abound about the fans that approached him on his Campground porch to sign one of his books. Invariably he accepted the book and the pen and stared thoughtfully into the middle distance for a good two or three minutes. His inspiration stirred, he would hunch over the title page and inscribe it with one of his inimitable drawings—a tree, a goat, a child with a collapsed kite—before scrawling his famous name beneath the complimentary work of art.

Legend had it that once you entered Shel Silverstein's circle of known souls, he was downright sweet. The trick was in surviving his hazing period. For me, it took a good six or seven years of smiling at the man when we passed on the street before his reflexive glower at last turned into a genuine smile. The smile said: Okay, I recognize you as a regular person about town.

I was a regular person about town a full seven years before he accepted me as such—perhaps he required proof of long residency before committing to a reciprocal grin. After all, a townie of only five or six years could easily move off island; far be it from Shel to extend himself to anyone without the grit to stick around.

Born in Chicago in 1932, he began drawing at an early age, simply because he could. He once told a reporter that as a kid he would have preferred to hit a baseball or to endear himself to girls but, failing at both, he pursued his one perceivable talent. In adulthood, when his opportunities for romance increased, he continued to draw and write out of thoroughly ingrained habit. The quest for female companionship went undiminished, apparently. Here on the island, whenever Shel's name came up, someone always chimed in, "He loves young women."

Not just "women," but "young women." (Hmmm—a successful and famous older man preferring the company of women decades younger. Is anyone surprised?) According to my Deep Throat in the vicinity, neighbors in the Campground were well aware of the coming and going of Shel Silverstein's nubile guests. (If this reputed predilection for young 'uns was true, it undoubtedly explains the seven years it took for the celebrated author to smile back at me.)

Best known for his children's books, all of which have been accepted into the canon of classics, especially *Where the Sidewalk Ends, Light in the Attic, Falling Up,* and *The Giving Tree,* he also created numerous plays, cartoons for *Playboy* magazine, and pop songs, the most famous of which was "A Boy Named Sue," sung by Johnny Cash.

The Vineyard was only one of his stomping grounds. He also had homes in Greenwich Village and Key West and a houseboat in Sausalito, California. But his cottage at 11 Forest Circle in Oak Bluffs, which he remodeled in an English storybook style, claimed most of the great man's time between June and November. During those warm months islanders were treated to the sight of Shel Silverstein tramping the beach roads and the byways. He shunned automobiles, seeing to it that wherever he lived he could get about on foot.

John Newsom, long-time resident of the Campground, chuckles to recall a trip to Key West where he beheld the same shabbily dressed, gruff-faced Shel Silverstein, shambling along that island's shore.

Another anecdote that Mr. Newsom recalls occurred during a winter some years back when Campground management was alerted to burst pipes in the house at 11 Forest Circle. Methodist ministers and administrators called a hasty meeting. As they stood around with sober and somber miens, someone asked if anyone knew where Shel Silverstein could be found. The board member who'd tracked down the author said, "He's at the Playboy Mansion."

Shel Silverstein took his last walk down in Key West. On May 11, 1999, two housemaids found him dead upstairs in his bedroom at his Florida home. The cause of death was never publicly revealed.

His books remain in print, and in their pages one can find many hints of the saintly being behind the bearded scowl.

Hail to the Chief

In the summer of 1993 the Vineyard underwent a change that was the stuff of sci-fi horror. Who knew that the arrival of a single personage would yield a climate shift that would plunge our old way of life under melting Arctic waters, as rustic island camps gave way to mansions the size of UFOs, glitzomaniacs overwhelmed our locale like alien pods in *Invasion of the Body Snatchers,* and real estate prices blew skyward as if our sandy, acidic soil contained all the plutonium any mad scientist could ever desire.

All thanks to President Bill Clinton, one year in office, with wife Hillary and daughter Chelsea in tow, who spent two weeks in August on our humble island. The biggest shock was how easily the Vineyard absorbed the invasion: In Oak Bluffs, the Wesley Hotel reserved fifty rooms just for the Secret Service agents. Real estate offices were deluged with requests for rental homes to lodge summer White House personnel and reporters from all the major news agencies. In Edgartown a car leasing dealership coughed up seventy-five Isuzu Rodeos, Amigos, and Oasis vans, while the Edgartown elementary school was transformed into a high-tech press center with satellites and extra phone lines.

You would think we'd feel as if a World War II Panzer division had rolled onto the island but, strangely, we responded with giddy joy. Hundreds flocked to the tiny country airport as Air Force One delivered the first family. Shops strung banners welcoming the Clintons. Stories abounded about the president's affability; not a hand was left unshaken or a baby unhugged as Bill sampled Primo Lombardi's peppers and sausage pizza on the porch of the Chilmark Store, shopped for tee shirts at Brickman's in Edgartown, and buried his face in a mound of mango madness ice cream at Mad Martha's in Oak Bluffs.

The charismatic prez could be counted on to add pizzaz to any event. At a fund-raiser in Edgartown he joined the orchestra, requisitioned a saxophone, and played "My Funny

Valentine" for a couple celebrating their thirty-fifth anniversary. He restricted himself to New England proprieties, however, and held back on his Elvis impersonation for more casual nights with down-home cronies. No reports exist of a pelvis-churning "hunka hunka burnin' love" fest on these shores.

Bill Clinton's vacation on the Vineyard attracted hundreds more people and vehicles to this tiny island, and yet brought no sense of extra crowding. Truth be told, the Vineyard in August is always frantically overcrowded, so hugger-muggerishly insane, with traffic backed up into all down-island towns and restaurants besieged. Finding an empty parking space is a laughably impossible dream. Adding another thousand bodies to the mix is the equivalent of sprinkling an extra shovelful of sand over one of our beaches.

Hosting a sitting president in our own backyard was an unexpected and euphoric bonus that crossed partisan lines. My friend Nancy Baron, visiting with her husband and two kids from Los Angeles, at first sneered at Bill Clinton's arrival; she hadn't voted for him, so she had no intention of reveling in his nearness. And yet one day as she was shopping for clothes in Vineyard Haven, she learned that Bill had entered the bookstore across the street. A mania to eyeball the man overtook her, reminding her of how she behaved at the age of eleven when she screamed to catch a glimpse of John, Paul, George, and Ringo at the Hollywood Bowl. She scurried across the street, only to run up against an army of gawkers mustering outside the store. She figured the secret service would spring their boss by the back door, so she charged around the building, jacked herself up a fence, and squatted in a tree with a bird's-eye view of the rear exit. Moments later the door flew open and the president emerged with his entourage. Nancy was flushed with excitement for the rest of the day.

The following two summers, 1994 and 1995, the Clintons opted to vacation in Jackson Hole, Wyoming, but 1996 saw them back on island. They continued to make a beeline here each successive August. By 1997 Vineyarders were jaded

Bill & Hillary Get the Old-Time Religion

The Clintons (along with Alan Dershowitz, on their left) take part in Rosh Hashanah services in Edgartown's Whaling Church (an island oxymoron if there ever was one!).

PETERSIMON.COM

enough to go about their business with less heed paid to the passing motorcades and strategic drop-ins at shops and eateries.

The mainland news services, however, sent the usual cadres of reporters with cameras; most of the time they slouched about wondering how to make a hot story out of a family having fun. The predictable fun included rounds of golf at Farm Neck, usually in the company of fat cat contributors to the Democratic ticket. In 1999, however, the press corps had something to write about: the president played golf with Prince Andrew of England that summer. His royal highness (or in the case of the second born, is he called his royal middleness?) had motored over from his yacht anchored in Vineyard Haven. As they strolled to their first tee-off, Bill remarked to Andrew that all of Martha's Vineyard once belonged to the prince's own royal family, before the American Revolution, of course.

On a whim the president turned to the press corps and quipped, "We're betting the island on this game!"

The entire entourage got behind the concept, and the collective adrenaline level shot sky-high as the prince moved ahead in round after round. By the fifteenth hole, however, an act of God spared the Vineyard from returning to British control as thunder boomed, lightning seared, and a hard rain drove players and spectators back to the clubhouse. By the end of the day, the stars and stripes still flew from the county courthouse in Edgartown.

Bill, Hillary, and Chelsea engaged in normal activities during most of the daylight hours—if you can call normal wolfing down eggs, sausage, and corn muffins at Linda Jean's restaurant in Oak Bluffs while surrounded by Secret Service, press aides, and legions of pumped-up fans. For the Clintons' more decorously scheduled social hours, the elite of Martha's Vineyard—a wag at the *Boston Herald* called them "island suck ups"—issued hundreds of invitations. The president and

first lady dined several times in the West Chop beach home of novelist Bill, and his wife, poet Rose Styron. The Clintons lolled on singer James Taylor's yacht, *Zorra*. News icons Mike Wallace and Walter Cronkite also spent quality time with the prez. Bill's birthday each August 19th struck the most resounding social bells of all. On a couple of occasions Vernon Jordan hosted the bash at his Chilmark home. Other summers, actors Ted Danson and Mary Steenburgen opened their island house to the birthday boy.

From 1996 onward, the Clintons stayed on the eighty-acre farmstead of Dick and Nancy Friedman on Oyster Pond on the southwest fringe of Edgartown. The main house is what we call quintessential Vineyard; commodious without being ridiculously large, remodeled within, its exterior an unpretentious display of weathered gray shingles. Windows sport original antique glass, and all five chimneys have been lovingly refurbished. Once a working farm, the property overlooks a sweep of the Atlantic Ocean and now houses a gentlemanly collection of horses, sheep, pigs, and chickens for the amusement of guests in residence.

The Friedmans—he a colossally successful developer in Boston—vacated with their baby to a house located far out on the point. Close to the mouth of the dirt road winding to Oyster Pond, a small army of government muscle men set up tents, mobile units, and a communications system. At night their lights—run by generators—burned with the intensity of a small factory in the middle of the wilderness. You could spot the encampment from the Edgartown/West Tisbury Road. Only the most insane autograph seeker or protesting crackpot would dare to cross *that* checkpoint.

Occasionally Bill's island idyll would be spoiled by a determined nonfan. On a sunny day in August 1999, a year after the president's ordeal with *l'affaire* Lewinsky, a woman paraded through the streets of Oak Bluffs with a black banner bearing an image of Clinton's face and the single word *Rapist*.

Another day, as Bill marched toward the tony restaurant Balance, in Oak Bluffs, he was accosted by a heckler. In a story filed in the August 24 edition of the *Vineyard Gazette*, it was reported that a young man was outraged because Boston police ticketed bicycle couriers for pedaling *sans* helmets.

"What do you intend to do about it, huh?" he yelled at the leader of the western world.

Clinton, rather than ignoring the ill-timed challenge, spun around and got right up in the young man's face. He told the courier that a friend of his, a Democratic fund-raiser named Dan Dutko, had died the month before in a bike riding accident: The man would be alive today, he added with the jab of a finger, if he'd been wearing a helmet.

The summer of '98, what with the Lewinsky mess and the whole deplorable impeachment process, was a decidedly low-key version of Clinton's champagne-corks-flying visits. That August we barely knew he was anywhere on island. No glitzy parties or gala touchdowns in any of the stores were heard about or seen. He was reportedly in the doghouse with Hillary; in fact, rumors were flying that she had refused to accompany him at all. We imagined him in the Oyster Pond farmhouse with only a few key associates hunched around the TV watching comedies in an attempt to take the man's mind off the tragicomedy his life had become.

Then, in a page taken from the movie *Wag the Dog*, where a fictional president tries to take the heat off a personal scandal by igniting a war, Bill Clinton made international headlines from the modest small-town venue of the Edgartown school. Once again the grounds had been furnished with all the cables and satellites required to reach the outside world. On August 21, the president announced the bombing of terrorist camps in Afghanistan and Sudan, declaring to news media all over the world, "I have said many times that terrorism is one of the greatest dangers we face in this

global era." Pretty prescient, huh? Maybe if Congress had been a little less anxious to nail the man for a bit of slap and tickle, as the English say, he might have been able to eradicate the Osama Bin Laden problem before a much less competent leader took office.

Since that summer of his discontent, Bill's visits to the Vineyard have been laid back. He's crossed the thresholds of so many businesses that any islanders who've still not met him are either living in caves or wearing sunglasses so dark they've missed the man's shock of white-gold hair, deeply burnished tan, and turquoise—I'm telling you, they're an unreal shade of blue—eyes.

The summer of 2003 Bill Clinton spent a quarter of an hour in my little bookstore in Oak Bluffs. At the time I was sharing the space with yet another outlet of the Black Dog, and it was into this emporium of tee shirts and black lab–bedizened gewgaws that the former president made his way. As he sauntered through the double doors, he glanced at me behind the register, nodded, waved, and called, "Howyadoin'?"

At first I wondered why a Clinton impersonator was browsing in the Black Dog, but then three buff young men clad in jeans and gaudy Hawaiian shirts followed in a tight triangle formation. They continued their surveillance from different angles as Bill put together a pile of clothes, handing them to the girl, along with his credit card, at the checkout counter.

The whole time I sat breathlessly waiting for the president to slap his forehead as he remembered his last notorious visit to the Black Dog. It was all over the news—the summer of 1997 when Bill bought a Black Dog tee (size Large?) for Monica. If he recalled this tiny smudge in his Vineyard scrapbook, he showed no indication of it. And then he wandered into *my* store.

Normally shy, I nonetheless had to grab my opportunity to meet the former head honcho. He held Hillary's best-selling memoir in his hands. I told him how briskly it was selling—more copies had flown off the shelves, in fact, than the similarly high-flying *Harry Potter and the Order of the Phoenix.*

"Really?" He asked, as if he truly didn't know that his wife's new book was the top-grossing nonfiction release of all time.

By the following summer, Bill's own autobiography had appeared, the long-awaited *My Life.* Although I personally sold more copies of Hillary's book, at thirty-five bucks a pop (and a heavy 800-plus-page pop at that), Bill's cinder-block–sized tome may have brought in more revenue.

But back to his visit to my store: He had enjoyed maybe ten minutes of leisure in the Black Dog, another three minutes of charming me, and perhaps another ten minutes to graze the mystery section. He perused at length the historical mysteries by such authors as Umberto Eco, Barbara Hambly, and Ellis Peters. But at last the buzz on the street triggered a noise level and a swarming of bodies like a billion cicadas descending on a field. The security unit had already ascertained that escape through the back would land the man knee-deep in garbage and a recent skunk dowsing. In what seemed like a single deft motion, the three men bustled Mr. Clinton out the front doors, onto the street, and into one of a convoy of three white vans that conveniently rolled up at that precise moment.

And I didn't get a chance to sell him even a paperback mystery.

Johnny, We Hardly Knew Ye ...

Much like Bill Clinton, John F. Kennedy Jr. had enough interesting things to say, and a sufficiently affable disposition, that the paparazzi could get their fill of him and leave him in peace. By revealing even a trace of substance, he avoided being a hidden hothouse flower like Princess Diana and his own mother.

Seemingly he liked everyone and carried no grudges. As a journalist, he once interviewed his dad's archenemy, Fidel Castro. He also sat down with Larry Flynt, publisher of *Hustler,* who some years earlier had printed topless photos of John's mother on Skorpios. Yes, John Jr. was thought to be an ordinary bloke, an ordinary bloke who also happened to be unimaginably rich, gorgeous, and *People* magazine's 1988 choice for Sexiest Man Alive.

A regular guy.

Not that on the Vineyard he spent any time fishing with locals or schmoozing down at the barbershop. Still, whenever he stayed at his mother's estate in Aquinnah, long-time neighbors grew accustomed to seeing him roller-blading down Moshup Trail or biking up to the cliffs or laying down a few treads of rubber in his convertible '66 black GTO, top down, music blaring. He waved at familiar faces. The consensus among Aquinnians was that John Jr.'s manner was indistinguishable from any other summer preppie's. One local even overheard the former president's son say to a local teen, "Dude, you got excellent skates!"

His reputation as a spoiled frat boy, tequila-and-beer-swilling slob, especially when he had his mother's house to himself and thirty of his nearest and dearest friends, gave way to a more mature version of the tall, devilishly handsome scion. He studied law and, although he failed the bar exam twice, ended up with a pass. He went on to work at the Manhattan D.A.'s office.

His dating style was that of any high-profile playboy: he was a modelizer and a starletizer.

Possessed with a reasonable amount of smarts, he founded a political magazine, *George.* In spite of Cindy Crawford posed as a bare-bellied George Washington on the very first cover, *George* never achieved the amusement level expected of it. In 1996 John Jr. married BU grad and Calvin Klein executive Carolyn Bessette. Within another three years, the deep blue sea had swallowed him and his slim, ultra-blonde wife.

A proclivity for danger, for thrills and chills, never quite left John Jr. There's an early snapshot of him at the age of three as he hurtles his tough little body at his daddy alighting from a helicopter. This shot of filial worship was apparently misleading. A faithful retainer to the First Family revealed years later that dad had actually just waylaid the toddler from scrambling onto the chopper.

Later, when John Jr. zoomed around the Vineyard in his vintage Pontiac, police chief Beth Toomey, of West Tisbury, told a *Gazette* reporter in August of 1999 that she often shouted out to him to slow down.

The fact that his Uncle Joe and his Aunt Kathleen had died in plane crashes failed to stop John Jr. in 1998 from taking flying lessons in Vero Beach, Florida.

Do we get the impression the Kennedys fly too much?

On the fateful night of July 16, 1999, John Jr. had been flying for a year. He had yet to qualify for piloting with low visibility, which in turn meant reliance on an instrument panel. But, defying common sense, and with hazy weather looming, John Jr. took off from New Jersey in his single-engine Piper with his wife and her sister, Lauren Bessette, as passengers. In an ironic twist, one of the last photographs of the beautiful pair shows Carolyn at the airport with her dashing husband, a flight manual tucked beneath her arm.

The plan had been to drop Lauren off at the Vineyard, then puddle hop over to Hyannis for a wedding. Some twelve and a half miles off the shore of his late mother's island home, John Jr.'s Piper blipped off the radar screen. A search and rescue team mobilized. A battalion of choppers circled overhead in ever-narrowing grids, with Coast Guard ships anchored off-shore. By the end of the following day, "search and rescue" had been changed to "search and recovery." No survival was possible after so many hours in 68-degree waters. John was thirty-eight, Carolyn thirty-three, and Lauren thirty-four. When the bodies were finally hauled up from the depths, the sisters' remains were shipped home to their parents. John was buried at sea—his closest associates maintained he would have wanted it that way.

Had the Kennedy curse followed John Jr. over the Atlantic, blocking his flight plan to the Martha's Vineyard airport? The curse might have had something to do with it, but so did his reckless piloting and his own youthful sense of invulnerability.

For weeks following the crash, with national and international news agencies fairly shrieking with the tragedy, islanders who stood for hours at the cliffs, eyes trained on the rescue effort, all commented that they could never again enjoy this view.

Given time though, an islander can't help but revel in the sweeping vistas from the westernmost edge of the island, just as we're more likely to recall John Jr. when we see a game of touch football—that sport so beloved of Kennedys everywhere—in a distant field or a riotous tossing of frisbees or someone on roller blades whooshing down Moshup or a guy driving just a wee bit too fast around a sharp Vineyard curve.

Murder Most Foul

An Examination of a Handful of Killings During 300 Years,
All of Them Bearing a Certain Vineyard *Je Ne Sais Quoi*

The First Recorded Killing

TYPICALLY, WITH CRIMES from so long ago, we retain little written information about the circumstances. On the books, therefore, the first murder trial on the Vineyard took place in 1650 when Chief Nohono of Aquinnah (the name changed later to Gay Head, and in recent years back to Aquinnah) showed up in the white man's court in Great Harbour (now Edgartown). The chief wore full Indian regalia complete with an impressive beaded headdress bristling with feathered insignia. He had come to answer for the killing of his wife, Celina.

No record remains of his sentence.

The Second Recorded Killing

AGAIN, WITH LITTLE to go on, we do know that in 1664 an Indian woman was discovered murdered at the western tip of the island, also in Aquinnah. The perpetrator was believed to be a Wampanoag named Pommatock, although he wasn't brought to justice until 1689, a full twenty-five years after the killing. Yet the Colonial judge presiding over the case could not have been more indignant about the crime if it had occurred the week before. He ordered that "Pommatock, Indian, shall be executed the 26th of September, 1689, for murder, done in or about 1664, until he is dead, dead, dead."

Now there's a magistrate without a shred of ambivalence toward capital punishment.

And Again in Aquinnah— Was It Something in the Water?

THE SCENE WAS LIKE something out of a crime novel: In the winter of 1823 an Indian woman named Mary Cuff was found dead on the beach. She was battered and bruised, her body smeared with the uncommon red clay of the cliffs. Suspicion fell immediately on a black man who'd joined the tribe a couple of years before. A free man of color, originally from New York, he'd assimilated himself—or so he must have believed—in the Wampanoag melting pot.

Unhappily for Richard Johnson, an argument with the victim from months earlier now surfaced to render him a favorite for the crime.

It hardly helped that on the day of the murder, he and the victim had again engaged in a public shouting match.

On the autumn day in question, Mary Cuff had wandered into the fields to gather bayberries, prized for their fragrance when blended with wax for candles. Mary had ended up with more than she could carry, so she hailed Richard Johnson as he passed by with his horse and wagon, hoping for a lift home. He refused. We can only guess he had his reasons. Perhaps Mary had been haughty in the past, and now was making nice only to procure a favor.

They hollered back and forth, their insults audible around the village. Mary trudged home with whatever bayberries she could haul in a pair of pails. When her husband, David, learned the source of her ill temper, he rushed out to confront Richard Johnson. When he found him, he boxed the man's ears. Johnson slouched away, swearing revenge on them both.

On Sunday morning, March 2, an hour before dawn, Mary, again in gatherer mode, had arisen to collect driftwood on the beach. Her body was discovered the following Tuesday. A one-cent oak club, splotched with blood, was later recovered five miles up the shore.

What no one found peculiar was that David Cuff had neglected to report his spouse missing until that same Tuesday morning. Did it normally take his wife more than two days to harvest driftwood from the beach? But the community of Aquinnians had grown up with David Cuff, and to turn on him was to turn on family. Far easier to point the finger at this recent arrival in their midst, this person of another race, this "stranger," Richard Johnson.

The black man was remanded to Barnstable County for custody. An excellent lawyer was appointed to defend him, one John Reed, of Yarmouth, who would later become lieutenant governor of Massachusetts. Mr. Reed demonstrated to the jury that all the evidence against the defendant was hopelessly circumstantial. It was not unlikely that in the mind of judge, jury, and every inhabitant of Aquinnah, the logical candidate for the crime was David Cuff, husband and late-responder.

We've seen enough *Law and Order* segments and read enough legal thrillers to know how Mary Cuff's murder would have been handled today. David Cuff would have spent untold hours in a fluorescent-lit interrogation room. Whether or not he confessed, his DNA would have been recovered from under his wife's fingernails, and some of his own blood might have ended up on that one-cent oak club.

But 1823 was light-years away from modern justice and forensics. Although Richard Johnson was acquitted, he left the Vineyard, never to return, and who can blame him? In time the questionable David married a second Mrs. Cuff, and we can only pray that she died of natural causes.

Who Killed William Cook Luce?

TWO NIGHTS BEFORE Christmas of 1863, out in the harbor of Holmes Hole (now Vineyard Haven) dozens of two- and three-masted schooners gleamed in the moonlight. Onshore, hundreds of sailors set up volleys of shouts and laughter as they drank and caroused their way through town. Down by the docks, William Cook Luce banged closed the shutters of his tiny grocery store. He wiped clean the counter and prepared to join his wife and three small children for seven o'clock dinner. He never made it home.

Two hours later, his worried wife dispatched two of her children to the shop to see what had detained their father. In the darkened grocery, they found him dead on the floor, a hatchet lodged in his skull. Somewhere between two hundred and five hundred dollars had been taken from his satchel.

Some assumed that one of the rough-and-ready sailors had robbed and killed him. In fact, the local constabulary arrested three sailors from a Bangor schooner, but soon discharged the men for lack of evidence. It may have dawned on the police that none of the scores of sailors thronging the town that night could be incontrovertibly charged with the crime. Easier to search closer to home.

The sheriff, John Luce (yes, he was the father of the slain man), mounted a campaign to depose alibis from every last citizen of Holmes Hole. Of everyone interviewed, a retired sea captain named Gustavus Smith, questioned on January 12, had the murkiest alibi, which is to say, none whatsoever. He had no recollection of what he had been doing on the night of December 23.

But—quick!—what were *you* doing twenty nights ago? Let's be honest: for many of us it's difficult to remember what we did *two* nights ago.

Here is the background for poor Gustavus (let's dispense with the more formal "Captain Smith" since the name Gustavus rolls so trippingly from the tongue): The retired sea captain's wife was an invalid. Gustavus hadn't the means to hire help, so he himself tended to her, gruelingly enough, night and day. At least once during every twenty-four-hour stretch of nursing duties, however, he yearned for a break—to take a walk, sniff the sea air, something. To this end, he asked the neighborhood women to spell him at his wife's bedside.

The wives began to resent his habitual requests, and soon, when they saw him coming, locked their doors and blew out the lamps. Who can explain this want of generosity? For the most part the Vineyard is known for its caring souls. It's hard to imagine that the town wouldn't have organized a posse to take turns with his ailing wife. Perhaps old Gustavus whined or demanded or neglected to thank those who helped him out. We can only assume that he'd made enough of a nuisance of himself that townsfolk following the murder jumped to the conclusion that Gustavus Smith had killed for the money to pay for his wife's care.

For ten full months before he received acoourt hearing, poor Gustavus was held in the Edgartown House of Corrections. During this time islanders divided into two camps: the pro-Gustavusians and the anti-Gustavusians. Fights broke up a great many friendships and dinner parties. At last the court in Taunton ordered the controversial prisoner brought to its district for arraignment.

The Edgartown jailer, Mr. Daggett, who was eighty years old and in frail health, appointed himself to transport Gustavus to Taunton. In the end the hardier and nominally younger prisoner escorted the deputy offshore. He hauled his keeper through snowdrifts lining the docks and helped him board the boat. Off island, Gustavus gave the jailer a boost onto the train to Taunton. Witnesses watching the two stagger over the snow believed that Mr. Daggett was the prisoner; they felt a wrench of compassion for his infirmities.

The Taunton judge listened to the evidence —or lack of it—and ruled that there was no possibility of convicting the retired sea captain. He released Gustavus on his own recognizance, ordering him to appear when wanted.

He was never wanted.

No record exists concerning what happened to poor Mrs. Smith, ailing for ten months without her husband's round-the-clock nursing. Perhaps the grudging neighbors had rallied 'round in the husband's absence, or maybe she had died with blessed speed.

And here's an interesting postscript: Following Gustavus's release, it came to light that an unnamed young man of Holmes Hole had been slated to marry the night that Mr. Luce was slain. At 6 p.m. he confided to his wife-to-be that he had no gloves with which to make himself presentable for the ceremony. She reminded him he was penniless, advising that he forget about the gloves. But as we all know, when a man has gloves on his mind, it's hard to shake him loose of his compulsion. He told his bride he'd go out and get his hands on some cash.

The wedding was to take place at 8 p.m. and for half an hour the bride and guests exchanged anxious glances. At 8:30 the groom finally appeared. He held up his hands to show off a new pair of burgundy red kid leather gloves.

As time went on and townsfolk mulled over the odd circumstances of the glove-crazed bridegroom in need of cash, they began to suspect him of Mr. Luce's murder. Not a single lawman ever followed up on the rumor, however. In deference to Mr. Fancy Glove's descendants, the family name was never disclosed in connection with the hideous crime. It's anybody's guess whose ancestor murdered the grocer, and whether or not a living descendant carries a pathological gene; after all, the mental health of anyone who would kill for a pair of burgundy-dyed kid leather gloves has got to be a bit funky.

Legend has it that the perpetrator confessed on his deathbed in a Connecticut hospital. But the family name still remains a secret. "Murder will out" is a not a surefire guarantee, but how nice it would be if, some one-hundred-forty-plus years later, poor Captain Gustavus Smith's tarnished family escutcheon might be shined up bright again.

"Rich Farmer Slain by Jealous Rival"

SUCH WAS THE LURID headline in a New Bedford daily in the early spring of 1904. On Chappaquiddick, the little island off the town of Edgartown on Martha's Vineyard, a forty-three-year-old gentleman farmer named Charles Pease was found murdered in a small grove on his property. He'd been shot through the mouth. His own rifle lay a few feet away from him. Suicide was ruled out when the coroner decreed that the rifle trigger lay too far from the man's fingers. He may have had the dexterity to fire with his toes, but he had died with his boots on.

His body was discovered on a Wednesday. He'd been married since the previous Saturday to a bride about whom Vineyarders knew absolutely nothing.

Family and friends of Charles Pease had always supposed the farmer would spend the rest of his days in his chosen role of confirmed bachelor. Well known and universally liked, he'd inherited a large tract of land in the area called Tom's Neck off Chappy's northern shore. He farmed his property just enough to subsist with a minimum level of comfort. In other words, he had the farm on early twentieth-century autopilot, which freed him up to fish to his heart's desire. He was a very Vineyard kind of guy.

But in early 1904 he began to talk of getting married. When his surprised friends and neighbors asked where he expected to find a bride, he replied, "Not around these parts."

And then one weekend, the aforementioned Saturday, as the first crocuses were beginning to push through the frozen ground, Charles Pease returned from a trip to the mainland with his freshly wedded sweetheart.

Vineyarders who caught glimpses of the lady described her as sensationally attractive, tall, blonde, about thirty years of age, and dressed in city clothes. Those who had a chance to exchange a few words with her said she was amiable but reluctant to discuss her background other than to say that she'd been a schoolteacher in Sweden.

During the next couple of days, neighbors observed the newlyweds as they toured the farm, she in her fancy clothes and lace-up boots. She clung to her husband's arm as he pointed out the many details of her new home, with which she seemed enchanted. His dogs rambled at his feet. The new Mrs. Pease carried a golf club and told everyone she encountered that she planned to teach her husband "the royal sport of Scotland."

Come Wednesday at noon, Mr. Pease left the house with a promise to be back within a quarter hour. By two p.m. his bride began to worry. A neighbor named Charles Beetle happened by, and the lovely Swede expressed her concern. Mr. Beetle told her it was not uncommon for Vineyard men to roust about away from home for the entire day, but the bride was still distraught.

"He's in danger," she whispered.

After an hour of searching the property, Mr. Beetle found the body of Charles Pease, dead by gunshot. As Vineyard authorities performed their usual lackadaisical job of hunting down the killer, they discovered a single intriguing fact: For several days, inhabitants along the Tom's Neck shore had observed an unknown yacht in the water. By the time the news of the murder spread, however, the boat had vanished.

And so had the new Mrs. Pease.

The police concluded—as did the newspapers—that a spurned lover of the bride's had followed her and her groom to the island, and in a rage of jealousy shot the farmer.

Again, we might ponder modern-day detection. A team of interrogators would have confined the Scandinavian lass to an airless room and grilled her until she gave up the names of past boyfriends. From there they might have matched up one of her husband's rivals with the owner of a particular yacht, and perhaps produced enough incriminating evidence to convict someone.

For years after the murder, the hundred or so inhabitants of Chappaquiddick exploited the story as an object lesson on the inadvisability of marrying off-islanders.

Just Another Killing in Paradise

THEY KNEW WHODUNIT, but no one had ever figured out why, and in that respect the murder of Knight Owen still lies shrouded in mystery. No one could have foreseen the violent end to the man's life, and nothing in the setting was, at least on the surface, disturbing in any way. It was the kind of killing that gives us a momentary shiver because it could happen to any one of us.

On a warm September afternoon in 1935, a small group of friends gathered in damp bathing suits on a secluded beach. Lazily, tipsily, they sipped highballs and debriefed each other about their afternoon bluefishing excursion. As they talked, they took turns with a .22 rifle, popping desultory shots at tin cans. (Typically, once the mainland press swooped in to describe the murder scene, this banal afternoon event was transformed into a glamorous cocktail party.)

Rustic plain-shingled dwellings with kerosene lamps for lighting and outhouses in place of indoor plumbing sat deep in the sands of this Tisbury beach, accessed from a long bumpy road that wound through the woods. Few of these "camps" remain today, but in earlier times they dotted our beaches. Four sat on this particular spit of sand where Herring Creek swooshed in and out into the wide embrace of Vineyard Sound.

Only one tenant spent every day of the year in this spot. Harold Look, fifty-four years old, with sun-weathered features, crinkly blue eyes, and dry Yankee humor, must have seemed, on the surface at least, like a twentieth-century Henry David Thoreau. He loved his solitude and considered himself both CEO and caretaker of this slice of paradise. As a manager for the Tisbury town waterworks, he also controlled the outflow of the creek. He knew the tides the way a gambler knows a deck of cards. For all his alone time, he was surprisingly sociable. His door was always open for Vineyarders who cared to grind the bottoms of their cars along the twisty road to hang out in his mildew-scented living room to drink beer and swap stories.

Born on the Vineyard, Mr. Look had spent time in the real world, clerking, patrolling, cleaning up, moving on. For the greater part of his off-island career he worked for the railroad. As Henry Beetle Hough, editor of the *Vineyard Gazette*, later described Harold Look's lot in life: "He was the man the traveler saw at work under a drop light as the train pulled into the station . . . the underdog, the restless, shifting, marginal worker."

When the Depression made finding and keeping nominal jobs ever more difficult, Mr. Look returned to the island and took up residence at the mouth of Tashmoo Pond's Herring Creek.

The railroad man turned beachcomber took a personal interest in the other dwellers of the camps—all of them summer people. He was especially fond and protective of an attractive New York socialite, divorcee Lydia Hyde, thirty-eight, who brought her four kids and handyman for indolent sun and surf days and low-key cocktail party nights. There was nothing to suggest that Mr. Look and Mrs. Hyde had ever engaged in anything approaching intimate relations. All that anybody had ever witnessed were the times the year-rounder dropped off a bucket of quahogs at the back door of the Hyde camp, or both of them lounged with mutual friends on someone's deck. In true Vineyard fashion, the New York sophisticate and the island hermit waived all social boundaries on the strip of sand they both adored.

Of course, no one knew what lurked in the depths of Mr. Look's regard for Mrs. Hyde. It seems clear in retrospect that he harbored for his attractive neighbor unbidden romantic urges. If he believed these urges were reciprocated, then, like so many so-called stalkers, he was delusional in the extreme.

It was noted that forty-two-year-old Knight Owen was more Ms. Hyde's friend than Mr. Look's, even though both men were descended from two of the island's original families. They had known each other for most of their lives. But the crotchety caretaker was blunt about his dislike for the more gently bred Owen, once declaring, "I could take Knight Owen and hold a sponge over his face or keep his head underwater until he drowned, and then tie him to a raft and ship him anywhere I liked because I know the tides." Outbursts like that elicited laughter from his listeners. "Oh, that Harold," seemed to be the reaction to such intemperate comments.

For, indeed, Knight Owen had an obnoxious streak, most of it exacerbated by alcohol. Mr. Owen's grandfather was Vineyard whaling captain Leander Owen, and his father was the William Barry Owen who invented the Victrola record player. Young Knight was raised with all the trimmings—boarding school followed by a degree from MIT. Life's slings and arrows winged their way to him, however, one right after the other: the loss of his family's fortune; a devastating stint in the air force during Word War I, when he crashed his plane in the North Sea and was left with a case of what they then called shell shock; a Boston brokerage career that disintegrated after the Stock Market Crash of 1929.

He'd returned to the Vineyard to write for the *Gazette*, but most of his two-dollar weekly earnings paid for his booze—a buck fifty could buy a lot more gin in those days. Some folks, when they drink too much, are considerate enough to pass out before they seriously bother anyone. When Knight Owen drank too much he kept on going like the Energizer bunny; he lurched into furniture, broke pottery, overturned lamps, cackled loudly, and told endless jokes and pointless stories.

That was precisely his form on that fateful afternoon in September when he turned up at Lydia Hyde's cottage while Mrs. Hyde and some visiting friends shot at tin cans on the beach. Mr. Owen's arrival provoked them into dispersing to their cabins in an effort to avoid him. Casting about for fresh company, he invaded Harold Look's space for the last time. Mr. Look followed Owen to his car, where, in full view of a nearby witness, he pointed a revolver and fired four shots, three of which pierced the drunkard's body.

Mr. Look tossed the gun into Tashmoo Pond, marched into Mrs. Hyde's cottage, and woke her from a nap. In front of her, her kids, and the handyman he announced, "I did what I said I was going to do."

"What are you talking about?" she asked.

He reminded her of an earlier threat that she'd scarcely taken seriously: that if she continued to allow Knight Owen to hang out with her and her friends on the beach, he would kill the man. Mission accomplished.

Mr. Look returned to his shack to change into his only suit and tie. He marched east along the beach toward town. The first person he encountered was a local doctor fishing the shore.

Harold Look told him, "I just shot a man. I want to give myself up."

Thinking he ws joking, the doctor thought suggested he borrow one of the rowboats nearby and row off in the opposite direction. Eventually the befuddled killer reached a paved road and surrendered to a passing patrol car.

The off-island newspapers had a field day with the murder story, with headlines going tabloidal:

RICH MAN SLAIN IN FIGHT OVER WOMAN

WAR ACE KILLED IN A BATTLE OVER WOMAN'S LOVE

BROKER SLAIN IN CAPE LOVE FEUD

LOVER KILLED, RIVAL HELD

At his trial, Harold Look was judged to be insane. He was sent away for lifelong incarceration in what in those days was called a loony bin.

Still, the story gives us pause. Many solitary retreatants live on this island, and on so many other islands, as well as tucked into all the backwoods of America. How many are modern-day Thoreaus and how many are Ted Kaczynskis?

Murder at the Rice Playhouse

IT WAS A DARK and stormy night. Truly, it was. In the wee hours of June 30, 1940, a northeast wind was smashing waves against the cliffs, and the foghorn tolled mournfully. In her dormitory room at the Rice Playhouse in East Chop, a seventy-year-old widow named Clara Smith had a date with a dark destiny.

The police reconstructed the crime as follows: Clara Smith lay sleeping in her bed. At approximately two o'clock in the morning an intruder thrust open the window and burst into her room. Mrs. Smith awoke, bolted upright and yanked the cord on the lamp by her bedside. Startled by the sudden light and movement, the intruder seized the woman by the throat and struck her three times with a heavy object. He may or may not have known that he'd killed her, but as his victim lay prone across her bed, he wrested a ring from her finger and a valuable watch from her limp wrist.

Several of the women in nearby rooms were awakened by Clara Smith's screams, but each and every one of them imagined a dorm mate was merely in the grip of a nightmare. They tossed and turned on their mattresses and lapsed back into sleep. Not that it mattered; the savage attack killed the woman with such swiftness that no one could have rescued her in time.

A devout member of the Christian Science Church, Clara Smith could not have been a more blandly innocent victim. She had hoped to take on a greater leadership role with her congregation and, toward that end, she'd decided a summer of elocution lessons at the Rice Playhouse would be just the thing to better read scriptures aloud.

The theater had been founded in the early 1900s by Broadway impresario Phidelah (another name not expected to make a comeback) Rice. Set above the seaward cliffs of East Chop, the playhouse lured summer audiences for the views as much as for the playbill. Only half a mile down the road, the summer resort of Oak Bluffs teemed with visitors eager for every form of entertainment. When they tired of strolling the boardwalk, nibbling taffy, and listening to the band in Ocean Park, they were happy to amble up the cliffs to catch a play fresh from New York and performed by an equity cast.

In time the success of the theater inspired Phidelah Rice to expand operations. Two dormitories were constructed along the cliffs, one for men and one for women. Other facilities were built for support staff and to provide dining facilities. By the time of Clara Smith's murder in 1940, the Playhouse encompassed a handsome and dignified campus much like a small Ivy League college. Theatrical celebrities such as Katharine Cornell, who had her own estate across the bay, lent her patronage to the playhouse.

Killer Performance

The Rice Playhouse, august theatre and academy (and site of an unsolved murder), once loomed over the sea in East Chop.
MARTHA'S VINEYARD HISTORICAL SOCIETY COLLECTIONS (env. 215)

Until that fateful stormy night, the theater's stock could not have risen higher. No one would have believed that the diseased mind of a murderer lurked in the halls of the Rice Playhouse.

The police clamped down on two suspects. One was Ralph Huntington Rice, fifty-two, drama teacher and brother of the far more illustrious Phidelah. His neurasthenic personality caused the authorities to suspect him. He fell apart the morning Mrs. Smith's body was found and the entire campus placed in lockdown. Surrounded as he was by stoic New Englanders accustomed to holding pat as ships broke up around them in a hurricane, Mr. Rice stood out as he paced the floor, pulled his hair, and vocalized his distress in gibbering English. The lawmen rifled through his room. They found out who his associates were, and one of them, several days later, unwittingly gave up an incriminating piece of evidence: On the morning of June 30, Mr. Rice had started a letter to a woman friend in Manhattan. On July 1—or so he later maintained—he added a postscript about the killing, remarking "I couldn't conceive of anyone coming into a dormitory and murdering an innocent woman like that." The New York friend, coincidentally, was also a Christian Scientist, and many turned to her for spiritual guidance, among them Ralph Rice. The postmark on the envelope of Mr. Rice's letter was dated June 30, at or before 11:00 a.m. This placed the suspect's news ahead of the time that anyone on the Rice campus knew of the murder.

Another suspect was arrested too, one Harold Tracy, an electrician and handyman employed full-time at the theater. His rooms, too, had been searched, and he was charged with possession of a concealed weapon, a revolver. The police learned that Mr. Tracy had served a ten-year prison sentence on a robbery conviction, that he was wanted for a jewelry heist in Kentucky in 1937, and that he had incurred a drunk driving arrest in Chicago a couple of years before.

Who was responsible for the crime, the nervous Nellie of a professor or an armed thug with a rap sheet?

Answer: Ralph Huntington Rice was the favored perpetrator, and was remanded to the Edgartown jail. Harold Tracy was packed off to the Barnstable House of Correction, a secondary suspect kept in reserve.

Ralph Rice's trial took place in September 1940. The defense cast doubt on the envelope that had purportedly contained the incriminating letter—the lady in New York had handed over Ralph Rice's correspondence without any clear indication of which envelopes, with their telltale postmarks, matched up with which letters. (It turned out that Mr. Rice wrote to his spiritual guide daily, or close to it.) His plea for spiritual direction began to look more and more like an S.O.S. from a deeply stressed man. He wasn't a killer; he was just a nervous wreck. The jurors sequestered themselves for a refreshingly brief forty-five minutes and returned a verdict of innocent.

During the testimony at the trial, it began to look increasingly as if the handyman and ex-convict Harold Tracy had killed Clara Smith. He'd been dating a beautiful young student named Marjorie Massow, who happened to inhabit the room next door to Clara Smith's. Furthermore, the older ladies in the dormitory, religious students like Clara Smith, had complained to the office about Mr. Tracy and Miss Massow keeping company, and the handyman had on at least one occasion expressed his ire toward "those bible biddies."

An assistant stage manager at the playhouse, a young man named William Everett Moll, testified that on the night of the murder Harold Tracy gave him a ride into town. The minute Moll climbed into the passenger seat, alcohol fumes wafted over from the driver. Tracy plied the foot pedals in fits and starts, and after a harrowing ride past the harbor, Moll asked to be let out, but not before he tried to persuade the driver to go home and sleep off his bender.

Tracy hollered as he pulled away, "I'm going out tonight and get a woman, and I don't give a damn if she's an Indian."

So now two facts had emerged: On the night of the murder, Harold Tracy was filthy drunk and uncontrollably horny (not to mention abominably bigoted). A possible scenario was that in this reckless and randy frame of mind, he decided to pay a call on Marjorie, who may or may not have satisfied his carnal needs. Climbing the exterior wall to what he believed was Marjorie's room, he plummeted into poor Clara Smith's quarters by mistake. When the woman flashed on the light, the vicious drunk realized that not only had he not surprised the luscious Marjorie, but he also had before him a spitting mad elderly Christian Scientist. Enraged, he lunged for her, bashing her head with whatever was handy—her lamp? His revolver? Then, seeing her unconscious or dead on the mattress, he made the best of the situation by filching her ring and watch.

The morning after the murder, Mr. Moll again encountered Mr. Tracy. At breakfast the man was ashen and hungover. He told the stage manager, "Something happened last night at Sumner Hall, and I am involved." Then he hung his head and nearly pitched himself into his Cream of Wheat.

Finally, in testimony at Ralph Rice's trial, Mrs. Mercer, a secretary at the playhouse, reported that on the night of June 30, afflicted with insomnia, she stood at her window to assess the storm and saw Harold Tracy scrambling away from the women's dormitory.

In Barnstable, Harold Tracy learned that the wheels of justice were grinding their way slowly but inexorably toward him. Within another ten days he would be remanded back to Edgartown for questioning by the grand jury. On April 25, 1941, he escaped from the Barnstable jail and disappeared into the hinterlands.

The wheels of justice continued to grind. Three times in Edgartown, Harold Tracy was pronounced, in absentia, guilty of the murder of Clara Smith.

Some fifteen years later, the Edgartown chief of police received a call from authorities in Kentucky. They had a freshly convicted armed robber in their custody. Records had revealed that the man, Harold Tracy, was wanted for murder on Martha's Vineyard. Would the chief care to have the suspect extradited north to stand trial?

Perhaps with so few murders committed over the past centuries, inertia all too easily sets in. After the Vineyard police received the news about the captured killer of Clara Smith, they apparently sat around the station scratching their heads. Had they lost the paperwork? Was the fishing derby in full swing? The police chief eventually got back on the phone with an answer for the Kentucky lawman: "Nah."

Too many years had elapsed since poor

Clara Smith had been snatched away from her bible studies and her elocution lessons.

There was another casualty of the crime. The unsolved—or at least not prosecuted—murder hung over the Rice Playhouse like the stormy night that had set the scene for the dastardly deed. Crowds dropped off. The big names of Broadway no longer wished to associate themselves with the theater that now reminded people of the House of Usher. By the end of the 1940s, the last of the staff at the Rice establishment pulled up stakes. Eventually the dormitories, the campus, and the theater itself met the implacable swing of the wrecking ball. Nothing remains today except a few ghosts and some distant memories.

An interesting postscript: After leaving the playhouse, Marjorie Massow moved to Hollywood and changed her name to Madge Meredith. She won a number of small parts in movies, enough to give her hope, but perhaps not enough to pay the rent. In 1947, at the age of twenty-seven, she and three men lured Miss Meredith's manager into a lonely canyon, where the victim was beaten and robbed. She and her associates were later apprehended. Madge Meredith received a sentence of five years to life in Tehachapi Prison, California.

Her crime resonates uncannily with the clubbing and robbing of Clara Smith. Was it possible this evil ingénue had urged an infatuated boyfriend to mug a nice old lady? Or had Marjorie herself perpetrated the crime, allowing first Ralph Rice, and then Harold Tracy to take the fall for it?

Who killed Clara Smith over sixty-five years ago on the East Chop waterfront? If it wasn't Harold Tracy, the culprit could still be alive right here on the island, a man or woman in his or her eighties or nineties, perhaps willing to expiate all sins in a deathbed confession.

Amateur criminologists on the island would love to finally put this cold case to rest.

Kindly Don't Bleed on the Carpet

IN THE LATE 1970s a killing took place in Edgartown that was truly too sad to contemplate.

So we won't.

Well, let me just say that a young man of questionable mental health shot his father, a minister, as the latter emerged from the lobby of one of the island's most beautiful inns.

Originally a whaling captain's home, this particular inn is sumptuous in the extreme, with Persian carpets going back to the Ottoman Empire, oak floors buffed to a high gleam, and wall sconces polished to the very core of their golden brassiness. Most patrons, upon crossing the threshold, suddenly wonder if they remembered to comb their hair, if their stockings are laddered, if the creases in their trousers have been suitably pressed.

After he fired shots into his father's torso, the young man fled, only to be picked up later and, eventually, remanded to a psych ward in Bridgewater, Massachusetts. Later he hanged himself in his cell.

A sad story, a sad, sad story, but here's the part that lifts the tragedy into, if not tragicomedy, then tragi-demifarce: When the wounded minister pounded on the inn's door for succor, no one ran to admit him. Now, perhaps no one heard his thumps for help. Perhaps the concierge was upstairs making beds or in the loo applying Chapstick. But still, word got out that the keepers of this exquisite country inn chose to bar the man from bleeding on their plush carpets. They had not wanted him to inadvertently smear gore on walls and candelabra. And in their defense, there was indeed a great deal of blood, all of it spilled on the front door stoop where the minister collapsed and breathed his last.

Customs of the Country

From Colonial Titles to Gravestones in the Garden:
Vineyarders Doing It Their Way

Island Royals

DON'T FORGET THAT before the American Revolution, the concept of democracy was about as serviceable as today's access to intergalactic travel. (Well, we suppose UFOs whizz around the universe, but we do not do so ourselves . . . yet.) We tend to think of American Colonials as rustic laborers in rags and patches. And indeed they were, for the most part. But during the first one hundred fifty years, England and all her hierarchical ways stood behind the Colonials, and bits and pieces of the old social order found their way to the New World. Aristocrats in the old country had little reason to cross the ocean: If you possess a castle in England and four hundred tenant farmers to run it for you, why would you wish to start over in a log cabin? But that hardly stopped them from taking land grants in the New World—sort of like stock options today—and selling them to up-and-comers eager to re-create the class system in this new wilderness.

And that is precisely what happened in 1642 when the Earl of Stirling and Sir Fernando Gorges in England sold their holdings to title and sovereignty of Martha's Vineyard, Nantucket, and the Elizabeth Islands to one Thomas Mayhew, an Englishman living in Medford, Massachusetts, who thus far had made a hash out of every business venture he'd tackled in the new country. However, a second marriage, to Jane, widow of Thomas Paine, brought Mr. Mayhew fresh finances, so he was able to muster the forty pounds necessary to purchase all that rocky real estate out in the ocean due south of the original Plymouth set-tlement. In 1659 Mayhew passed along his rights to Nantucket for thirty pounds sterling and two beaver hats—one for himself and one for his wife. He sent his son, Matthew, ahead of him to the Vineyard to roll up his sleeves and convert the Indians to Christianity—the better to ease their land away from them—and to make some headway laying down the law with the dozen white families already settled in Edgartown, then called Great Harbour.

When a few years later Mayhew, Sr. arrived on island, the law was precisely what he continued to lay down. As far as he was concerned, his payment of forty pounds granted him

"I am monarch of all I survey. My right here is none to dispute."

absolute power over the one hundred settlers dwelling there. Vineyard historian Charles Banks summed up Thomas Mayhew's attitude by attributing to him the following sentiment: "I am monarch of all I survey. My right here is none to dispute." And now he could get to work conferring upon himself and his family all the airs of a peer of Great Britain.

In 1684 Matthew Mayhew, Thomas's grandson, was made Lord of the Manor of Martha's Vineyard, and his wife, Mary, was therefore Lady of the Manor. The L of the M of MV eventually sold back the title but was allowed to remain L of the M of Tisbury.

And so, inevitably, class consciousness reared its head on the island. Early Vineyarders marked their social level with a prefix before their names. The Mayhews as the ruling family were addressed as Worshipful. Next in social gravitas held the title of Mister, Master, or Missus, denoting a person of gentle birth and a scion of an established family. After that came the nomenclature of Goodman and Goodwife, with the abbreviated Goody; these were the yeomanry or peasantry of New England. The lowest on the rung had, regrettably, no title whatsoever. A Thomas Burchard of Edgartown was recorded as Mr. in 1653, Goodman in 1663, and plain Thomas Burchard in 1673 when he fell into disfavor with the Worshipful Mayhews. At feasts and funerals, food and beverages were dispensed according to social rank, with wives and children securing the status of husbands and fathers.

After the American Revolution all men were called Mister, and not a moment too soon!

Naked Brides

IT WAS AN OLD English rite practiced on the island in Colonial times: The father of the bride was expected to present his future son-in-law with a dower of land. A dowryless bride was held to be naked of worldly goods, and, in order to symbolize her penury, was obliged to wed in the nude. This quaint custom was designed to allow the husband to avoid taking on his wife's family's debts.

Of course we're talking about Puritan days, so the poor and humiliated girl was allowed to wear a shift at the ceremony. We can only hope that none of these smock weddings, as they were called, were carried out in the dead of winter.

It would be nice to think these ceremonies were honored more in the breach than in the observance, but the last on record occurred in Edgartown as late as 1757.

Prenuptials, anyone?

Yesteryear's Glitz

THE VINEYARD WELL TO DO of the late 1600s had the barest of luxuries to set them above the hoi polloi. Candles made of bayberry wax instead of tallow were one. In addition, a well-to-do person possessed at least one book, invariably a heavy theological tome. A respected landowner named Samuel Sarson of Tisbury died in 1703 with a scant four books in his estate.

Early homes were log cabins with mud roofs. No glass was available for windows; light was admitted through oiled paper or bleached cloth set in wood frames. The wealthiest islanders possessed a single Venus glass, otherwise known as a mirror. Beds were the single grand feature of the home, four-posters with feather mattresses, downy pillows, and top knobs draped with valences. Early Vineyarders apparently loved sleep, along with any other activity performed on a mattress. With beds so luxurious, no wonder they figured prominently in last wills and testaments.

On the subject of wills, these documents were, to our minds today, laughably picayune. It's easy to understand why, with the scarcity of worldly goods, mothers denoted which petticoat went to which daughter, and clothing, hats, and shoes were disposed of by name. Houses were often carved up by rooms, with this one inheriting the east front room, that one the bedroom and adjoining buttery, this one the cellar, and another the barn. A man named Samuel Bassett made this bequest to his wife: "All the wood that she shall have occasion for or improve during her natural life and no longer." We can only wonder what he hoped to prevent her from doing with the wood after she died.

Health Care, Colonial Style

IN EARLY TIMES the chief medical treatment for almost every ailment was bloodletting. Until the end of the 1600s, no physicians could be found on the island, so innkeepers stepped in as healers. They dispensed drafts, clysters (an old-fashioned term for enemas), large pills called boluses, and herbs. They set fractures and, most important, let blood, which may also have marked the last procedure inflicted on the patient, considering what we now know to be its dubious side effect—that is to say, death.

Some practitioners of early healing arts sought help from Wampanoag pawwaws (the island term for medicine men). From the beginning, though, the island bestowed upon its citizens a general healthfulness; it has for centuries been called a natural sanitarium. When strolling through our ancient cemeteries, visitors are often struck by the longevity displayed on so many of the tombstones; countless Vineyarders lived into their eighties and even nineties.

Of course even the healthiest specimens cannot avoid death indefinitely, and islanders had their special ways of dealing with their dearly departed. To avoid what in the old country smacked of popery, the dead were buried without prayers or service. The minute the patient ceased to breathe, a pine coffin was hastily cobbled together, and neighbors showed up to carry it on a bier to the cemetery. The well to do had a black velvet pall with tassels, which surely made it more agreeable for them to be dead.

Because of this desire for quick interment, burials often occurred at night by torchlight, a tableau that summons up visions of old vampire movies, though, to the best of this writer's knowledge, no vampires have ever been encountered on Martha's Vineyard.

The Golden Age of Vineyard Whaling: 1830s–1860s

WHALES WERE DRAGGED or harpooned, and oil was expressed from their carcasses. A fortune was made each time a ship returned to its berth in New Bedford, Martha's Vineyard, or Nantucket. In the course of a three- or four-year excursion around the globe, a ship either rode out furious storms or failed to ride them out. Of the New England men who shipped out to sea, three out of five would one day perish in the drink. Whaling was agony. It was also the most glorious of enterprises, offering daily adventure, money for all, and a continuous opportunity to see the whole wide world.

Once a Vineyard captain neglected to kiss his wife good-bye at the wharf. When later his first mate reproached him for this omission, the captain responded, "Why? I'll only be gone six months."

Here's a typical whaling schedule in 1837: the Vineyard bark *Emily* had been at sea twenty days out of Talcahuano, Chile, when Captain Luce finally had time to open the letters received back onshore. He learned that his wife had died six months earlier. The *Emily* arrived in New Bedford three and a half years later with more than a thousand barrels of oil fetching forty-three thousand dollars—the equivalent of several million today. A foremast hand would have received two hundred fifteen dollars for forty-two months labor, before supplies drawn from the ship's slop chest were deducted. Captain Luce, with his "lay" of six percent, would have received two thousand five hundred eighty dollars for the voyage. The owners earned twenty-eight thousand dollars, less overhead and fittings, which they notoriously scrimped on at the expense of human life. On the other hand, if the ship went down, the owners lost every cent of their investment.

A Vineyard boy could sign on between the ages of fifteen and eighteen, and after several grueling years at sea could advance in rank to mate by the age of twenty, and make captain in his mid-twenties. He could retire by the age of forty, fabulously rich by the standards of the day, and become the proud owner of one of the Gothic Revival mansions grouped together like antique tract house developments in the hearts of Vineyard Haven and Edgartown.

A show-off tip: To wow friends and family with your architectural savvy, stand before a Vineyard whaling captain's house and remark in an authoritative voice, "Now there's a handsome example of Greek Revival." How do you identify one? First off, on the island, Greek Revival captains' houses are almost all one-and-a-half stories high, with the second floor delineated by sloping, garret-like rooflines, and they present to the street facades of white clapboard and black shutters. Look for fanlights under the steeples, a front door bracketed by plain Ionic columns, and finally—here's the key part—two windows on one side of the door, only one on the other (or three on one side and two on the other—the important bit is the asymmetry). If the house displays equal numbers of windows on both sides of the front portal, then it's emphatically not Greek Revival. It could be a Cape, a Georgian, a Federal, or even a deconstructed Victorian, but there's no need to bone up on these other styles, as you will have already impressed your companions with your Greek Revival acumen.

Getting back to whaling families, in a nineteenth-century best-selling book, *Yankee Whalers in the South Seas*, the author, A. B. C. Whipple, maintained that master mariners had wives and children in far-off ports of call. Whipple described a typical captain as spending a year or two at home in New England with his original wife and children before sailing off to whatever South Seas Island he used as his base of operations. For the ensuing three- or four-year length of a classic voyage, the captain would cozy up to his Polynesian family as habitually as he chased whales.

New England historians deem this a maritime myth. Whalers had to follow wherever the whales led them, which would have precluded flitting home to a particular native wife for her sago-and-yam pancakes. Also, captains were continually struggling to keep their crews from defecting to paradise; hence, the fewer trips ashore the better. As late as 1893 Captain Gilbert Smith, of Vineyard Haven, recorded in his journal at San Carlos: "Six men deserted, three caught and jailed. Crew found swimming to shore put in irons."

And how did the wives, daughters, and sons of whaling captains fare when the man of the house was off at sea? Well, according to the daughters of Captain George W. Eldridge in their book *The Captains' Daughters of Martha's Vineyard*, published in the early 1900s, life was better when Papa was away. When a man is accustomed to acting the dictator aboard his vessel, he'll continue to run a tight ship while at home. Captain Eldridge frowned at the idea of his daughters doing well at school because it revealed they were slacking off in more important areas such as helping Mother with domestic chores. He hated the sight of homework and forbade any scrap of it under his watch.

The girls bathed once a week in a big tin-lined tub in the kitchen. They entertained seldom, their want of a social life exacerbated by Mother's snobbery. Mrs. Eldridge refused to let her daughters play with the girl across the street because one of her many aunts had long ago borne a child by a sailor. She also frowned on the nearby Hillmans because they worked in the harness factory and were descendants of refugees from the 1847 Irish potato famine. Socailly, the most acceptable families were Methodist, with Baptist families ranking second. In high school the Baptists were known as the other crowd.

And so life clattered on comfortably enough until Father came home again. Speaking of which, there is one piece of whaling lore that needs to be refuted: The so-called widow's walks, those railed platforms at the tiptops of captains' houses, were rarely used to train anxious eyes to sea to spot returning heroes. Instead, much more prosaically, they were designed to make it easier to douse chimney fires. At the first hint of trouble, an occupant of the house could dash up the stairs to the rooftop, water bucket in hand, to splash out errant sparks. If in doing so she raised her eyes to behold her husband's vessel gliding into port after a four-year hiatus, well, so much the better. Or not.

Those Wacky Early Methodists

THE FIRST METHODIST camp meeting, six frenzied days and nights with more than twenty-five thousand participants letting rip, took place in 1801 in Cane Ridge, Kentucky. The noise boomed for miles around like the thunderous shock waves of Niagara Falls. People fell into mystic trances, lying in rows like soldiers slain in battle. Others barked, danced, ran, and hollered in tongues. It was, when all is said and done, a religious Woodstock.

These ecstatic services alarmed the sedate Puritan groups entrenched in this country, and they made every effort to block this new-fangled religion. We mustn't forget that, contrary to what we learned in grade school, the Puritans who left England to escape intolerance had come to the New World for the freedom to be intolerant themselves. In Provincetown in 1795, the town voted that the thirty Methodists in their midst must tear down their new meetinghouse. When the Methodists refused, a group of vigilantes pulled the structure down for them. The Methodists rebuilt, so there. The Puritans desisted from another teardown, but they lobbed fish heads at anyone heading inside for services.

Gradually people realized the Methodists were here to stay, and their presence gained acceptance. Eventually the fiery camp meetings sponged up converts like ants on a sugared drainboard, and Puritanism faded away like a bygone virus.

On the Vineyard, camp meeters encountered the same pattern of abuse, then acceptance, though in milder form. In 1787 two former Virginia slaves arrived as Methodist lay speakers and preached for several years. Other circuit riders visited, without much long-term effect on the vice-ridden ports in Edgartown and Eastville. In 1880 a minister named Erastus Otis won over enough converts to attract persecution. Townsfolk got up a petition to drive all Methodists from the island. The petitioners feared Methodists' influence over children and "weak-minded persons."

By 1820 the island was host to a new preacher every year or two, each one more charismatic than the next. Soon, enough residents were converted at camp meetings to turn the tide of sentiment. In 1844 the Methodists built the Whaling Church in Edgartown, that great, gorgeous, and not-too-pompous Greek Revival structure in the center of town. Other churches followed, and by the mid-nineteenth century virtually every island soul, weak-minded or otherwise, was a Methodist.

The program would get rolling with a preacher contrasting human depravity with the hope of salvation through grace. Penitents would descend to the circle below the pulpit where lay practitioners would pray and sing until redemption washed over the converts.

It was an optimistic creed in a time when death and every other form of catastrophe threatened all islanders. Nearly every Vineyard family had a member on a lengthy whaling voyage from which it was likely he would never return. Loneliness and deprivation hovered around men aboard ships and families isolated on land. The need to pack up all this stress drove some to alcohol, immorality, and violence—certainly the Edgartown and Eastville answer. The camp meeting answer was pretty much the opposite: Bring your troubles to God. Have faith that God will sustain you, come what may. Here He comes, lifting you up, even as you lay your troubles at His feet.

Other, more cynical opinions existed about the appeal of camp meeting conversions and the promise of sublime madness. A Unitarian minister visiting in 1830 blamed the nervous temperament of islanders on too much coffee. Fewer cups of java would eliminate all need for salvation. This minister also opined that islanders were prey to a particular mental condition brought on by too much inbreeding, especially up island. (He was right!)

More About the Sublime Madness

THE FIRST METHODIST camp meeting took place on the shores of Squash Meadow in August 1835. Volunteers cobbled together a rough board structure for the preacher's tent and the congregation sat on plain wooden benches. And, oh, sweet success: sixty-five souls were saved during the weeklong retreat. As the Methodists rode the crest of victory, they voted to build a permanent structure.

Annually for ten years, during the last week of August, a meeting was held in the grove of ancient oak trees. In the first ceremony, called the Love Feast, congregants gathered at the preacher's tent and gave testimonies of religious experience. Then, in the Parting, they walked in procession, singing hymns and passing in rows to clasp hands and bid one another farewell, their faces haloed by the amber glow of candles and lantern light. So inspiring was the sight that, before long, flocks of tourists were assembling to watch the show.

Often the pilgrims would sit out the night to sing and pray and, with any luck, fall over in a dead faint of redemption. The greatest number of tents was forty, accommodating a little more than one thousand people. The greatest head count came in at three thousand. In 1840 the site was christened Wesleyan Grove. In 1846 and 1847, the camp meeters tried an off-island event, but the experience was a flop.

One and all, they missed the ancient oaks of Squash Meadow, recognizing it for what it was—holy ground.

In the second half of the nineteenth century, the crowds of onlookers swelled from three thousand to twelve thousand, and by 1858, the numbers of tents increased to three hundred twenty. This settlement of white canvas tents came to be known as the White City. Imagine the enchantment of an August night in the grove: Whale oil lamps lit the paths and infused the tents with an ethereal glow. Later, after the invention of electricity—which, for all its convenience, removed a whacking great quantity of beauty from the world—camp meeters tried to re-create the early magic during a single evening in August known as Illumination Night, when paper lanterns are strung between the cottages and in long lines extending to the tabernacle. But in the mid-1800s, every night in August was illuminated by the warm glow of lanterns.

Devotion to this spot inspired people to convert their tents into board structures, a combination of wood and cloth. In 1865 the trustees purchased the twenty-acre grounds for thirteen hundred dollars, and in 1869 the iron tabernacle was built. The Wesley Hotel in the summer was lined with booths and bazaars as a central promenade for throngs of visitors.

The first camp meeters and their attendant spectators were also the first summer people in

America, though they would have been shocked by the term. They were in the vanguard of Americans taking vacations: Lock up the farm, honey, we're going to Martha's Vineyard!

The Deal on Victorian Architecture

ANYONE CAN IDENTIFY a house as Victorian or gingerbread style, but for those who wish to sound a drop more educated, two words will do the trick: Queen Anne.

Queen Anne means a hodge-podge of styles in a shameless stew of excess; more is more is definitely more. Look for irregular rooflines on a single house—a steeple spiking above a gambrel motif with gables popping up like mushrooms. The overall style is European, romantic, with nary a flat facade; bring on the bay windows, balconies, and cupolas.

In Oak Bluffs, both in and out of the Campground, the Queen Anne cottages were festooned (many still are and many, deconstructed, have been restored) with jigsaw scrollwork, a specialty of island carpenters. Gothic windows and doors with pointed arches evoked the Middle Ages when faith in both God and church ran strong. Some of the homes have more rounded, Romanesque designs, but the tribute to churchiness remains.

In the 1800s the cost ran from six hundred dollars for a smaller cottage to twelve to fifteen hundred dollars for the larger models. Lots were available for long-term lease, costing from one hundred to four hundred dollars. (Today, if you purchase one of these dollhouses for five hundred thousand, that's considered a steal).

The shingling we see in modern times was added to the exteriors in the twentieth century, and architectural purists believe they distort the Victorian tone. Front porches were added in the 1880s and later, but they look so jaunty and provide so much pleasure that no one, not even those staunch purists, is willing to turn up a nose at them.

The Greased Pig Race of 1888

IN THE FESTIVAL TOWN of Oak Bluffs, in the last quarter of the nineteenth century, town planners wracked their frontal lobes to come up with new events to keep the summer folks entertained. In August 1888 someone had the bright idea of inaugurating a Greased Pig Race.

A dozen or more volunteers—strapping young males, strong swimmers all—were assembled on a barge about one hundred yards offshore. From a nearby farm a frisky pig was appropriated for the event. A pair of jolly good sports dipped bare hands in a bucket of lard and smeared it over the pig's head, legs, and torso. At the blast of a whistle, the lubricious pig was tossed into the water and the contestants lined up along the barge in their long, baggy shorts and tank tops. At a second toot of the whistle, they dove in after the slippery hog.

No one, however, had explained the rules to the commandeered pig. Furthermore, the animal was smarter than all the human players.

The point of the contest: The person who successfully wrestled the oily oinkster to shore would be the winner.

No one, however, had explained the rules to the commandeered pig. Furthermore, the animal was smarter than all the human players; it turned one hundred eighty degrees and began paddling its porcine heart out toward Cape Cod. The men turned and swam after it and after it and after it. The hundreds of spectators lining the bluffs could see absolutely nothing.

The pig's bacon was saved, and the event was scrapped, never to be attempted—or even mentioned—again.

In the Days When When Blue Was Red

IN THE 1870S, one hundred fifty year-round families lived on the island, mostly in Oak Bluffs, and mostly they were farmers and fishermen from the Azores, an outpost of Portugal. These first Portuguese settlers turned sandy soil into rich gardens and provided produce for summer cottages, hotels, boardinghouses, and restaurants. Thanks to these growers, an abundance of flowers packed every porch and yard.

Spring and summer jobs were available for every able-bodied Portuguese. Summer ladies hired on the basis of whether or not the worker was Republican. Applicants learned to answer in the affirmative, and they went ahead and entered the voting lists as a solid Republican bloc.

This tradition has faded away in the past few decades. Today we're blue, blue, blue, baby, with but a few lonely reds hiding out in isolated pockets of the island.

A Slower Pace

THE ISLAND PHONE system in the first half of the twentieth century had everyone on common battery. If your number was thirty-three, for example, you would know the incoming call was for you if you heard three long rings followed by three short ones. When you stop to think about it, this must have meant the telephone in one's house jingled all the livelong day.

The party line was going strong in the 1940s when clothing merchant Al Brickman planned a sale. He decided to allocate a small budget to a promotional campaign, and he called a professor of advertising in Boston for advice. The expert told Mr. Brickman he could dispense with paid publicity. In his small-town setting, all he needed to do was to mention his sale over the party line: When he heard the seventh click, he'd know his sale was going over.

Here's a little anecdote, passed down through generations, that emphasizes the separateness of the six island towns in those days: Roger Allen of Chilmark, a respected local builder, was asked by a summer client if he could complete his house by April. "Not without I import labor," was the reply.

"Where would you import it from?"

"West Tisbury."

A few years later, a fifth-grader at the Tisbury School, assigned to write about Julius Caesar, began his paper: "Julius Caesar was an off-islander . . . ."

Nudity Is Nothing New

JUST ABOUT EVERYONE coming to the island with any sort of savvy about the place has heard of Lucy Vincent Beach in Chilmark, renowned for its nude bathing opportunities. The site is populated by superannuated hippies, up-island crunchies and sophisticates, and a certain internationally known attorney who prefers his birthday suit to Armani. They play volleyball, yak on cell phones, and romp in the surf, with nothing to cover themselves but sunblock (one can only hope applied with strategic finesse).

The splendors of this clothing-optional locale have been in vogue since the freewheelin' 1960s. But what makes us suppose that sunbathing *au naturel* is a relatively modern sport on the Vineyard? It's not. Lucy Vincent Beach has an antecedent:

In the year 1900, a Dr. Walton Brooks Daniels strolled with friends along the cliffs below Nashaquitsa Pond, in Chilmark, and stumbled upon a sight that both shocked and upset him.

In an August 1900 letter to the *Vineyard Gazette* Dr. Brooks wrote: "We came upon a score of morning bathers of both sexes, quite as naked as when Nature chiseled them. Even the quick glance that New England prudery permitted revealed that their sculptor had not always done well by them."

So, you see, nothing's new in nude beaches, not even the range of pulchritude—or lack thereof—on the part of naked-as-jaybirds bathers.

Psycho Croquet

At the end of every major war, Americans can count on an era of pure silliness. After World War I we had flappers; after World War II, the explosion of the suburbs; after Vietnam we had a decade of disco. Following the Civil War, the biggest surge of zaniness was . . . croquet!

The croquet invasion on Martha's Vineyard began in the Methodist campground in the 1860s. The game had hit these shores after a test run in England and France where it was first introduced as a royal sport. In August 1866 the *Vineyard Gazette* weighed in on the fad exploding on the island's sacred land: "Instead of giving attention to the earnest words and practical zeal that so successfully wrought out the work of grace and goodness, we hear the merry jest and see the rallying around the croquet ground . . . a game, we are told, that tends to the softening of the brain but which, at least, we shall pronounce absurd."

During the many decades that croquet ruled the island, no group ever took to it with more gusto than the camp meeters. Only one rule prevailed within the perimeter of Wesleyan Grove: No croquet on the grass surrounding the preacher's stand. But infraction of this rule was guaranteed not to offend the preacher himself because, most likely, he was busy elsewhere thwacking ceramic balls through enameled wickets. Yes, clergymen were among the biggest enthusiasts, inviting another critic to write to the *Gazette* in 1869: "The only development liable to lower the moral standard of the camp is croquet. This is played incessantly for weeks before the meeting." It was reported that ministers were often late to services, held up by a rousing croquet competition.

The same indignant writer goes on to berate the ladies of the croquet wars: "We have yet to witness a game in which cheating and lying are not common occurrences, especially among the fair sex, we deeply regret to say. It is the general practice of the ladies to push balls into more favorable positions when unobserved, and if detected to deny it. We have ministers' daughters do it time and again."

Yikes!

In truth, women had the advantage because their voluminous skirts could easily settle over their ball, and with a little fancy footwork they could redistribute said ball to a more advantageous location.

A general rule decreed that on any given day a croquet course could be monopolized by whoever was the first to put down wickets. A minister recalled how once he awakened at one a.m. and rushed from his tent to stake his claim, only to discover that another minister had beat him to his favorite plot of croquet land.

When secular housing went up all around the Campground, all of the new developments were implanted with a great many parks, and the croquet virus spread as quickly as new grass could be seeded. Newcomers to town were warned to tread carefully over open ground for fear of tripping over wickets. All over Cottage City, the normal sounds—melodies from the bandstand, birdsong, the bells and whistles from the harbor—were accompanied by the constant clack of mallets hitting croquet balls.

Clerics continued to be criticized for their participation in the sport, but the editor of the *Vineyard Gazette* noted that the men of the cloth "saw no inconsistency between croquet and their Master's business." In other words, what would Jesus do? The answer was obvious: He would play croquet.

The sets cost one dollar. Although a dollar went farther in those days, the sum nonetheless was still low enough to make the game accessible to everyone since no other equipment was required. Other fads waxed and waned, skating and bicycling most notably, but nothing had the staying power of croquet.

In 1882 a National Croquet Association was formed, and a number of devotees in Cottage City joined. In 1899 a handful of men from the island met with other croquet maniacs in Norwich, Connecticut, to come up with a higher tech version of the game, which they called Roque. The wickets were narrower, and permanent courts were fashioned from hard, smooth materials with borders to stop balls from caroming away. Looking back, it was perhaps the development of this more formal, professional version of the game that robbed all able-bodied citizens of any age or gender the pleasure of their own low-key enjoyment.

In 1935 the Martha's Vineyard Roque Club held its fifty-fourth—and last—annual tournament. As ever, a number of ministers turned out to compete in the game.

Don't Believe Everything You Read

IN THE 1930S, when Henry Beetle Hough took over editorial duties at the *Vineyard Gazette* in Edgartown, he and his wife, Betty, noticed that strangers rambling past the newspaper's fence were picking blackberries and stuffing them in their mouths. This seemed rude, so Mr. Hough made a sign and nailed it to the front gate: "WARNING: These vines have been sprayed with Nu-Homolleptica."

The following day, visitors from a nearby hotel chanced to walk through from the back of the Gazette's property, munching blackberries all the way to the sidewalk. When they reached the gate, they read the sign and were appalled. They pounded on the front door, but the office was closed.

They copied down the term *Nu-Hommelleptica* and scurried to the library to look it up in the medical dictionary. They failed to find it, though they ransacked every other reference book in the building. Anxiety mounting, they rushed to the doctor's office, where they were obliged to wait an hour—even as the Nu-Hommelleptica coursed through their intestinal tracts—before they could be seen.

The doctor looked at the name of the so-called poison. Perhaps he knew about Mr. Hough's dry sense of humor. He handed the note back and told the couple to go home and quit their bellyaching. Later Mr. Hough heard the couple had actually muttered about suing the newspaper before they left the island.

Getting Things Done (Not!)

IT IS A TRUTH universally acknowledged that of all the locales where it's difficult to induce workmen to show up, the Vineyard has the most laid-back, procrastinating, and downright disappearing carpenters, painters, plumbers, and electricians of all.

I know of a contractor who vanished one February in the middle of a big McMansion job. When he and his full crew returned sporting tans that had "Florida" written all over them, he told the irate homeowner without an ounce of chagrin that he and his men had been battling the flu with the help of vitamins, orange juice, and sunlamps.

The month-long fishing derby, running annually from mid-September to mid-October, sucks up islanders like the black holes of outer space. During the derby weeks of 2005 I needed phone lines installed in the new building intended to house my newer, bigger bookstore. A lone Verizon guy showed up to inspect the premises. As he stood in the basement, he nodded sagely at the designated spot for the new interface, then mumbled something about grabbing tools in his truck. I didn't see him again for two and a half weeks. Apparently the blues were biting out at Paul's Point.

It was the same situation with my friend Everett, a builder who'd agreed to install some vital shelving in my store. In spite of all his other bigger projects, he had promised to appear the minute my facility was ready to receive his services. On the Friday before the derby commenced, I put in my green-light call to him. He left word that he'd trot 'round momentarily. Thus began my own production of *Waiting for Godot*. A week later I left him this message: "You have no intention of calling me until October 15th, have you?"

Agreeably enough, he declined to get in touch with me.

After another ten days elapsed, I sent him an e-mail with words loosely borrowed from Bob Dylan:

Oh, where have you been, my blue-fished one?

Oh, where have you been, my striped-bassed young man?

I've stumbled on the side of twelve Boston Whalers

I've walked and I've crawled over six crooked dinghies

And it's a hard, it's a hard, it's a hard, it's a hard—it's a hard fish a-gonna fall.

Sometime later my errant builder e-mailed back: "I take your hint. Will leave a fresh catch in your fridge."

The stories of workers' intransigence and their absolute unconcern in the face of indignation get better all the time. My friend Bob George, who lives with his wife, Bonnie, down the dirt road leading to Quansoo in Chilmark, told me this tale of an encounter he witnessed first-hand in the parking lot of Alley's Store in West Tisbury:

A pickup with the name of a construction company painted in fading letters on the side pulled into the lot. Moments later a gold Mercedes 420 with New York plates swooped in from the road and squealed to a halt directly behind the pickup, blocking it from any immediate exit. A driver in jeans and a crisp new black tee shirt hopped out of the Mercedes and hailed the contractor slowly easing from his truck.

"I've been looking for you all over Chilmark!" cried the New Yorker. "I just want you to tell me how much more time it will take to finish my house!"

The contractor, a tall, handsome guy in a raggedy gray sweatshirt, had a faraway look in his eyes as he pondered the question.

Finally he said, "I'm thinking eleven more days."

Mercedes Man was overjoyed. "Great! That's great! So you're saying it should be finished a week from Thursday?"

The contractor scratched the stubble beneath his jaw line. "I'm thinkin' I can give you a day next week, two days the week after, and then in a month or so . . . "

He hadn't meant eleven *consecutive* days.

The rule of thumb is this: If a contractor tells you he'll complete your project in November, ask him, "November of which year?" A lot of people have been misguided by failing to nail down that last little bit of vital information.

Gravestones in the Garden

WE HAVE AN inordinate number of people on the Vineyard who prefer to plant their dearly departed in the backyard. Strictly speaking, this isn't legal anymore, although I know a man in his sixties with a waterfront home on Senge-kontackett whose mom and dad *requiesat in pacem* under a pair of handsome marble tombstones just to the left as you turn in the drive. They couldn't have died more than thirty to forty years ago, so either some sort of waiver was obtained from the town, or the sentimental son thought he had enough acreage to get away with it.

For the most part, at-home gravesites date back to earlier times when it was customary after someone died to grab a shovel and dig someplace where you need not sacrifice your peony bushes. The home burial, too, might have stemmed from New England frugality so survivors could avoid springing for a plot in the municipal cemetery. And, occasionally, risk

Quiet Neighbors

Vineyarders' penchant for burying their dearly departed in the garden is on display in this Edgartown dooryard, where six seventeenth-century tombstones are set back only a few steps from the sidewalk. The woman in the picture is the author during a brief stint as a blonde.
AUTHOR'S COLLECTION

of contagion existed, say from smallpox, the tendency was to chuck the body in the ground ASAP, no band of mourners.

The poshest byway in Edgartown, South Water Street, which runs along the harbor, has for more than three hundred years hosted the interment site of Governor Thomas Mayhew's immediate family. Three large graves and three small graves denote, presumably, three grown-ups and three little ones. In the 1980s the family that owned the property rather liked the look of their six ancient tombstones set only twenty feet back from the sidewalk, and in stark contrast to the beige power-washed shingles of the house. The unsuspecting traveler, out for a stroll, would come upon this miniature cemetery and cry out, "What the—?"

The present family planted hydrangeas and allowed them to overgrow most of the gravestones. (These latest homeowners had originally planned to haul the ancient markers to the landfill until the historical society informed them they had another think coming.)

By the way, Governor Mayhew himself, along with his wife Jane, are buried without headstones or even plaques in the middle of this same front lawn. After purchasing the Vineyard in 1642, Mayhew ran the place with a club in one hand and his own rulebook in the other; Mussolini could have taken a pointer or two from him. Historians believe that Mayhew on his deathbed realized his enemies might not forgive him, even after he breathed his last. The anonymous burial was his way of keeping the townsfolk from digging him up and slapping him.

One story stands out in our stock of do-it-yourself burials: In the early 1990s an up-island real estate broker offered a tour of a deluxe property to a couple from New York. If you had the money—which they did—you would be hard put to find anything more sumptuous than the restored antique manor house on one hundred waterfront acres on the cliffs of Chilmark. The buyers were ecstatic and ready to sign the paperwork. They continued to roam woods and meadows, hill and dale, stopping short beneath an aged oak tree. At the base of the tree was a single gravestone, and on that wind-pocked surface, three initials marked the name of the long-ago departed.

The woman's face turned white.

The broker said, "Heh, heh. These old tombstones are considered quaint in these parts."

What the woman failed to find quaint was that the initials were her own. She considered this coincidence to be a bad omen, so the couple left to mull it over. After several days of keeping the real estate agent on tenterhooks, they called to announce they would, in fact, purchase the property.

It was only after they moved in that they learned about the ghost . . . (But that's another story. You'll find it in the "Windy Gates" chapter of *Haunted Island: True Ghost Stories from Martha's Vineyard,* by yours truly.)

The Self-Sufficient Couple

IN THE LATE 1970s, Steve and Marilyn were living off the "fatta the lan'," as Lenny expressed it in *Of Mice and Men.* Almost painfully reclusive, the scrappy pair nonetheless accepted a rare dinner invitation from a friend of mine, actress Linda Kelsey, who rented to them several acres of arable property in West Tisbury northwest of Thimble Farm. There Steve and Marilyn grew sufficient crops and managed enough livestock to feed themselves. They lived the old-fashioned way, without plumbing or electricity, which meant that an outhouse and a supply of kerosene took care of their personal needs. The couple's sole income derived from a generator-run poetry printing press, which produced twenty-five hundred dollars annually.

"That's all we need to get by," said Steve— tall, broad-shouldered, and prematurely grayhaired—as he snapped his suspenders with no small amount of pride.

Neither husband nor wife were missing any teeth, nor were their sentences devoid of perfect grammar. Both came from upper-middleclass backgrounds and possessed college degrees. Their pursuit of a simple life was bred of pure idealism. You might say they were living the life of Thoreau times two.

Marilyn was tall and lanky, with dark hair worn in braids and soulful, Modigliani features.

"Every season we teach ourselves something new in order to remove us one more notch from consumerism," she told us. "This week we're making soap from hemp oil and lye. I'm having a blast with different scents like lavender and basil—grown in our yard, of course."

Steve said, "The soap will save us an extra twenty-five dollars a year in provisions."

Marilyn added, "The next step is making our own candles."

The pair had married only a few months before, the ceremony conducted in Linda's driveway in the company of Linda, her husband, Glen, and their two daughters, Sophie and Margit. Steve had sent away for a divinity degree after completing a correspondence course in ministry, so they'd actually married themselves. (Whether or not this was strictly legal was possibly of no great import to a couple who spent virtually no time in the so-called civilized world.)

The last we heard, Marilyn and Steve had given up their West Tisbury digs to manage fifty acres in Mississippi, where their families had chipped in to buy them their own homestead. Whatever they're doing, we can bet they've continued to subsist without a single store-bought item, but it was the Vineyard that furnished them their apprenticeship, on Fatathelan' Farm.

Those Pesky Skulls and Bones

IT'S ENOUGH TO make any new homeowner wonder when he's going to catch a break. After a lot of wrangling, he's got his permits, and he's hired a crew that actually deigns to show up. A bulldozer starts to break ground, and what do the workers find? The bones of a three-hundred-year-old Indian, that's what.

For thousands of years before the white man trickled to the island, Native Americans settled the land. They hunted and gathered and left not a shred of litter or any other kind of despoilment behind them. Even when they died, aside from a respectful pile of rocks, Vineyard Indians buried their dead without markers. When you come right down to it, gravestones, from the humblest plaque to the most obnoxiously ornate marble monument, are but a final ego trip.

Thus it is that, down through the last three and a half centuries, Vineyarders have been digging up human relics when and where they least expect to. The possibility is so pronounced that there are few builders who fail to brace themselves whenever a hydraulic shovel sets steel teeth to a virgin plot of soil.

In the old days, Colonials simply transferred these bones to the nearest refuse pile. This occurred all along the Edgartown harborfront, where, for eons before palefaces arrived, Indians had enjoyed the sparkling views and safe haven from gale-force winds. Today this sweep of shoreline is packed cheek to jowl with Federal-style and Greek Revival homes, each hosting its resident ghost (or ghosts!) as a result of long-ago builders disrespecting the human remains that once reposed beneath the cornerstones.

I know, I know—this hardly passes the test of good science. But as Hamlet said to Horatio . . . well, you remember that squib about stuff in heaven and earth undreamt of in his philosophy? Take it from a veteran ghost hunter, this factor of desecrated gravesites figures prominently in many of the bios of chronically haunted houses. When you encounter an old New England house that appears to be riddled with occult static and you do a little digging in the historical records, you'll find that long ago Ezekiel Workman, excavating a basement for Captain Whaling Dollars, came across a skeleton or two or three—possibly an entire tribe's worth of reliquary—and tossed the lot in a faraway field (there to create further havoc for anyone attempting to dislodge the bones a second time.)

Nowadays laws are strict about reporting uncovered human remains. If they're "fresh," so to speak, then naturally law enforcement steps in to investigate. If the bones pass the age test, archeologists are summoned to ascertain just what we're dealing with here—is it a lone graveyard deposit or are we sitting on an American Herculaneum?

A case came up in the early 1990s where a contractor opted to take the middle ground. A cardiologist from Boston had purchased twenty acres along the northern shore of West Tisbury, and his architect had drawn up plans for a neo-chateau complete with towers and turrets. On the day the basement was due to be excavated, the workers hit the wrong kind of pay dirt: a fully preserved skeleton of a long-dead aboriginal Vineyarder. The contractor made a snap decision: He tossed the bones into his trunk and brought the old gent home to be stashed under a pile of tools and boxes in the garage. When the house was finished, some nine to ten months later, the contractor made a full disclosure to the Law. For his transgression, he was fined ten thousand dollars. The bones were vouchsafed to tribal authorities in Aquinnah who took it upon themselves to consecrate the remains in sacred ground.

(The above facts were published in both the *MV Times* and the *Vineyard Gazette*. Reading between the lines, one could conclude that the Boston doctor was well aware of the skeleton on his property. We can imagine the emergency call placed to the homeowner's townhouse, with the contractor perhaps offering to take the fall if the doctor would subsidize the fine. Did they conclude that the important thing was get the starter chateau built, then they'd worry about the consequences of grave robbing later?)

The doctor is a charming man. I made his acquaintance after his house had been in existence for a couple of years, and he'd decided to make it available for summer rentals. I recalled the story about the skeleton and asked him if there'd been any repercussions.

"Repercussions?" he asked.

I got straight to the point: "Is the house haunted?"

He looked thoughtful for a moment (perhaps wondering about this deranged rental agent into whose hands he was putting his summer home), but then replied, "No. Nothing that I've noticed."

Was he hedging? Had someone *else* noticed . . . something?

I was soon to find out firsthand that all was not quite right with this spanking new chateau. For the coming August I rented it to movie star Michele Pfeiffer, and her husband, David Kelley, screenwriter and creator of the TV series *Allie McBeal*. Although I prefer to think I'm not easily star struck, I found myself going the extra distance for these famous visitors. David Kelley had leased a van for the month, and I offered to take delivery of it myself, collect the Pfeiffer-Kelleys at the airport, and convey them to their castle.

I brought my son Charlie along for the ride. He was then an exceedingly cute, short, bespectacled nine-year-old. I mention Charlie's adorableness to contrast it with Ms. Pfeiffer's frosty demeanor: If a celebrity's aversion to strangers causes her to be unfriendly to the poor working stiff going out of her way to transport a van to her, she might at least spare a smile for the working stiff's fourth-grader. Ms. Pfeiffer was, after all, in full possession of her own maternal hormones—her young adopted daughter sat at her side, and a recently

born infant was strapped into a child's car seat. Afterward, Charlie remarked on the actress's "mean face," and neither of us has enjoyed watching Michelle Pfeiffer movies to this day. (Of course, two fewer fans will hardly cut into her box office receipts.)

The morning after the Hollywood family arrived, I received a call from David Kelley at my office. "Do you have any other rentals available?"

"Oh, dear. What's wrong?"

"It's a lovely house, but something about it is giving us the willies."

"You mean—?"

What the Backhoe Turned Up

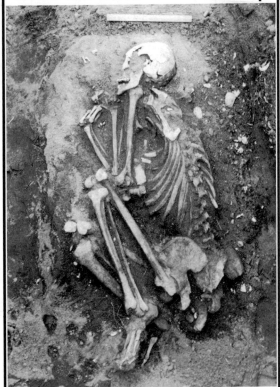

Ancient Native American skeletons dot the subterranean landscape of the island, such as these remains found in the aptly named Indian Hill area of Edgartown.

MARTHA'S VINEYARD HISTORICAL SOCIETY COLLECTIONS (env. 390)

"Last night we heard a thump against the outside wall, and then a few more thumps on interior walls."

"Um hmm."

"Also . . ." he hesitated. "Someone kept running up and down the stairs. It sounded like a child, but our daughter was fast asleep in the bedroom adjoining ours."

Those were bona fide ghost pranks, but first I got down to the brass tacks of business: So sorry, but there were no other rentals to be had at this last minute, particularly not waterfront homes with deluxe amenities. And if such a rarity had existed, he and his wife would lose the twenty thousand dollars they had already paid for their present rental; an indigestible sum even for movie stars. (I kept that last little editorial to myself.)

Then, my voice softening, I said, "Give it another couple of days. The spirits in the house will subside. They just need to be assured that you're taking good care of it."

(And it would help if your wife were less of a sourpuss.)

August played out without another call from the Pfeiffer/Kelleys. We can only conclude that no more disturbances of a supernatural nature spoiled the serenity of their vacation.

The following summer I learned they had taken a rental on Nantucket.

A Guide to Star's Homes (Or, How to Decide Which Environ Is for You)

PLANNING ON MOVING to the Vineyard, either in the economy class of year-round living or in the ritzier vein of taking on a summer home? It pays to know ahead of time where you'll feel the most comfortable, with neighbors who share your tastes and interests, and with celebrities who happen to be your perfect soulmates. The wrong geography can mess you up bigtime. We've seen this happen in the last ten or fifteen years when *nouveau riche* summer folk realized their original installation in Edgartown left them on the low end of the trend-o-meter. In a faintly comical mass exodus, these social *fashionistas* sold their Edgartown properties and made their way to *luxe* homesteads in Chilmark and Aquinnah.

So here's a breakdown of the island *arrondissements* . . .

Edgartown specializes in W.A.S.P. breeding going back many generations. You'll feel most at home if you've got a Boston Brahmin in your background—or, better yet, one of those Mayflower connections that are taken seriously only by people with early Pilgrim pedigrees of their own. Edgartown apparel has calmed down a bit, but you'll still spot elderly yachtsters ambling along the wharves in pink, green, and turquoise plaid pants. (My friend Margaret was set upon at an art opening last summer by an Edgartown gentleman wearing very very very purple trousers). Gin and tonic is still the drink *du jour* (as much *du jour* as *de la nuit*, in fact), and the celebrities are of an older, more dignified vintage: Walter Cronkite, Robin Cook, and actress Patricia Neal. Surprisingly enough, Dave Letterman makes his summer home at the Herring Creek farm estate in the southern plain of Edgartown called Katama. You'd think he'd have more highjinks with other comics of his generation—Larry David, Dan Akroyd, and Ted Danson—all based in Chilmark, but perhaps Letterman secretly harbors a personal preference for Star Sapphire Bombay gin and purple pants.

Oak Bluffs also has its share of multigenerational preppies, especially in the East Chop area along the northern shore, but the town has long attracted African Americans of the professional and artistic classes, the most famous being filmmaker Spike Lee, senator Edward Brooke, the late Dorothy West, and writers Jill Nelson, Bebe Moore Campbell, and Stephen L. Carter, author of *The Emperor of Ocean Park*. A few celebrated palefaces live in Oak Bluffs as well, most notably Tom Clancy, who recently built a humongous yellow house on every last square inch of his small in-town property. The preferred Oak Bluffs intoxicants—well, anything! And if you'd rather smoke it than sip it, that's fine, too. This is the one island town where you can wear anything, be anything, say anything, and for that reason it's hard to imagine writers, artists, and other species of bohemians living anywhere else, though a few of them do.

Vineyard Haven has an outward reputation for being a wholesome, family, year-round town, but it has long claimed a hidden glamour. Starting with theater actress Katherine Cornell and her star-studded parties on the northern shore of Vineyard Haven, the rich and famous have for years nestled along the sands of Tashmoo Lake and West Chop: Mike Wallace, Art Buchwald, Lillian Hellman, Dashiell Hammett, and William Styron. As with the Edgartown illuminati, you're dealing with an older group of heavy weights with a more elegant body of work under their belts. The Vineyard Haven drink of choice is whatever you've imported from the other two down island "wet" townships, though here you're likely to find another brigade of gin-and-tonic guzzlers, gaudy pants, and more tennis than you might find healthy in a well-rounded life style: There are pre-tennis meetings for coffee, rounds of tennis itself, and preprandial, midprandial, and postprandial analyses of that day's tennis games. Clearly not for everyone.

The emerald fields and lush forests of West Tisbury are just as pastoral as those of Chilmark, but the people are much less status conscious, and therefore property sells for only a million per square foot as opposed to Chilmark's billion. Even the celebs here are

lower key: the late Washington *grande dame* Katherine Graham, opera diva Beverly Sills, Carley Simon, and prize-winning historian and author David McCullough. Mr. McCullough, for instance, is assuredly much too busy researching distinguished Americans' bios to chase after the weekend's hot party. The West Tisbury drink would be a good Tuscan vintage red wine; these people know what to eat, drink, and read (the *New Yorker,* of course, and the latest Nathaniel Philbrick).

At last we come to Chilmark and Aquinnah, where the socially motivated have staked their claims. From what I've been able to acertain, the summer rolls out for these people with a rash of annual parties, much as Mrs. Astor and her friends used to plan their elaborate entertainments in Newport, Rhode Island. In this part of the Vineyard, a particular well-heeled couple will host a yearly Fourth of July bash, another will adopt Bastille Day, another President Clinton's birthday, and yet another couple might

> *In Edgartown you'll still spot elderly yachtsters ambling along the wharves in pink, green, and turquoise plaid pants.*

plan a blow-out anniversary bash to fend off divorce for another year. Speaking of divorce, in Chilmark and Aquinnah circles I wouldn't be surprised if in some pre-nuptial agreements, the Party of the First Part has obliged the Party of the Second Part to cede to the former the Danson/Steenbergen annual August barbecue invitation. Everyone's mad to have Mary and Ted, the Alan Dershowitzes, and the Larry Davids as guests of honor, though I've heard through the grapevine that the Davids will appear only if they're entitled to handpick their party mates. (It's easy to imagine a segment of *Curb Your Enthusiasm* where Larry David grouses, "Why should we have to go to any party where there's anyone we don't already know or like?!")

All of this jockeying for position creates a band of secrecy around many of the parties. Those who haven't made the guest list are likely to feel miffed, though of course they're free to retaliate by themselves not inviting the not-inviters when it comes time to throw their own big hoedown. Basically the up-island scene works for anyone who misses the social fireworks and meltdowns of high school.

The up-island drink of choice is anything expensive and, preferably, a trifle rare. Bottles of absinthe smuggled in from the Slovak republic would do very nicely. And of course, drugs of the narcotic variety are helpful in these locations, since it's often difficult to stay serenely in place when all shops and restaurants are a forty-five-minute drive away and you've got to cool your heels until the next party some three days off.

So, if you're moving to the Vineyard, take your pick and take your chances. The worst that can happen is that you'll be stuck in Chilmark with the sudden realization that what you really hanker for deep in your soul is an open-mic banjo night at a dive in Oak Bluffs. At least, if that's your bag, you're not going to mind that the Larry Davids left you off their guest list.

And where do the regular folk live? The plumbers and schoolteachers and pharmacists? All over, actually. Before our sandy soil alchemized into pure gold around the turn of the millennium, people could still swing the mort-gages. Also, many islanders have inherited houses from antecedents who bought, for example, a Campground cottage for the grand 1933 price of nineteen hundred dollars. Nowadays none of these people could afford to buy their own houses.

The situation has now reached the tipping point: Property taxes huff and puff against our humble abodes like the big bad wolf. For those trying to support themselves on modest salaries or pensions, the temptation to sell their run-down little capes for 1.2 mil and move to Costa Rica or Des Moines is compelling. Many have already left. You run into people on the ferry who hold their thumb and forefinger a quarter-inch apart and say, "We're *this* close to leaving."

And then there are the legion of renters who are required to move out of their homes every summer to make way for tenants willing to pay four thousand a week for the privilege of moving *in*. Those of us with year-round rentals lucked out only because our digs are too shabby for landlords to get away with leasing them to the well-heeled in July and August.

The whole thing is just too sad to relate, so I will now prepare to shut up about it—except to add this: Does there exist on island a billionaire with umpteen acres of waterfront property who'd be willing to cede over a little piece of it to a quiet, non-smoking woman who'll build a hermitage, read, write, meditate, and send good vibes out over the shore? This is the sort of arrangement we need to keep nice poor people on the Vineyard.

Eccentrics, Human

On an Island Where Everyone's Looped to Their Tonsils,
a Handful of Vineyarders Nonetheless Stand Out

Miss Nancy Luce, Tourist Attraction

BACK IN THE nineteenth century, our citizenry was much less sensitive to a person's infirmities, both physical and mental. People with extra body parts or excessive weight or frightening demeanors were employed as spectacles in so-called freak shows. Today all but the most primitive among us try for supreme tact at all times. If today a kooky lady who writes poems about her chickens lived nearby, stories about her would be circulated, to be sure, but you would never find tour buses lumbering up to her front door.

Nancy Luce might strike some as a sort of Emily Dickinson without the education and without the devastating talent. Like Dickinson, Miss Luce followed fairly normal patterns up through early adulthood. Dickinson enjoyed parties and dances with young men. Nancy Luce delighted in riding horses through the West Tisbury countryside, past the old mill, over squelchy, wet pastures, and along crumbling stone walls. But both young ladies, in their early twenties began to sequester themselves. The belle of Amherst took solitary rambles in the woods, wrote poems in secret, and saw no one but her immediate family. Nancy Luce, after her parents died, lived alone in a weathered cottage dark with low beams and massive slabs of Victorian furniture. Fearing for her health, she decided it would be expedient for her to drink goat's milk—lots and lots of goat's milk.

She bought a goat, named it Aljigana, and subsisted for months at a time on Aljigana's milk alone. When her pet and meal ticket died,

Nancy was inconsolable. In her grief she sought a replacement in two bantam hens that she named Ada Queetie and Beauty Linna. Many more hens followed, and their names grew increasingly imaginative: Teedie Tainie, Letoogie Tickling, Teppetee Tappao, Pondy Lily, Tealsay Medoolsay, Ottee Ophete, and Tweedle Dedel Bebee Pinky.

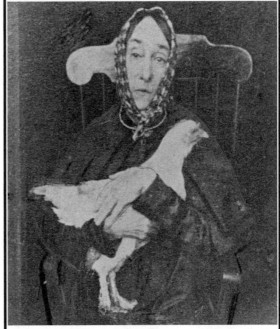

Lady with Chick

Poet, notorious eccentric, and tourist attraction Nancy Luce poses with one of her beloved chickens, circa mid-1860s.
MARTHA'S VINEYARD HISTORICAL SOCIETY COLLECTIONS (env. 745)

In her adoration for her chickens, Nancy began to write ditties about them, and it wasn't long before the poet laureate of West Tisbury became known to the rest of the island. (Today we are still able to marvel at her words thanks to Walter Magnes Teller, who gathered Nancy's verse into a volume called *Consider Poor I: The Life and Works of Nancy Luce*, published by the Dukes County Historical Society in 1984.) By the 1860s, visitors to the camp meetings in Wesleyan Grove piled in wagons and made a merry two-hour pilgrimage to Nancy's brooding cottage and the pack of poultry that lived inside her four walls with her.

Of these visits, Nancy wrote:

> Good behavior of foreign folks
> From camp meeting,
> They behaved well
> And bought books of me.
> I cannot live without them.

At other times, however, her guests were less well-mannered. They taunted and jeered for the sake of getting a rise out of her, and once she took their bait, her tormentors teased her all the more. Of these she wrote:

> Every time my head is wounded,
>   with noise,
> I never get over it,
> I wish I never been in this world,
> I undergo so much with my head.

For all her melancholy and gentle madness, Nancy possessed a streak of business cunning as well honed as that of any shopkeeper hawking souvenirs on Circuit Avenue. She negotiated with a printer in Edgartown to have photogravures of her hens printed in batches, along with pamphlets of her fowl poetry, all of which she sold to the folk who came to gawk at her, whether politely or impolitely.

Just as today visitors flock to the island and buy Black Dog tees, so in the 1860s through the 1880s travelers commemorated their island vacation with a keepsake from Nancy Luce's homestead.

As time went on, the growing number of hens' gravestones in Nancy's backyard added to the homestead's appeal as a tourist attraction. Among the first chickens to die, inevitably, were the original duo, Ada Queetie and Beauty Linna, of whose passing the poet lamented:

> They died with old age, over twelve
>   years ago . . .
> O my Poor deceased little Ada Queetie,
> She drew such a sight and her love
>   and mine,
> So deep in our hearts and her under-
>   going sickness and death,
> O heart rending! . . .
> No tongue could express my misery
>   of mind
> She had more than common wit
> And more than common love,
> Her heart was full of love for me,
> O do consider my Poor little heart.

At last, in April 1890, Nancy followed the way of her dear departed hens. Her first and last wish was to be buried with her feathered adoptees, but authorities pressured for her to be interred in a proper cemetery in West Tisbury. Strangers bought the homestead, and the chicken grave markers were recycled as doorsteps. Somewhere along the line, the tiny tombstones were donated to the town library.

So by sheer force of nuttiness, the memory of Nancy Luce lives on. Her poetry does as well:

> Be good and kind to all that breathes
> Act up our good saviour's laws
> Have tender feelings in your hearts
> For all the poor harmless dumb
> creatures.

The words lack the scope and resonance of Emily Dickinson's "I died for Beauty but was scarce adjusted in the tomb/When one who died for Truth was lain in an adjoining room," but Nancy's poems, over the long reach of time, still carry a freight of kindly advice.

Old-Time Doctor

IN THE FIRST quarter of the twentieth century, a Dr. Terry of Edgartown kept up appearances by going about in a tall silk hat, an Edwardian topcoat, and striped trousers. He never left home without them. In his role as country doctor he had also taken it upon himself to bring telephone service to the island, the better to be available to his patients, and in the same tall-hat getup he often serviced the poles himself. So, sauntering home from treating a farmer with influenza, he might spy a tangled line overhead and, without hesitation, shimmy up the pole—top hat and all—to straighten things out.

He employed one service man, a young fellow named Frank. One time Frank was working high overhead as the good doctor stood below calling out instructions. At last Dr. Terry told Frank to come down; he had an appointment to keep. The service man replied he only needed a few more minutes to complete the repair. The doctor insisted he cease and desist that minute, but Frank kept working on the line. Patience was not in the doctor's repertoire, so he picked up an ax and chopped at the bottom of the telephone pole. Frank scrambled down in one helluva hurry.

Dr. Terry had a compulsion to swat flies on the porch of his drugstore. Swatting flies outdoors is perhaps a bit of a lost cause, but we may realize by now that this country doc was as mad as the hatter who made his silk top hats. Nonetheless townsfolk were accustomed to observing the doctor leaping about, sawing the air with his swatter, coattails flying.

About his medical abilities, he was known as much for his acerbic style as he was for his fairly high number of cures. Once a woman came to him with a sob story about her pregnant and unwed daughter.

"I don't know how this could have happened!" she wailed.

"Simple," said Dr. Terry. "Immaculate conception."

And then he picked up his swatter to run out and kill more flies.

"Marooned with Maniac on Island"

IN THE EARLY 1930s on Noman's Land, when a vital little community of fishermen and farmers still populated that now desolate island due south of Aquinnah, a shocking event occurred that made the headlines of big city newspapers.

A man named Frank Crapo had worked for the Wood family for three years. He was willing and able, and the Woods had long appreciated his help. The villagers enjoyed his good company. According to son Bertrand Wood, who later wrote about Frank Crapo in his book, *Noman's Land Island,* "He was a big, powerful man, with muscles made hard by heavy work out-of-doors, but was a heavy drinker when off the island."

On September 19, 1931, Crapo returned from a week's vacation in New Bedford. He was withdrawn and disoriented, but it wasn't until three more days elapsed that the islanders noticed a new, disturbing sign of instability: Crapo's temper was on a short fuse, and when it blew, he became violent. Bertrand, Bertrand's father, and the three other men on Noman's, armed themselves with shotguns. They cornered Crapo in the field and marshaled the man into his garret room over the Woods' kitchen and locked him inside.

During the night the Woods were kept awake by their worker's screams. He pounded on the wall, demanding to be liberated. He hallucinated that someone named Walter was in fierce pursuit of him. At last, his paranoia giving him superhuman strength, he broke down the door, pushed past the armed guard downstairs, and tore off into the moors. His shouts could be heard drifting over the fields.

During a quiet interim, the deranged man returned to the Woods and pleaded with them to lend him a shotgun to defend himself against his imaginary enemy, Walter. The Woods remanded him to his attic room and rebolted the door. They convened in the kitchen with the other villagers to decide how to deal with the raving lunatic. Someone had to sneak away to the bigger island to get help.

On the fourth morning of the madman's siege of Noman's Land, Mr. Wood Senior stole down to the dock and climbed into his powerboat. He rowed away, careful not to start the engine until he floated on the far side of the breakwater. But even with that precaution, the sound of the throbbing engine set Crapo off on one of his rampages.

Once again he broke out of his room and charged down the stairs. At the foot of the stairs, two armed men held him at bay with their shotguns pointed at his chest. Crapo's last shred of sanity took note of the fact that if he descended one more step he'd be shot. He retreated back to his room, but continued to shout at Walter and to batter the walls.

Bertrand Wood wrote, "After what seemed an eternity, we heard the sound of motors and saw a seventy-five-foot Coast Guard patrol boat coming toward the island."

Soon enough, Wood Senior led eight strapping Coast Guardsmen from the docks to his home. They huddled in conference to plan an attack. Two of the men took a ladder from the shed and placed it below the madman's window. The others climbed the stairs to the attic, a dory oar held before them as a battering ram.

At a prearranged signal, the two men outside clattered up the ladder. They pounded on Crapo's window. The inmate lunged at the window at the same time that the men wielding the oar burst into the room. Crapo seized a chair and slashed at his attackers. They thrust the oar at the chair, breaking it in pieces.

Standing in the doorway, Bertrand Wood beheld the terrifying sight of the crazed and cornered Crapo tossing men at the walls as if they were rag dolls. It took all eight guardsmen to hold the man down. "He had the strength of insanity," wrote young Wood.

When at last the man was subdued, he shook his head and calmly asked for a cigarette, as if he and the other nine men in the room had only just finished a round of gin rummy. He was handcuffed and transported to the Taunton Insane Hospital.

Bertrand Wood's uncle went along to sign the commitment papers. After the formalities were taken care of, the doctors who examined Crapo told the uncle that the few remaining residents of Noman's Land were lucky to have escaped this episode with their lives: The patient's disorder was one of the most dangerous types known to modern psychiatry.

Paranoid schizophrenia? Whatever they called it, the unfortunate Mr. Crapo disappeared into the insane asylum system of the day.

Johnny Sea View

MANY YEARS BACK, my (now ex) husband Marty and I were driving north on Barnes Road, heading for Oak Bluffs, when we passed an older guy with his thumb extended on one hand, and a chain saw clutched in the other.

"Will you look at that?" I cried. "Who in his right mind would pick up a hitchhiker with a chain saw?"

"Oh, that's Johnny Sea View," said Marty. "It's safe to give him a ride." And we did.

In his 70s, a twinkly little man—he was once a jockey—with blue eyes, lanky white hair, and a raspy, persnickety voice like a Damon Runyon racetrack tout, Johnny Sea View picks up tree-trimming jobs, hence the chainsaw.

When you have time to shoot the breeze with Johnny, he'll be happy to tell you war stories. You don't believe them, because how could any one fellow during World War II have been in so many locations engaged in so many perilous missions? According to Johnny, he flew with the Air Force in England, penetrated enemy lines with the French Resistance in northern France, and parachuted into Sicily.

One day at an Edgartown cocktail party, I found myself talking to a dentist from Boston who had also glided into Palermo by parachute in 1944.

"You didn't happen to know Oliver Perry, did you?" (Johnny Sea View's real name, before his sobriquet took hold).

"Oh sure. We were on the same squad of paratroopers."

Holy cow! If Johnny's tales about his derring-do days in Sicily were true, then all the other stuff might have actually happened as well!

Johnny maintains a gallantry that disappeared with powdered wigs. When I run into him in a store or office, he takes one look at me, spins around on his heels, and hustles himself outside again. But wait! He is by no means taking flight. A couple of minutes later he returns and thrusts a bouquet of dahlias or rugosa roses at me.

"Freshly stolen!" he announces.

Heaven knows what chain of circumstances brought Johnny from jockey fame to rolling back the Huns in World War II to snatching flowers from Vineyard gardens. There was a time when an old seen-better-days hotel on the waterfront in Oak Bluffs housed a honky-tonk bar stocked with island characters. The blowzy owner, Loretta, who once donated a trunkful of mink coats to the thrift store, presided over the bar with her big whisky laugh. Philosopher fishermen, amiable boozers, and lone Johnny with his war stories enjoyed her company and the bar. So much a fixture was Johnny in this dive that he was rewarded with Sea View—the name of the old fleabag hotel—as a nickname.

The Sea View in its old incarnation is long gone. Today the three-story structure is a refurbished neo-Victorian townhouse of posh little condos. But Johnny is still very much intact, hitchhiking around the island with his chain saws, reliving his war days, and gladdening the hearts of island women with ragged bouquets of stolen flowers.

The Landlady in the Shed

AND THEN THERE WAS Carole (not her real name), who owned a three-story house that rears up over the sea on the bluffs of East Chop. In her sixties, an erstwhile composer, she found that the only way she could make ends meet was to rent out her oceanfront home to summer visitors. However, her ends wouldn't meet enough to provide her with a rental of her own. So when summer and her first tenants arrived, Carole took up residence in the shed on the street side of her house.

A copse of Russian olives screened the shed from the main house, and Carole stayed quiet enough that no one ever stumbled onto the fact that their landlady lived right outside in the back yard.

In the dead of night, Carole would clean up in the outdoor shower. No one ever cared to ask—or to know—what she did for other bathroom facilities.

We do know where she slept, however. The shed was crammed with a baby grand piano upon which she composed new pieces, playing softly enough not to rouse her tenants. At night she unfurled a bedroll under the piano and crawled beneath for a good night's rest.

She found that the only way she could make ends meet was to rent out her home to summer visitors.

Carole sold her house a couple of years back, and a Boston developer gutted the inside. He took what looked like a dozen machetes to the overgrowth in back. The shed is gone, and the house is spiffed up on a shaved-to-the-ground arid bluff, but many of us miss Carole and her cockamamie summer living arrangement.

It's Mo!

MAN OR WOMAN? Saint or sociopath? Cultural ornament or the island's biggest mooch? It's impossible to know exactly, but this bewildering individual is, without a single doubt, entirely lovable. For purposes of anonymity, we'll refer to this island character as Mo Putney.

Mo's sexual orientation is as mystifying as comedian Julia Sweeney's character Pat, of *Saturday Night Live* fame. Ultimately Sweeney brought the androgynous character to the silver screen in *It's Pat*, a movie whose plot revolves around Pat's friends and neighbors devising all manner of tests to determine Pat's gender. Although the actor playing the part was female, she guarded the secret of her alter ego so superbly that even in the end we're left guessing.

Mo revealed that she had grown up as a young lady named Penelope, an eater of cucumber sand-wiches from a patrician family.

Our own Pat, i.e., Mo, is probably a woman of sorts. I only know this because some years ago in an interview with the *Vineyard Gazette,* Mo revealed that *she* had grown up as a young lady named Penelope, an eater of cucumber sandwiches from a patrician family. All that fancy background has gone by the board. Now in her sixties, Mo lives in a tiny government-subsidized apartment in Vineyard Haven. She gets about by bike and bus and wears well-worn dungarees, sneakers, and ancient baggy sweatshirts. Her hair is a more-pepper-than-salt bob, her face has never held a lick of makeup, and a missing front tooth completes her smile. Her voice is pitched low and, subsequently, some islanders will swear up and down that Mo is male.

Whatever.

Mo is a highly specialized breed of pack rat who manages to stash all her holdings in other people's domiciles. All over the island, homeowners long ago agreed to store boxes, bundles of paperwork, and canvases—Mo is an artist—in their attics or basements, only to find that years later they're still holding the goods. Mo is possessed with some kind of compulsion to leave a habitat trail behind her.

Last March I planned a month's trip to Italy, and I asked Mo to stay in my cottage to babysit my dog and cat, pet- and house-sitting being one of her many occupations. Before I returned, I called her from Boston and asked if she'd mind clearing out before I arrived home; after weeks away, I longed to come back to perfect solitude. When I opened the front door, Mo was gone, but her stuff was very much in residence: four weeks' worth of the *New York Times* stacked halfway to the ceiling, a dozen boxes of jigsaw puzzles, rucksacks of personal goods, books galore, paper sacks filled with unidentifiable projects, piles of old clothes, and a month's worth of food preparation stuffed in freezer and fridge.

Normally Mo's lack of a car might have accounted for her leaving mountains of gear behind, but on that particular weekend she had the use of an SUV provided by the West Chop lady whose Pekinese Mo was sitting concurrently with my pets.

Over the course of the next four weeks, Mo paid me a weekly visit to return casserole dishes she'd borrowed to whip up one of her masterpieces. Each time she handed me an item of cookware with whatever food it had contained, she'd say, "Sorry it's dirty. I don't have a dishwasher."

"And you don't have a sponge?" I finally asked.

Mo Putney is not one to sit at home. Chances are, were you a fly on the wall of Mo's living room, you would rarely see her. At any time of the year, at any island event—art opening, book signing, symposium—Mo is there, provided complimentary food and drink are served. I've bumped into her at events way up in West Tisbury, where, having scoffed up free booze, cheese, and grapes, Mo will ask me if I'm heading down to Edgartown, where another "do" promises cake and fruit punch. Between the two functions, Mo will have covered all the major food groups.

Part of her reason for inquiring after others' plans is that Mo is continually in need of a ride. For a time, up in Chilmark, some local ladies whiled away winter's cold doldrums by organizing a monthly film society, held in different Chilmarkers' houses. Dinner was always potluck. Somehow Mo Putney got wind of the festivities, and spent the requisite three hours changing from the Edgartown/West Tisbury bus to the final Chilmark hinterlands run. After the movie had been viewed and the buffet of luscious comfort foods consumed, the ladies began to disperse. Mo asked if anyone was headed back to Oak Bluffs.

"We all live up here in Chilmark," she was told. (A forty-minute drive from Oak Bluffs.)

"That's okay," said Mo, her adorable, tooth-missing face brightening. "I'll spend the night!"

The hostess herself drove home the Woman Who Came to Dinner.

Mo's inevitable presence at an event is mainly a happy addition to the occasion. She's a sparkling conversationalist and well informed, all those *New York Times* editions having been crammed into her cute gray-bobbed brain. As much of a freeloader of food and booze as she is, she is also palpably generous herself; she would give you the shirt off her own back if for some strange reason you fancied it. She is also a veritable Mary Poppins to many islanders' pets. Once, when she arrived on my doorstep with yet another soiled casserole dish, she bent down as my cocker spaniel charged up, deliriously happy to greet her.

"It's Auntie Mo!" I cried.

Mo straightened up with a sudden disquieted look on her face. "*Cousin* Mo," she corrected.

Are we absolutely certain she was once named Penelope?

A Living Legend

WHEN YOU FIRST move to the island you hear Trina Kingsbury stories.

Like the time she knocked six cops on their keisters.

Or when she wrenched the urinal from the men's john at the Lamppost and banged it down between the bar and the tables.

And what about the time she hijacked an Air New England flight so she could bring her sick pig to the vet in Hyannis?

"Oh, lord. I don't know who invents these scenarios," chuckles Trina when I meet her for tea and talk at her quaint farm called Swolley Hole at an undisclosed location in Chilmark. "Not that some of them don't have a germ of

truth," she said, with a fond gleam in her periwinkle blue eyes.

These days Trina hardly looks like the bar-busting Valkyrie of what she herself calls her hell-raising days. Now her once dark hair has turned a uniform golden gray. She wears gold-wired glasses. Dressed in a hand-knit vest over a long country skirt, she more resembles the poet/artist/farm lady of her feminine alter ego.

Not that she's unable even nowadays to hurl a guy across a room. "What sets me off is being groped in female places," she told me. "Anyone who knows me also knows: You get fresh, you go flying."

In her younger days, the Vineyard native, six feet tall with flowing dark hair and what an island male with a long memory described as a "formidable figure," was quick to throw a punch, particularly after she'd spent the warm-up part of the evening drinking. Looking back, she realizes she had set herself a mission: "Girls in bars were always thought to be looking for sex. I taught people that we had a right to enjoy a drink undisturbed. I was like the Carrie Nation of sex in barrooms, bringing in an ax to put a stop to boozing molesters."

Trina's brawling reputation devolved from her dad, the larger-than-life Craig Kingsbury, known to the world as Quint, the character played by Robert Shaw in *Jaws* (see "A Shark Named Bruce" in the "VIPs" chapter). "My dad taught me how to fight and how to throw people without hurting them."

> *"Girls in bars were always thought to be looking for sex. I taught people that we had a right to enjoy a drink undisturbed."*

Although today Trina looks, if not fragile, then smaller than the Amazon warrior of her youth, she maintains she still has the musculature to give someone a good pounding. "I first built up my strength from shoveling out barns at my parents' farm."

Trina's gentler qualities came from her mother, the late Gertrude Tereski Kingsbury, long a nurse at the Vineyard hospital. The split between the yin and yang influences of her parents can be seen in Trina's yearly contributions to the Agricultural Fair: On the one hand she competes in the chainsaw- and ax-throwing competitions. On the other hand, she invariably wins blue ribbons for her knitting, crocheting, and sewing. Her crow-quill pen-and-ink prints of island wildflowers and island butterflies have adorned houses all over the country for years. Trina is also understandably proud of her lifelong certification in the British Horse Society: "I grew up on the back of a horse."

As we mull over some of the tall tales of Trina's Bunyonesque youth, she puts together the pieces that yielded the sick-pig/hijacking whopper:

"I had to spend some time in Maine, so I left my Swolley Hole animals with a critter sitter. I had these two pigs, a boy named Boris and a girl named Mildred. I got wind that a pack of vicious dogs had attacked both my pigs. Boris was dead, torn to shreds, and Mildred had run away. I was frantic to look for her, so I chartered a plane to come home. Well, I'd been partying, and the pilot had to think twice about taking off with me. Then he decided once we were up in the clouds, I'd pass out and everything would be hunky-dory. I didn't pass out, so the back-and-forth shouting from the cockpit to the cabin must've sounded sort of raucous to the air-traffic controllers. They told the pilot to abort the flight over Bangor, and when we landed, cops swarmed onboard to arrest me. I kept yelling about having to get back to my poor sow, so the papers had a field day with headlines like 'Girl Hijacks Airplane to Find Pig.'"

Over the years Trina faced many stern judges, but for the most part they were charmed by her folksy manner and her own brand of logic that often put an appealing spin on her wild behavior.

While she never yanked a urinal from the Lamppost john (that she recalls), she acknowledges that she waged her share of barroom battles that ultimately got her banned from Oak Bluffs taverns—although, given the passage of time, it's safe to assume she's been granted a tacit amnesty. One episode she told me about took place at the Ritz: "I was raising hell, and they asked me to leave. When I got outside, I remembered I'd left my keys in the bar, but they wouldn't let me back in to get them. I zipped up my windbreaker, pulled the hood over my head, and walked back inside through the plate glass window. *Crash! Bang!* I didn't get a scratch.

"Another time a bunch of us were up here at the farm, raising hell, drinking Napa Sonoma Manana—it cost eighty-five cents a half gallon. My pals were starting to get on my nerves, so I told them all to get out before I went berserk. Then I went berserk anyway and heaved this bottle of Napa at the coal stove. When I looked up, the bottle was intact, but the coal stove had split in half!"

The simplest statement falls from Trina's lips with a zinger tacked on. A discussion of a long-ago operation causes her to recall, "And the surgeon had to spend some extra time removing shrapnel under my ribs from the time I got shot on Nashawena Island."

Nowadays Trina's acreage resembles something out of a Beatrix Potter painting. A miniature windmill stands near a sylvan pond, and wind chimes tinkle from aged oaks. A tiny gravel pathway leads up to a storybook kitty-house with hand-painted *trompe l'oeil* shutters and a wooden owl standing sentry duty just outside the door. Although at the present time no pigs live with Trina, her dog Alice Von Wolftrapp, a Portuguese rabbit hound/German Shepherd mix, trots down the path to greet all visitors. His orangey-gold coat is nearly matched by Doc, the cat, with apricot fur on his big-boned body and round, green-eyed mug. A second cat, Cho, is absent on the afternoon of my visit.

These days Trina's escapades are romantically pagan. "Instead of all-nighters drinking and carousing and sleeping it off in jail, I like to pull moonlighters. I do this with my pals on full-moon nights. We drink everything from tea to Gibsons and wander around the meadow in our jammies."

Just as long as no male moonlighter lays a hand on her, Trina has definitely mellowed with age. Should someone be so ill-advised as to try, he would surely end up (in her words) "ass over-teakettle" in the pond.

Eccentrics, Animal

All Creatures Great and Small, Heroic and Looney-Tunes,
Stinky and Adorable

The Island's Rin Tin Tin

FOR THOSE OF US with island dogs too stupid to answer to anything but the dinner bell, the following tale of canine heroics will bring renewed hope regarding doggy I.Q.

On February 1, 1815, citizens of Martha's Vineyard received word that Great Britain and the United States were suing for peace in the wake of the War of 1812. In those days Vineyarders must have felt greater solicitude for their sister island, Nantucket, and immediately a call went out to bring the news to those siblings farther out to sea.

Only one problem, and it was the same old predicament that has stymied people in these parts from time immemorial: Stormy weather. A bitter wind was shrieking down from the Canadian tundra. Charcoal clouds glowered over the water. In Edgartown the harbor was frozen silver-blue solid all the way down through Katama Bay to the Atlantic.

Nonetheless two valiant islanders agreed to attempt the perilous crossing—Allen Coffin and his cousin, Joseph Thaxter Jr. At the last minute, two Nantucket whale men, eager to return home no matter what the adverse conditions, also volunteered. They grabbed an open boat fortified with iron runners for easy gliding over the ice. As they pushed off from town, Mr. Coffin's dog—unnamed in the chronicle, but why don't we call him Freddy—trotted at his master's side. Repeatedly Coffin ordered Freddy back to the village, but the loyal, albeit disobedient, dog persisted in padding along behind the men and the boat for a full four miles across the ice.

At last the four men and the dog reached South Beach, only to find some of the water clogged with icy porridge. They hopped aboard and set sail through the partially frozen sludge. Gradually they made their way across Muskeget Channel, but as they closed in on Nantucket, their vessel crunched up on the shoals. Enormous chunks of ice walloped the open boat. Water squirted through leaks. Frantically the four men bailed the water back over the gunwale. Without warning, from either side two giant ice floes converged on the boat. A geyser of water shot up from the depths. The vessel sank in minutes, taking the two men from Nantucket down with it.

Coffin, Thaxter, and Freddy were pitched onto an ice floe. They labored to their feet and trudged across the icy sandbars to Nantucket's western shore. Coffin's heart went out to his freezing dog; he plucked him from the ice and bundled him under his coat for warmth, and the body heat was reciprocated as it rose from Freddy's furry little form. Tragedy struck again, however, when Coffin looked back to see that Thaxter had expired from the cold and exposure. The lone survivor knew he had only minutes remaining before he too would succumb to the elements.

At last Coffin reached the beach of Nantucket, where he collapsed in the snow. With a final gasp he ordered Freddy to go find help. The dog bounded off across the fields. Two miles inland, he arrived at the Obed Marshall farmhouse. In the style of the phenomenally brainy Lassie and Rin Tin Tin, Freddy barked and barked until the farmhands realized they were being asked to mount a rescue.

The Obed Marshall boys, with Freddy still vocalizing, set out with a sleigh. They recovered the fallen Vineyarder, and clambered for home, but not before they dispatched the genius dog out onto the frozen sandbars to search for survivors. Some time later Freddy returned to the farmhouse with a hatchet in his mouth.

Perhaps he thought the simple-minded humans needed a reminder to chop logs to build a fire and thaw out his master?

Coffin recovered, and his trusty dog lived to a ripe old age.

We can only pray that Freddy's descendants frolic on Vineyard soil today.

The Last Heath Hen in the World and Maybe Even the Whole Milky Way

A BIG VOICE lived in this little chicken body; the mournful call of now extinct heath hen was not unlike the blare of a foghorn. The sound emanated from a pair of orange sacs the size of tennis balls. The last members of the clan subsisted on the Vineyard during the first third of the twentieth century. The heath hen was a cousin of the prairie chicken, and its meat was equally tasty—a factor in its demise.

The abundance of heath hen in early New England was such that historians attribute the Pilgrims' survival during their first winter more to the wild American chicken than to the much touted turkey. Heath hens were absurdly easy to shoot; they were sluggish runners, and their flying ability resembled the takeoff of a drunken duck. The plenitude prompted people to complain about a diet overdependent on heath hen: Servants in Colonial households demanded no more than two helpings of heath hen per week.

The combination of vulnerability and deliciousness, in addition to a tendency for hunters to kill even the juveniles of the flock, depleted the stocks within two centuries. By 1870 no heath hens remained on the mainland. Census takers soon discovered that the sole surviving heath hens on planet Earth dwelled on Martha's Vineyard. At the time of this discovery, two hundred birds presented themselves for roll call. Six years later, fewer than one hundred remained.

Here on the island we owe a debt of gratitude to the heath hen because the heroic efforts to save them yielded today's Manuel F. Correllus State Forest. In the 1880s, to protect the dwindling ranks of the soon-to-expire bird, six hundred acres in West Tisbury were set aside as a preserve. When the park was put in place, only fifty birds remained, and those were treated like the celebrities they had become. A warden was hired to watch over their welfare. Fire barriers were dug, and special crops were grown to feed the birds. Extra food was distributed in winter, and all hawks, owls, or feral cats were shot on sight. Had extra funds been available, it's a sure bet the trustees would have provided the heath hens with heated condominiums, but short of that, everything was done to enhance their chances of survival.

The project worked. By 1915 heath hens were flourishing on Martha's Vineyard—more than two thousand of them by official estimates. Ornithologists and ordinary tourists arrived from all over the world to witness the birds' theatrical mating ritual: As the females stood on the sidelines, the cocks put on a magnificent show. They strutted, they hopped, they danced a gavotte, and they staged mock battles, all the while blasting forth with their macabre *WHOO-OO-OO* cry.

It looked as if full recovery was assured, but then tragedy struck.

In May 1916 a fire funneled through the underbrush of the preserve, demolishing nesting grounds. So fierce were the heath hens' maternal genes that they sat stalwart on their eggs in a blaze of self-immolation much like the ancient Indian funeral suttee, only this one performed for future chicks rather than past husbands. For the few remaining heath hens, the following winter brought with it an invasion of goshawks, a fierce predator of slower, earthbound birds.

In the census of the spring of 1917 only one hundred fifty heath hens remained on the island, and disastrously, as a result of the conflagration in the nesting grounds, almost all of those birds were male. The flock dwindled still more.

By 1927 scientists counted thirteen heath hens, only two of which were female. And then the last heath hen stood up to be counted: In December 1928, one lonely little guy, named Booming Ben by the press, was left to trumpet *WHOO-OO-OO* over hill and dale in search of a soul mate that never materialized.

An effort was made to interest the sole survivor in a sexy lineup of plump prairie hens, considered to be close genetic cousins. Booming Ben turned up his snobby beak at them, and continued to wail *WHOO-OO-OO* for an illusory love.

In 1931 ornithologists trapped and banded old Booming Ben. He was spotted three more times, the last sighting taking place on March 11, 1932. Four scientists watched the little fellow fly, clumsily, of course, into the mists, never to be seen again.

The Tipsy Pig

LORD EMSWORTH, of the P. G. Wodehouse novels, who revered his big, fat prize-winning sow, the Empress of Blandings, almost as much as Joe DiMaggio loved Marilyn Monroe, would also have worshipped seven-hundred-pound Helen of Chase Road in Edgartown.

Helen came to the Morgan household—to mom Anna, dad Jesse, and son Stephen—in the late 1970s. At that time Helen was merely a conventionally tubby pig destined for several rounds of ham sandwiches. But when the family discovered their new porker was pregnant, they gave her a reprieve, a kind of farmyard maternity leave. Soon after, Helen wiggled and waddled her way into their hearts, and continued to pile on an impressive number of pounds, much of it derived from beer calories. Who knows what prankster first introduced Ms. Piggy to the pleasures of America's favorite alcoholic beverage, but soon beer became part of Helen's daily nutritional regimen until she was holding up her end like the most dedicated of fraternity kegsters.

Helen's favorite snack was poison ivy, which ended up being a tremendous boost to the family. Son Stephen during this period told a local reporter, "She sucks that stuff up like spaghetti."

It's hard to say whether poison ivy is fattening when eaten in bulk, but it's clear the Morgans could have made a fortune by turning the big gal over to other islanders to rid their yards of itch weed.

When you have an animal that weighs a third of a metric ton, all hell breaks loose on the rare occasions that she roams free. Once on an early autumn day, Helen escaped from her pen and trundled off to visit the neighbors. The dwellers of Chase Road nearly fainted when, all of a sudden, with a snort as loud as thunder, a massive face with apple-sized nostrils jammed into their screen doors.

On another occasion Helen connected with the grille of a neighbor's car. No injury came to Helen, but damages to the vehicle amounted to one hundred forty-six dollars. The Morgans covered the cost with their homeowner's insurance, though, as Stephen said, "It needed a special note."

A barnyard specimen so monumental attracts similar-sized attention. Island children clamored for their parents to drive them past big Helen's little farm. And in those days before signs marked many of our roads, Missy Fatstuff made an excellent landmark for visitors new to the Vineyard: "Turn left at the blue mailbox, follow on past a split rail fence, and when you see the biggest pig in New England, hang a right."

Paula Catanese, now of Oak Bluffs, used to live on Chase Road at the same time that Helen reigned supreme. Paula had learned that the big girl loved LifeSavers candy. Accordingly, Paula would visit the pig and lay a row of the multicolored disks on her trough.

"She was so methodical about it," Paula told me. "She always ate the cherry-flavored ones first, then grape, orange, and last the lemon. It was hilarious to see this huge animal nibbling so delicately at the candies. It completely changed my mind about the term 'pigging out'!"

In her tenth year of fame and obesity, Helen developed an intestinal blockage. (Too much poison ivy with beer chasers?) Her vet made a heroic effort to save her, but on a day in early November 1988 the jumbo pig was given a last couple of beers for the road before she was put to sleep.

Lord Emsworth would have led the entire village in mourning.

Raising a Stink

YOU NEED ONLY disembark from the ferry for the briefest of visits to learn, within thirty minutes of your arrival, that skunks predominate on Martha's Vineyard. That ferocious odor, like no other rank smell in the universe, oozes forth from the underpinnings of buildings, from sites of roadkill, from patches of lawn or shrubs, or along split rail fences where an offended skunk has sometime earlier in the day or night been alarmed enough to raise its tail and open fire.

The problem is that we have no natural predators of skunks, aside from the tires of speeding autos. In all of mainland America, coyotes cull the stock of these black and white stink bombs, but here we're far enough out to sea that a coyote would need to be an extraordinary swimmer to make it this far. We could, arguably, import coyotes, perhaps a Noah's Ark male and female duo to get the breed established, but that would shock and appall the thousands of cat lovers on the island, in addition to the owners of small dogs, as pampered pets make tasty snacks for the likes of coyotes.

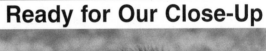

Ready for Our Close-Up

These cuddly-looking baby skunks are looking sassy enough to kick up their legs, Rockettes-style—they know they've got the run of the island, with no natural predator in sight.

VINEYARD GAZETTE PHOTOGRAPHIC ARCHIVES, EDITH BLAKE PHOTO

Here's a modest proposal: We alert all pet owners to keep small animals indoors for one full year, then we bring over a team of hungry coyotes, all of one gender so they won't be making coyote pups. We strap electronic tags to their legs to ensure our ability to round them up once all the skunks on the island have fallen to their prehensile claws and slavering jaws.

The thing is, the island skunk population had been totally eliminated some four hundred years ago. When white settlers began trickling over here in the 1630s, Indians reported a lifestyle complete with skunks, foxes, raccoons, beavers, and bears —all of whose ancestors no doubt migrated here in a primordial time when the island was connected to the mainland, before some glacial earth mover shoved a cleft between the Vineyard and Cape Cod. Early on in the settlement period, the island's early sheep farmers exterminated beaver and bear. They also killed off all the deer, though some wash-ashore deer swam over from Naushon Island in the early nineteenth century and the Rod and Gun Club brought some in for their own dark purposes. Now we have enough deer to keep the planet in venison patties for the next five decades.

For a full six decades the scent of piney woods, wild grapes, and honeysuckle went undisturbed.

As for foxes and skunks, they were fully exterminated in 1900 in a poisoning campaign waged by another set of enterprising sheep farmers. They failed to kill every last raccoon, however—these we have in abundance, all of them eager to make our acquaintance over our garbage cans. But the skunks disappeared for a full six decades, sixty-plus years during which the scent of piney woods, wild grapes, and honeysuckle went undisturbed. The stench of a skunk's own brand of chemical warfare had been eliminated.

Speaking of which, if you've never smelled a skunk's payload up close, it's a hundred times worse than the stink that assaults you briefly on the highway—it makes your eyes water and actually hurts your teeth. At one time my bookstore in Oak Bluffs shared space with the Black Dog General Store. Twenty-four-year-old Nate Polaquin, manning the Black Dog counter, happened to be standing outside the front double glass doors one fall day in 2004 when a startled skunk squeezed off a neutron bomb of its foul juice in the narrow alley alongside our building. Nate barreled back into the store, his jacket wrested across his nose and mouth.

"We've got to get out of here!" he shouted.

At the same time, the skunk's murderous vapors flooded the air shafts. The stench whooshed into the room, invading every cell, penetrating every cranny. It was the work of a moment to grab my keys and flee the building with Nate hauling tail in the opposite direction. I was inside the "skunk house" for all of ninety seconds, and hadn't of course been directly targeted, but all the same, when I arrived home, having aired out my clothes with a ten-minute bicycle ride, my son wrinkled his nose and asked if I'd been skunked.

So, for more than sixty years, the island was blessedly skunk free, and then, in the November 1969 issue of the *Dukes County Intelligencer,* the following report was filed: "There is probably now a small resident breeding population of skunks."

What happened? Where had they come from?

For years urban—or rather rural—legend had it that island hell-raiser Craig Kingsbury (previously showcased in these pages) brought this new swarm of skunks to our sweet-smelling rock. Mr. Kingsbury died a few years ago, but in the spring of 2005, his daughter Kristen Henshaw published a collection of her dad's tales, compiled from hundreds of hours of tape recordings of the wily man's adventures.

And sure enough, without a trace of remorse, he claims he carted a cage of three hundred skunks to the Vineyard and set them free in the woods. By his account, he brought them over in his ox cart, telling the ferry guys that the critters were rats (not that rats are a whole heckuva lot better!).

Why did he do this? After you've read *Craig Kingsbury Talking*, you understand that this man was a prankster of mythic proportions. The tales of his childhood leave you stunned and pitying his poor parents, who raised him in Trenton, New Jersey. By Mr. Kingsbury's own account, there was no strawberry patch not pillaged, no bird unruffled by BB guns, no bull not taunted when young Craig was in the vicinity. He was Spanky and the gang all rolled into one deranged hooligan. Throughout his early years people peppered his backside with rock salt shot in attempts to eject the little sociopath from their property.

The fact was, Craig Kingsbury never grew out of his love of mischief making. Maybe the stench of skunk never bothered him. A few chosen souls exist who don't mind it, including Walter Wlodka of Chilmark, the man you call when you need some black and white beasties trapped and eliminated. Mr. Wlodka once, after removing a family of the offending creatures from under our house—mama and three little ones—remarked that the smell has never bothered him, in fact, he kind of likes it.

That's what he gets the big bucks for.

So the skunks are back like never before—Mr. Kingsbury has set aside for himself one odiferous memorial—and if we don't come up with a plan real soon, a new black-and-white striped icon will replace the black dog on our leading tee shirts.

And Speaking of Tee Shirts, What's the Story of the Black Dog?

WHAT IS THE MOST frequently asked tourist question on Martha's Vineyard? It used to be, "Where's the bridge?" or "Where's the tunnel?" or "Where's that little bridge where Ted Kennedy—?" Nowadays, though, befuddled travelers want to know, "What's the story of the black dog?" They recognize they're in the midst of some kind of sartorial phenomenon, but they're in the dark about its origins.

The thing is, even longtime Vineyarders are hard pressed to understand how it came about that on a sunny summer day, they can look around them and observe every last person decked out in a tee shirt, of whatever size or color, with the silhouette of a black labrador emblazoned over the wearer's left nipple. A visitor from another planet might even make the logical assumption that this island is one big summer camp with every member issued an identical tee shirt upon arrival.

One point worth making is that no Vineyarder would be caught dead with a single item from the Black Dog catalogue, just as in Paris you don't see the natives donning garments that advertise the Eiffel Tower. At Christmastime we might pop into a Black Dog store to buy goodies for off-island friends and relatives, knowing they share mainlanders' appreciation for the doggy icon, but try giving a pair of Black Dog socks or boxer shorts to a Vineyarder, and they'll get passed along to an unwitting bystander like the proverbial holiday fruitcake.

Here's what happened: Years ago a homey tavern on the Vineyard Haven waterfront came out with a tee shirt, just as cafes and retail stores all over the country sell their own one hundred percent cotton tees to encourage human beings to shell out twenty bucks for the privilege of flashing ads on their backs. A waitress at the Black Dog Tavern, a budding art student, had doodled a black dog graphic on the back of her pad, and the management picked it up for use on the menus.

By the time the tee shirt appeared, the waitress was long gone, back at school in New York. Some years later she learned her scribble had turned into megabucks for what was now becoming, thanks to the success of the tee shirts, an exploding enterprise, with new stores opening and a spiffy inventory of everything  from shirts to shot glasses to dog collars. The waitress/ artist hired a lawyer and, in an Edgartown court of law in the late 1970s, won a settlement for an undisclosed amount of money. In return, the artful doodler had to promise she would take the money and, if not exactly run, then go away and stay away.

Let us hope the artist transformed her earnings into a fruitful career for herself, since her cute little graphic has continued to provide fortunes for many people.

So who or what is the black dog, besides a figment of an artsy waitress's imagination? Was there an actual dog to breathe life into the legend? Apparently.

Before Captain Robert Douglas opened the doors of the Black Dog Tavern in the 1960s, the love of his life was—and still is—the topsail schooner *Shenandoah,* a reproduction of a nineteenth-century ship that for decades has been the jewel in the crown of the Vineyard Haven harbor. When people see the stately lines of the graceful schooner gliding across the sound under full sail, they stop what they're doing and run to snap pictures or stare in awe.

According to Black Dog lore, Captain Douglas lived alone on the Vineyard Haven harbor. Like many Yankee sea salts with terse

vocabularies and an inward nature, he valued his solitude above all things. Then one dark and stormy night, in the teeth of a winter nor' easter, a buddy of the captain's dropped off a sopping wet black puppy he'd rescued from a muddy puddle. "Gotta catch the ferry," said the friend. "Try to find a home for her. If you can't, just drop her off at the pound."

As related in the children's book *The Story of the Little Black Dog,* by J.B. Spooner and illustrated by Terre Lamb Seeley, you can see it coming a mile away—the grumpy captain adores the pup from Day One but doesn't realize it until . . . well, here's a synopsis of the tale:

Pup pees on carpets and chews old boots and smashes valuable antiques. Come spring, and to spruce up the *Shenandoah,* the Cap brings the pup to prevent her from further annihilating his land home. In short order the pup gets her sea legs and learns which portholes lead to which bunks neatly spread with navy wool blankets. She makes herself at home in the dining saloon, where "two long, shiny, gimbaled tables rocked gently back and forth while the kerosene lamps overhead moved with the same rhythm."

It hits the captain like a bolt of lightning to the mizzenmast: *This here's a sea dog!*

Other adventures await master and pup, and to read the Spooner/Lamb Seeley book is to fall in love, as did the master mariner, with this excellent specimen of a [sea]man's best friend.

Is any part of this story true? Well, the last time I hooked Captain Davis up to a polygraph machine, he passed with flying colors.

The original Black Dog has long made its way to that section of heaven reserved for nautical canines, but her silhouette lives on—gracing tens of thousands of tee shirts, coffee mugs, and bags of candy.

So what's the real deal with the Black Dog? It means that if you're walking down a busy street in Hong Kong, and you see someone approach with a Black Dog sweatshirt on his torso, you'll know he's been to Martha's Vineyard. It's an affordable status item, plain and simple.

But it's also that sea salty dog aboard the *Shenandoah*—and riding in the backs of pick-ups—and snuffling along *Rosa rugosa*–lined trails—and romping on beaches with tiny tots. The black lab is, after all, the Vineyard's premier breed and is dear to islanders' hearts.

The Cat and the Custody Battle

THE REAL NAMES will need to change because the events that occurred fully fourteen years ago still create pangs of injury in both parties. So we'll give them the *noms de plume* of Cindy and George, and the cat a *nom de chat* of Benny.

In the 1980s, on a magical peninsula extending out into the depths of a cove, Cindy, her husband, and their two kids lived with their two cats, Cecil and Benny. In the fall of '91, the family moved to a house in town, nine miles up island. Cecil settled comfortably into his new digs, but after two months Benny, a short-haired brown tabby, up and disappeared. Cindy hunted for him over field and dale, to no avail. At last she gave him up for dead.

In August of the following year, Cindy ventured back to her old stomping grounds at the cove in search of the wild mint that grew near the water's edge. As she filled her basket, she heard a rustling in the bushes. All at once ol' Benny jumped out of the underbrush. He plopped at her feet and sent up an audible purr in greeting. Tears of joy and amazement rolled down Cindy's cheeks. She scooped him up and drove him home.

Turned out that Benny had been taken in by a man named George who'd become attached to the plucky young feline. When he realized his adopted pet was missing, he placed an ad in the paper. A couple of days later, Cindy saw the ad and called George to thank him for caring for her pet during the time of his absence.

And they all lived happily ever after.

Except, they didn't.

Twelve days after Cindy retrieved her cat from the field of wild mint, that inimitable Benny hightailed it once again. Two days later he showed up on (you guessed it) George's doorstep. This time the man decided to keep the cat for its own safety. Clearly the tabby was attached to this area above all other locations. To expose it to another perilous trek down island, across creeks and farms and roads, was to risk all nine of its lives, six or seven of which had been used up in the first long march home.

The Party of the First Part took the Party of the Second Part to small claims court for the return of her pet. The judge of the Martha's Vineyard District Court ruled that Benny be remanded to his original owner. George refused, again citing the animal's safety. The judge threatened the man with thirty days in jail for contempt of court. Still the P. of the S.P. held firm. He hired an animal rights lawyer and took the case to an appeals court in Boston. This new judge ruled that George could keep the cat until the matter was settled in court the following year.

No one knows how the issue was resolved. A secret verdict was handed down, a gag order was instituted, and the saga of the cat with the world's best navigational skills became nobody's business.

Presumably Benny is dead by now. In cat years he'd be one hundred and twenty.

Let us hope that Cindy and George worked out a policy of joint custody. Of course, Cindy would have had to tell Benny, "You are grounded, mister!"

The Sailin' Schipperke

IT WAS A SMALL, black ten-year-old dog, an odd little fellow called a Belgian Schipperke, which in Flemish means "skipper," a tribute to the breed's centuries of guard duty on canal boats. The pooch and its owners spent the summer of 1941 in Oak Bluffs on one of the finger streets east of the harbor.

In those bygone times, townsfolk were less conscientious about confining their pets, so the schipperke spent many hours of the day running around on his own. His ancient genes throbbed with the memory of Belgian canals, and thus he often made his way down to the wharves.

A number of times the dog boarded the ferry; he was small enough to scrabble up the gangplank unseen. Only after several crossings would the sailors realize the frisky fellow had been hanging around for fully half the day. Eventually someone would recognize old Schipp and return him to his summer cottage. His owners would welcome him back, perhaps wishing he could tell them all the adventures that had befallen him during his time at sea.

The Pig That Ate Vineyard Haven

THE HOG NAMED Fern was the size of an over-stuffed couch. She lived up a winding dirt lane called Hay Path off Stoney Hill Road in Vineyard Haven. Much like the beer-guzzling Helen of Chase Road in Edgartown, Fern had endeared herself to her owners past the age when you would have needed to whisper the word "bacon" in her presence. Thus she'd grown beyond bulky. Yearly she gave birth to a pile of piglets that looked unusually tiny cuddled up to their Godzilla of a mom.

Fern had plenty to eat in her giant shed behind her family's home. What she missed, when her owners occasionally traveled off island, was human company. Couldn't get enough of it. If the family's absence coincided with stormy weather, and the electric fence that kept Fern penned shorted out, the love-handled hog would light out for fresh territory. It was then that Sharon Rzemian, animal control officer, was brought in.

Slim, brunette Ms. Rzemian on first sight looks like no match for a big bruiser like Fern, but the animal control officer told me in an interview that she had only fond feelings for the runaway. "The distress calls that came in for me to come get Fern were often from men who were terrified of her. They thought she might bite them."

Or sit on them and press the life out of them?

Sharon recalls a midnight hour several years back in December when footloose Fern had stretched herself out across the entrance to the NSTAR parking lot. "There was a horrific nor'easter blowing, so the guys had been called out in the middle of the night to mend fallen lines. Once Fern crashed across their driveway, however, no one could maneuver his truck around her, plus no one wanted to get close to her to move her away."

Sharon, who patrolled Oak Bluffs at the time, and Beth McCormick, the animal control officer in Vineyard Haven, were summoned from their toasty beds on this gale-tossed night to deal with the stubborn sow.

"The minute I arrived, the NSTAR guys, all of them huddled on the loading dock, jeered at me for thinking I could get anywhere with the big beast. I called out 'Fern!' and she lifted her big hammy head and gave me her *honk! honk! honk!* greeting."

Sharon and Beth got the hog up and moving down the bike path toward home. "With an animal that size, in the middle of the night, there's no vehicle big enough to transport her, so we had to walk her the several miles back to Hay Path."

Both animal control officers shivered inside their windbreakers and heavy boots. Sharon had fashioned a rope for Fern's neck, but her highness hated being pulled. The officers took turns plowing into the pig's pillow of a derriere with their chests, each bump good for a twenty to thirty foot ramble before Fern stopped for a breather.

"She was ten years old by that time, and had a bum leg," says Sharon. "Sometimes she would pause to regroup, but other times she would sink to the ground for a good piggy snooze. At this point Beth stretched out on her stomach facing the pig, chin in her hands, and she'd try to reason with her, 'Fern, come on. We're freezing our butts off out here. You know we love you, but it's time to go home.'"

On a couple of occasions when Fern made a jailbreak with her current crop of piggies, Sharon wound up having to bring the whole brood home. "That was easy. All I had to do was to get Fern moving; the babies trotted along behind her."

Fern finally died a few years back. "I couldn't blame her for wanting to roam," says Sharon with a bittersweet smile as she looks back on her adventures with the pig. "She wanted company."

We all know how lonesome it gets here in the winter.

Yoplait Skunks

SHARON RZEMIAN has another memory of an animal getting into a repetitive jam: "Skunks are always nosing around in dumpsters, of course, and they poke their way into every last grimy can and carton, but there's one item they can't shake loose from: Yoplait yogurt containers. There's something about the conical shape; once the skunk snuffles into it, a vacuum forms, and the container seals tight around its head," she told me.

Sharon maintains that islanders enjoy a love/hate relationship with skunks. People who would normally be badgering the officer to come trap and slaughter the skunks in their yard are the same folks who, once they spot a poor critter with a banana-mango Yoplait container on its head, place mad calls for rescue.

Once Sharon approaches the benighted skunk, she steals up slowly, avoiding any contact with its tail. She reaches for the Yoplait container and wrenches it up and away in the motion of a baseball batter swinging a hard line drive. The momentum pitches the creature free of the yogurt cup. After somersaulting a few times, the skunk stops and looks back at its liberator. Then it shakes its head and scampers off into the undergrowth. All Sharon needs to do at this point is look for a trash receptacle for the crinkled container.

"Animal welfare activists have been writing to Yoplait for years to ask them to redesign their cups," Sharon explained to me. "They do have a small warning on the side to urge customers to flatten the container before they discard it, but how many of us stop to read the small print on a yogurt carton?"

Certainly not the skunk population of Martha's Vineyard.

Crime Capers

Or, Is Martha's Vineyard Just One Big Barney Miller *Set?*

The Stolen Church

OUT ON NOMAN'S LAND, the little 628-acre island due south of Squibnocket, a bustling community of fishermen and farmers once existed. These days it's a barren chunk of dirt, for many years an improbable hybrid of bird sanctuary and military testing ground. We can only imagine flocks of highly agitated birds, twitching as they wait for the next detonation.

In the nineteenth century, a sea captain named Hiram Luce lived on Noman's, and made himself an integral part of the tiny church that graced the island. Well, "graced" may be too gracious a word. The church was the size of a fishing shack, with two small windows, one on each end, and a door made of weathered barn planks. But the rousing character of the services more than compensated for the humbleness of the building.

Captain Hiram was proud of his mellifluous voice, and it was his that soared over those of all the other churchgoers as they sang. His monopoly on the hymns led him to co-opt the sermons as well, and pretty soon he was preaching in the same stentorian tones with which he'd once hollered for his crew to "Lower all stove boats!" The big, ornate Bible from which he drew inspiration has for years been exhibited at the Chilmark Public Library.

The church sat on land belonging to one of the farmers, and eventually the farmer got the bright idea of claiming the church as private property, since for years he'd paid taxes on the land beneath its rotting planks. What he planned to do with his church ownership is not part of the historic record. Charge admission?

Restore it to a functioning tool shed or convert it to a three-hole outhouse?

We can only theorize that living in so small and so unimaginably insular a community turned many a man into a lunatic, because common sense would have told this farmer that laying claim to the church would rile up the other Nomanites. His hostile takeover was the cause of much wrangling.

The farmer refused to budge.

One day when the "church thief" had left the island, a group of strapping sailors positioned logs beneath the shack of worship and rolled it clean away onto neutral ground. The farmer took his case to court. The judge fined the leader of the moving crew two hundred dollars for "stealing a church."

It could certainly be argued that the farmer actually was the first to steal a church, but as all of this happened a long time ago, we can assume St. Peter has already taken up the matter with him.

Adultery as Felony

HAVE ISLANDERS EVER been charged and imprisoned for infidelity? Yes! But it's comforting to know that it only happened once in all the years from 1789 to 1873. (No record exists of what incident of cheating occurred in 1788, but it must have been juicy.)

In 1873 a sixty-three-year-old retired Tisbury merchant, one Thomas N. Hillman, whose wife and ten relatives lived with him in his far from spacious home, was arrested in tandem with one Mehitable Norton, thirty-five years of age. (There's a name we won't see coming 'round again with a fresh generation of baby girls.)

Mehitable was released the following day. In the dark ages of our Puritan history, she would have had to endure, if not outright hanging, a day or two in the stocks. But islanders have never been fond of that brand of public humiliation (certainly not today, when the entire court report is published weekly in the papers). By the time the suave 1870s had rolled around, when Thomas and Mehitable were caught in the act, island law was downright magnanimous:

Adultery meant engaging in sex to someone other than your spouse. Mehitable was single, so technically she had committed no crime, or at least not The Crime.

The most definitely married Hillman, however, was guilty as charged. He drew a stiff sentence and was shipped off to spend three long years in the New Bedford House of Corrections. Even today there are probably countless sixty-three-year-old gentlemen who would gladly assume the risk for a night of illicit love with a sexy Mehitable.

Another Quaint Law on the Old Books

IN MID-1800S America, "lunacy" was considered a reason for imprisonment. In any given penitentiary in those days, six percent of the clientele had been booked as lunatics. If they failed to snap out of it—and of course, back in those days, no Thorazine or Lithium or even Prozac was available to help patients back from Neverland—they were transferred from prison to an even more punitive insane asylum.

On the island we've for the most part kept our crazies among us. After all, it would be logistically impossible to ship the majority of year-rounders to psych wards off island. But during that era when so-called madmen and madwomen were swept off the streets with regularity, it was common enough to hear or read about a few poor deranged souls who'd been sent to some distant mainland "hospital" and were never again seen on these shores.

Copycat Arson

DESPERATE TIMES CALL for you-know-what measures.

In the 1890s in Oak Bluffs, a businessman named Augustus Wesley owned the Wesley Hotel across from the harbor. He reaped a fortune each summer when tourists poured onto these shores to observe the religious ceremonies in the Methodist Campground and/or to sample the saloons, brothels, and madcap festivities of town.

Mr. Wesley was in need of fresh scratch. He was building a mansion on Ocean Park and—well, you know how mansions are. It was costing more than he had budgeted for, even more than he had in his bank account.

What to do? Hmm. How about burning down the Wesley House and collecting the insurance? With any luck he'd receive enough money to finish the mansion and rebuild the cash-cow of a hotel. Pure genius!

His first mistake, on that August afternoon in 1894, was to tiptoe out of the tabernacle halfway through services. Puritan righteousness still ran deep in the New England psyche, and dozens of worshippers disapprovingly noted his impious exit. They watched as the businessman, looking unmistakably furtive, scampered to a back door of his hotel. He glanced to the right and he glanced to the left, and then right and left again, as if preparing to burglarize his own premises, before disappearing inside.

Minutes later, a plume of black smoke

billowed from the rear of the Wesley Hotel. Inside the tabernacle, someone rang the bell to summon the fire brigade. Horses dragged a fire wagon through the maze of Campground lanes, and soon men in yellow slickers were aiming hoses at the funnel of flames. Poor Mr. Wesley must have watched with a sinking heart as the fire was extinguished before it could do more than singe the walls of the storage room where the blaze had started. The beautiful Victorian summer inn had been saved.

What rotten luck.

Unhappily for Augustus Wesley, he'd launched his caper at a time when the citizens of Oak Bluffs were already ratcheted up to an hysterical pitch about arson in their midst. Since August 1892, catastrophic fires had destroyed two luxury hotels, the grammar school, and a number of cottages (see "Serial Fire Starter" in the "Scandal City" chapter). Every last soul in town waited in dread for the next random arson assault. No one had slept peacefully during the past two years.

So far no arrests had been made, and townsfolk had come to that paranoid state where they distrusted their neighbors, their mothers, their pet hamsters, even themselves.

No one thought for a minute that Mr. Wesley had set the other fires. But his willingness to add to the chaos by running a scam of his own won him no allies. The judge presiding over the trial shared that view, and he sentenced the former pillar of the community to five years in a serious mainland penitentiary.

The moral of the story: Never sneak out of church early to perpetrate a crime.

The Good Old Days of Rum Running

TODAY THE BIGGEST drain on island fishermen's incomes is not red tide or overfished stocks, but the long-ago repeal of Prohibition. Prior to that, during the Roaring Twenties—well, those were the days when fishermen hauled in a mighty lucrative catch, and stowed it under a camouflage layer of ice and fish.

Smart men that they were, Vineyard fishermen saw an opportunity and grabbed it. Whereas bootleggers in sleek motorboats were too conspicuous to avoid being busted, the funky, battered old family fishing boats could chug through a fleet of U.S. Coast Guard interceptors without raising a single red flag—at least in the beginning.

The Feds had pushed the legal limit from three miles to twelve miles out to sea. No biggie. The foreign contraband warehouse boats simply anchored a few clicks past the line and waited for customers. On dark-of-the-moon nights, our gallant island fishermen motored alongside the wholesalers and loaded on as many burlap bags of booze as they could fit in the hold. A topping off of ice and a shovelful of fish, and—*voilà*—you had a nice smelly diversion for prying Federal noses.

Big city bootleggers were eager to utilize Vineyard fishermen. Any owner of a fishing vessel willing to pick up more money in a single booze run than he'd made in the past two years could apply for the privilege. A bootlegging rep would be sent down to him, clad in rubber boots and ragtag clothes. By day the rep would drag lines and haul in squiggling catch with the fishermen. At night, the disguise came off. The bootlegger gave orders all the way from pick up to delivery onshore, where a truck would be waiting at an isolated cove.

Eventually the coast guard got hip to the fishermen's trick. One night in April 1927, a New Bedford fishing schooner called the *Etta M. Burns,* loaded with spirits, chugged into Vineyard Sound. The helmsman, who may have been sampling his own cargo, fell asleep at the wheel. The *Etta M. Burns* crunched onto the beach along the north shore of the Vineyard.

At dawn a beachcomber stumbled upon the stranded boat, then legged it home to call the rescue squad. A coast guard vessel steamed into the cove. Megaphone in hand, the skipper ahoyed the *Etta M. Burns*. He offered to dispatch a cutter to pull her from the sand. The knot of fishermen on deck hollered back that their vessel was taking on water. Their captain was in town summoning help, and they'd be fine on their own, thank you very much.

It might be safe to say that fishermen haven't the minds of hard-core criminals: It would have been wiser to accept the helping hand of the coast guard and be towed back out to sea at taxpayers' expense. Their refusal triggered suspicion in the skipper. He came aboard, and when he saw no signs of leakage, he rowed back to his boat and radioed in for backup.

A brisk wind arose, and the coast guard boat had to bide its time offshore. During the night, the gale pushed the *Etta M. Burns* parallel to shore. Waves broke over the deck. The crew deserted into the woods. Behind them, the schooner broke apart, its countless bottles of Old Mac Scotch Whiskey thrown every which way into the surf.

When daylight broke, Vineyarders swarmed the beach snuffling after free bottles of hooch. One Vineyarder had a different agenda, however: Mr. Chester Pease, a devout Prohibitionist, smashed every bottle he found.

Islanders who sampled the Old Mac said it should have been labeled simply "firewater." And it turned out they were correct. The coast guard traced the shipment to a rusty steamer anchored twenty miles due south of Montauk, Long Island. The steamer housed in its hold its own distillery, right down to bottles, fancy labels, and canvas sacks, ready to hand off to the middlemen of the fishing classes. The primary ingredient turned out to be Belgian alcohol, so there was nothing Scottish about this scotch, not even a single kilted marketing man bestowing his blessings on the product.

After the debacle with the *Etta M. Burns*, island fishermen found it harder to trawl for cod and whiskey at the same time.

The Bow and Arrow Robber

IT'S ONLY IN THE movies that crooks are brilliant. In real life they seem inept enough to make you wonder what else they could possibly do for a living.

In Edgartown one morning back in the early 1970s, two men sat parked in a car in the driveway of the Daniel Fisher house. Both men had visited community services, which was then lodged in the gracious old dwelling. The driver had offered the passenger a ride home "Right after I run a quick errand. Okay, man?"

The errand happened to be robbing the Dukes County Savings Bank.

He entered the bank and approached the teller. He brandished no weapon, but he'd scribbled a mean-sounding note. The clerk was sufficiently alarmed to fork over a couple of thousand dollars. The robber demanded the return of the note; he was smart enough to recognize it as Exhibit A in incriminating evidence. Cash and note in hand, he hurried back to his vehicle and waiting passenger.

As he motored from his getaway site, the robber hung a left on North Water Street, then another left on Morse Street, then a few more lefts. (Those familiar with the screwy one-way lanes of Edgartown will know how intricate a process it is to leave town.) The robber and his hapless companion at last arrived at the road running alongside the Edgartown Commons. It was here that the robber handed his stickup note and a butane lighter to his unwitting accomplice.

"Burn it, will ya?"

Sometimes a flick of a Bic isn't good enough. It pays to note that the passenger was physically handicapped, and try as he might, he was unable to ignite the lighter. *Click! Click!* Nothing happened.

Annoyed, the driver grabbed the note and chucked it out the window.

Big mistake.

You can rob a bank on Martha's Vineyard, but woe to anyone who litters.

Actually, the heist had been duly reported to the police, who were out in force to apprehend the perpetrator. But it wasn't until he tossed paper from his window that any of the authorities took notice of him.

The note sailed to the pavement. Down a side street, Sergeant Joe Arujo in a patrol car observed the blatant act of litterbuggery. Bingo! The sarge switched on his blinking lights and swerved to pull in behind the vehicle.

Had the perp possessed the sangfroid to sit tight and accept a ticket for littering, he would have been able to ride home with his two grand, undetected—at least for that particular heist.

But our bank robber was not a man to let moss grow under his behind. He put his foot on the gas pedal and fishtailed out of town. Sergeant Arujo gave chase. Simultaneously he called all units; it hadn't taken him long to fig-ure out that he had more than a litter-happy twerp on his hands.

The bank robber led the cops a merry chase west along the Edgartown/Vineyard Haven Road, spinning out to make a left onto Barnes Road, which runs alongside the state forest. With Sergeant Arujo on his tail and howling sirens bearing down from West Tisbury, the robber screeched his car to a halt. He grabbed a hunting bow from the back seat and bailed out into the forest.

Meanwhile, the abandoned passenger sat in dazed shock. For many hours afterward he had a lot of "splaining" to do back at the station.

The robber legged it into the woods. Sergeant Arujo of Edgartown, Sergeant Dan Flynn of Oak Bluffs, and a couple of West Tisbury cops pounded hard after him. All of a sudden, the robber stopped, pivoted, yanked back on his bow, and zinged an arrow at his pursuers. The arrow barely missed the shoulder of one of the West Tisbury cops. *Now we're angry,* was their united response. They charged ever harder, and tackled the wannabe Robin Hood, forming a football heap over him.

And thus was the Bow and Arrow Robber brought to justice.

To Key or Not to Key

IF YOU READ the mystery novels of Vineyard authors Philip R. Craig and Cynthia Riggs, you'd think we score at least two murders per annum on the Vineyard. In reality, what you really need to worry about are extra zucchinis being deposited in your car in August.

This sense of shelter from the storm, especially in the off-season when we're down to seventeen thousand souls, makes us fairly laid back about locking our houses. Many of us, too, are cavalier about leaving keys in our cars, mostly because our island junkers are too rusted and busted for anyone in his or her right mind to swipe them.

For those who hail from the city, this is a difficult concept. My friend Larry Mollin, a screenwriter from L.A. with a summer home in Aquinnah, once asked if he could leave his car with us for a weekend off island. Now, this car was an '88 Citation with more rust than paint on its sides. The driver's door didn't open from the inside, so whoever sat in the passenger seat had to circle around to liberate the driver.

So Larry parked the car, and sauntered over to tell my son, Charlie, and me, *sotto voce,* where he'd cunningly concealed the key. Charlie and I burst out laughing.

"Larry!" Charlie said, "You could tape your keys to the front windshield and no one would steal that car."

I chimed in, "There are heaps in the Chappy junkyard that look better than this one!"

A few years back, I worked at a real estate office in Oak Bluffs. When it was time to leave one day, I walked out the front door and halted in my tracks. My old canary yellow Dodge Colt was gone. A dread feeling washed over me—that sense of having been violated. I staggered back into the office to call the police, then realized I hadn't the heart to make that extreme gesture. Instead, I returned to the street to see if maybe the dang thing had rolled somewhere.

Glancing to my left I saw, four doors down, the gaudy yellow hood of my Colt parked in front of the Oyster Bar restaurant. I ran down the street as a sous-chef in a spattered white apron alighted from my car and started toward the double doors.

"That's my car!" I yelped. "Why have you taken it?"

Up until now I might have thought "hopping mad" was a cliché, but in my rage and incredulity I literally bounced from foot to foot.

The sous-chef looked chagrined. "My boss told me to go get his car from up the block," he explained. He said it was the one with the key in the ignition."

"You dingbat!" I cried. "*Every* car on the block has a key in the ignition!"

A Legion of Naked Joy Riders?

As I SAT in the office of Police Chief Paul Condlin recently, he mused about how odd it was that from time to time people are apprehended driving with no clothes on. He recalled two cases in particular.

A few years back, a rash of car break-ins occurred in the Slough Cove area of Katama, near the beach. Late one night, a patrolman noticed a car with two people in the front cruising slowly enough to engage his suspicions. He popped on his blue lights and wrenched his wheel around to pull up behind the vehicle. The driver hit the accelerator and took off. The cop gave chase.

Suspects and pursuer peeled onto the main road, then blazed east onto the tarmac at the Katama Airfield. The lead car slammed to a halt, both doors thunked open, and two men, both stark crackin' naked, hit the pavement running, bare feet slapping the tarmac.

"It didn't take long to catch them," said Chief Condlin. "What stumped us, though, was that there was not a stitch of clothing in the car. It turned out the two men lived some seven miles away, in the Ocean Heights area, so what were they doing driving buck naked around the beach in Katama at two in the morning?"

Is there a law against cruisin' in the nude? It seems to be one of those murky areas. It was definitely illegal to take flight from a policeman, and once the perpetrators hit the airfield, they were clearly flouting some kind of No Public Nudity law. One way or the other, the two birthday-suited riders spent the night in the town jail. Let's hope the cops had some jailhouse sweats or PJs to give them.

On another occasion, Chief Condlin received a report that the victim of a motorcar fatality also had taken clothing to be optional. The chief and I spent some moments pondering whether these chance discoveries of naked drivers suggest that on any given night a small percentage of people are driving around bare-assed on the dark roads of Martha's Vineyard.

The Maine Connection

WAY BACK IN 1980 some marijuana traffickers operating out of Portland, Maine, had a bright idea for hauling their product down Massachusetts way. First they smuggled it in—all eight tons of it—by mother ship to a private cove on Martha's Vineyard. At the appointed late-night hour, a fleet of vans pulled up to the beach and workers unloaded the cargo from boat to vans. At daybreak the caravan rolled down the highway, careful to maintain the legal speed limit, to the ferry terminal in Vineyard Haven where a reservation for all eight vans awaited them. (Whoever concocted these plans had the same gene as the man who designed the extra squiggles in the paisley design or those overly intricate labyrinths from which no one ever emerges.) The convoy of vans rolled onto the ferry where the usual assortment of steamship guys signaled them into adjoining slots.

And then the plan fell apart.

Even with the vans' windows rolled up, that smell of three acres worth of marijuana wafted out through the cracks and vents of the vehicles. Within minutes the entire cavernous hold of the ferry reeked with the telltale fragrance of America's favorite illegal smoke. It only required another few minutes for squad cars to swoop down to intercept the captive vehicles.

All in a day's work.

Why the original boat couldn't have just conveyed the weed to a more convenient mainland cove is a deep, dark mystery. Again, it says a great deal about the missing gray cells in many criminals' brains.

Cute Little Jail

JUST WHEN LAW and order on Martha's Vineyard is beginning to sound like the backdrop for a musical comedy, we have, on top of all this lovable criminal activity, one cuddlesome house of corrections.

You'll Find It in Fodor's

The national press has referred to the Edgartown House of Corrections as the Bed and Breakfast and the Posh Jail, among other terms of endearment.
CAPTAIN J. SANTOS

Built in 1873, it sits at the corner of Main Street and Pease Point Way in Edgartown, another captain-style home with white clapboard and black shutters. A white picket fence and a pleasant garden complete the look of a dwelling to which parents might comfortably dispatch their kids for trick or treating on Halloween. Inside the clink, the food is consistently tasty—the legacy of a former inmate who, in addition to his criminal talents, happened to be a chef of the *nouvelle cuisine* school. So on the whole, time done in this particular joint falls on the easy side. (In an amusing coincidence, the lane running behind the jail is named Easy Street.)

Recently the jail received the equivalent of a Michelin Guide upgrade: In November 2005, a twenty-three-year-old Saudi prince, one Bader al-Saud, convicted in Boston of a DUI manslaughter charge (he struck and killed a man crossing Charles Street in the wee hours of the morning), through family connections finagled a transfer to our own dear little jail to serve out his one-year sentence. All of a sudden the national press got hold of the story, and headlines were rife with qualifiers such as "bed and breakfast" "charming New England" and "posh" applied to our local lockup. Vineyard law enforcement officials were quick to point out that the accommodations were demonstrably shabby.

Whether shabby or luxe, the house of corrections is laughably easy to escape from. Bars guard the windows of the upstairs cells, yet breakouts are routine. None of the prisoners are ax murderers, so security tends to be lax. Plus the authorities find the escapees sooner rather than later; convicts have an uncanny tendency to hightail it straight to their girlfriends' homes in nearby towns.

The way the prisoners fly the coop varies, but normally they're able to jimmy a window frame or scamper off into the bushes during outdoor rubbish collecting detail (not forgetting to discard their telltale orange vests). On a few occasions inmates have dismantled a brick fireplace—the same one, as a matter of fact; the mortar must be old and crumbly—and crawled out through the opening.

On one occasion, however, in a direct reversal of the trend, another crook with spotty IQ transcripts broke *into* the jail. It was a moonless night, and a burglar new to the neighborhood thought the house of corrections was just another family home. He tapped a window-pane, popped a catch, and let himself into the darkened downstairs chamber. It happened to be Chief McCormick's living room. Awakened by the noise, the chief overpowered the burglar, hauled him upstairs, and tossed him into one of the cells. It was the easiest bust he'd ever made—hadn't even needed to change out of his jammies.

Field of Dreams

ONE TIME BACK in the 1970s a guy stole a tractor trailer and chugged off down the West Tisbury Road. A patrol car got wind of the heist and gave chase. The thief plowed onto the shoulder of the road, scrambled out of the truck, and bolted into the hills and dales of the state forest. The two cops in the pursuing unit gave chase, also on foot.

The suspect charged into a field of shoulder-high shrubs. The police pulled up short, entirely forgetting the suspect, who disappeared into the thousands of conserved acres. The cops realized they'd straggled into a vast field of marijuana, all of it growing on government land.

Considering that the officers salvaged the truck and uncovered one gigundus pot field, they may have decided the fleeing crook had actually done them a favor.

And Just When You Think Our Criminals Can't Get Any Dumber...

THIS ONE FOR the idiot books happened a couple of years ago. Late at night a cab pulled up to the sporting goods shop on State Road in Vineyard Haven. The guy who'd hired the cab instructed the driver to wait as he slipped out of the back seat. In ten minutes he was back with a load of tennis rackets and skateboards. He gave directions for the cabbie to take him to an address in North Tisbury.

Not only was it easy to trace the thief through the cab company, but the crook also shared a rental house with several fellows, one of whom happened to own the sporting goods store. The latter was surprised to see a selection of his own merchandise being carried into the house long after store closing time.

Gang Bangers Take a Chilmark Rental

THE FOURTH OF JULY had fallen on a Friday that year in the 1990s, so the island had sizzled with lots of festivities, some of which left a number of rental houses with beer-soaked upholstery and broken plates, windows, and chairs.

Over the weekend, a friend of mine at the real estate office asked me if I'd do her a favor. She handled sales and I transacted rentals. She had on the hook a couple from New Jersey eager to buy a house. Like so many owners of second homes, they would need to meet the yearly nut by renting the place to summer vacationers. Only problem was, they hated to think of their newfound property resting in the hands of strangers. My friend asked me to show them a typical rental—a nice one, of course—to reassure them that the house could take the weekly traffic.

Immediately I thought of the Socha house in Chilmark. Spanking new, it had bleached wide-plank floors, a soaring fireplace, sun-flooded windows, and gleaming appliances. It was the kind of house so sparkling and impeccable that even damp swimsuits strewn on the floor along with a raft of beach toys would not have besmirched its handsomeness.

I made a date to take the Jersey couple out to Chilmark on Sunday during the hours when the cleaning crew would be turning the house over for the next week's renters.

We crunched into the secluded drive. At first nothing seemed out of place. Confident that the couple would adore the place, I led them up to the front door, all the while merrily chatting about the nice middle-class families who rented Vineyard dwellings.

We made an appreciative pass through the living room with its Crate&Barrel furniture, green marble fireplace, and cathedral ceilings. All was well and good. The kitchen too, welcomed us in its usual pristine condition. From the back yard, however, came the sound of some kind of ruckus: men shouting to one another, outdoor furniture being heaved along the ground, and the thud of sneakered feet jumping from grass to wooden deck.

We wandered outdoors to find a dozen men in faded jeans and sweatshirts prowling the property: an undercover unit sent down from the Boston Police Department.

The lead officer wore a Red Sox cap, and he filled us in on the reason for their presence. A notorious group of gang bangers from the mean streets of Dorchester had rented the Socha house over the July 4th weekend. The bangers had planned a three-day party advertised on flyers posted all over Boston. A live band was promised, along with a private shuttle bus running for a straight seventy-two hours from down-island towns to the isolated Chilmark property. So isolated was the location, in fact, that none of the surrounding neighbors had been bothered by the hip-hop band (slyly enough, the gang had stationed the musicians in the basement).

The lead cop told me and my horrified clients that his team had been investigating this particular gang for trafficking in automatic weapons. And if this wasn't alarming enough, he added that they chiefly funded themselves through sales of heroin. The gang members had left the night before, and the squad was now combing the grounds for such residues of lawlessness as discarded hypodermic needles and spent shotgun shells.

My clients and I wandered back through the sliding glass doors into the kitchen. The couple from Jersey looked as if they needed a trip to the hospital for a blood transfusion.

I looked around the shimmering white kitchen and said, "You know, on the plus side, they left the place immaculate!"

And it was true! For all their devilish goings-on, these "gangstas" cleaned up better than most of the nice middle-class families who'd ever rented homes on Martha's Vineyard.

Scandal City

From Ornery Redcoats to the Kennedy Car Wash:
More Than Two Centuries of Vineyarders Misbehaving

Lousy Limeys

IT IS A DAY that lives in infamy in the annals of Vineyard history:

On September 10, 1778, an Englishman named General Gray, in control of eighty-two battleships and ten thousand soldiers, raided Martha's Vineyard. His men carried off every last sheep, pig, cow, and ox they could find, leaving islanders in a condition of severe deprivation for the coming winter.

Before the pillaging began, the general promised to pay for the appropriated livestock, provided the islanders put up no resistance. As his men herded three thousand sheep and other assorted farm animals onto their boats, General Gray startled island officials by saying, in effect, "Oh, you don't expect money *now*, do you? You must apply to British officials in New York."

Then he sailed away to wage war on the mainland.

Shortly thereafter, an islander was dispatched to New York to collect payment. The officials on the scene sent word to General Gray to confirm the transaction. The commander professed no recollection of sailing his eighty-two ships into Vineyard waters and requisitioning enough sheep to feed and clothe the colony of Vermont for a full year. The Vineyard emissary returned home empty handed.

Over the next couple of years, Colonel Beriah Norton of the Vineyard made two separate trips to London to apply for reimbursement. He was given a special hearing in Parliament, but not a single farthing was ever dispensed to the Vineyard for General Gray's war crime.

My suggestion: Island retailers should put out jars on our counters with labels reading "Gray's Raid Reparations Fund." We get a lot of English tourists here in the summer. By and large they're about the nicest people around, so they may feel a strong urging from their conscience to chip in and make good on their ancestors' perfidy. In today's coinage, the monies owed for the stolen livestock would amount to tens of thousands of dollars, enough to pay for a municipal swimming pool and a round of drinks for everyone at the Ritz bar.

Seaside Fleshpot

THE MOST VITAL civilizations have been forged by a clash of opposing ideas, cultures, and goals. This clash is what made Oak Bluffs the exciting town it's always been, generation after generation. The sacred and the profane are beautifully braided in Oak Bluffs, but for those who stand too far to one side of the spectrum or the other, the best advice we can give is to get out of town!

In 1692 John Daggett purchased five hundred acres around today's Oak Bluffs harbor, then called Squash Meadow. His son, Joseph, aged twenty, married an Indian woman, and together they farmed the property. Their marriage set an example for centuries of racial blending.

The first community to flourish in that area was an eighteenth-century seaside sin city.

Half a mile west of the East Chop lighthouse lies a stretch of shore called Eastville.

Long ago it devolved into a peaceful strip of beach houses, but back in 1730 this snug little cove so perfectly sheltered from gales was where the Claghorn family built a tavern for sailors. Officers of the ships anchored offshore ferried directly to Vineyard Haven—then known as Holmes Hole—for their refreshment. All the noncommissioned seamen headed as fast as their rowboats could glide them to the village founded by the Claghorns.

You get the picture,

Eastville was overrun with pleasure-crazed sailors with no supervision. None whatsoever. After months at sea, getting bullied—even flogged—by stern officers, is it any wonder that they were ready to cut loose?

In record time Eastville boomed with taverns, inns, and ship chandlers. And above these early American taverns of the scruffy seaport variety, there lurked a prostitute or two, or more, to comfort the lonely sailors. These ladies, clad in lacy caps and showing ample cleavage, hung out of upstairs windows and called down to the passing sailors:

"Got half a dollar, luv? Come on up!"

Before long Eastville was known up and down the Eastern Seaboard as America's Barbary Coast.

How ironic it is that in less than one hundred years, a plot of ground located only a mile west from Eastville would become a destination for religious pilgrims.

Nathaniel Hawthorne's Own Scarlet Letter

NOBODY THOUGHT he would amount to anything. At the age of thirty-two, Nathaniel Hawthorne wrote stories that no one had, as of yet, cared to publish, and no other plans for advancement in the world had caught his interest. Deep depression had dogged him from childhood, confining him to a solitary way of life. At the same time, his heart longed for enduring love.

Hawthorne's uncle, Sam Manning, kept his mopey nephew gainfully employed by putting him in charge of the horses for his Salem Stage Company. The summer of 1836 brought Nathaniel to Martha's Vineyard to procure fresh mounts. He stayed with the Gibbs family at their inn on North Water Street (now the Edgartown Inn), and it was there that the depressive, brilliant stable hand fell in love with eighteen-year-old Eliza Gibbs.

That they loved deeply is an undisputed fact in Vineyard historical circles. The pair were as star-crossed as any two lovers down through the millennia, however. Eliza's father, Andrew Gibbs, was white, and her mother, Priscilla Coombs Gibbs, was Native American. Father

farmed and Mother managed the inn. Their days were busy, their evenings preternaturally quiet as their mixed marriage had caused the family to be ostracized by Edgartown society.

When it came time for Nathaniel to ask Mr. Gibbs for his daughter's hand in marriage, the latter refused on the grounds that the young man was a struggling writer and a horse peddler from off island. And even had Mr. Gibbs accepted his suit, Nathaniel must have known his own family would oppose a marriage between their patrician-born son and a half-breed island girl.

Yet Eliza and Nathaniel had the whole of that summer idyll to express their passion, in secret, of course. We can only imagine where they might have escaped to lie in one another's arms; a garret room at the inn, a field of wild daisies and asters down by the shore, in a dinghy on a moonless night out in Katama Bay.

Eliza's devotion kindled in her lover a season of inspired writings: three tales, all destined to be classics, each studded with Vineyard characters. *My Kinsman, Major Molineux* drew on Edgartown banker Ichabod Norton, who charged twelve and a half percent interest for his loans and from this financial base built up a fortune in whaling ships and island farms. In *Clippings with a Chisel* he brought to life an Edgartown tombstone carver and his clientele. *The May-Pole of Merry Mount* illuminated the young writer's real-life love affair in the characters of Edgar (named for the town of his summer stay) and Edith (a name with obvious similarities to Eliza).

By the end of the summer, Nathaniel was obliged to bring the horses back to Salem and once again take up his duties at home. Mr. Gibbs remained averse to any marriage between his daughter and the boarder. Nathaniel left the island broken-hearted.

In the spring of 1837 Eliza journeyed to the house of her cousins, James and Salome Coombs, in West Tisbury. It was there, away from the prying eyes of the Edgartown society that had never given her the time of day to begin with, that Eliza gave birth to a daughter. Sadly, the following December, the child died.

The years brought improved fortunes for the shattered lovers: Nathaniel's fifty-six tales were at long last published (with the covert help of his friend Horatio Bridge, who, unbeknownst to Hawthorne, underwrote the twenty-five hundred dollar expense for Osgood and Company of Boston to produce the book). *Twice Told Tales* eventually became a worldwide success. Five years following his affair with Eliza, the budding author married a Salem woman named Sophia Peabody. Their first child, a daughter named Una, was born two years later. In a letter to a friend and legal adviser, Hawthorne mused that he now had one daughter in heaven, and one on earth.

As for Eliza Gibbs, eight years after Nathaniel left the island, she married an Edgartown tailor named Sylvester Fisher. When he died a few years later, the couple had borne no children. Deacon Fisher is buried under a tombstone bearing his name in the Edgartown cemetery. Interestingly, it was Eliza who had purchased the small family plot, and she herself

is interred there, albeit with no marker. A few years ago, inquiring minds with an historic bent were eager to know what secrets this grave site might disclose. An excavator was hired to take a look. He found, buried in the left-hand corner beside Eliza Gibbs Fisher's coffin, the tiny casket of an infant.

The most enduring legacy of this island liaison was Hawthorne's masterpiece, and America's number-one classic novel, *The Scarlet Letter*, published in 1851. Hawthorne biographers believe that the character of Hester Prynne, valiant unwed mother and victim of Puritan prejudice, was based on the author's lost love, Eliza Gibbs. He must have been all too painfully aware that, had his daughter lived, Eliza's predicament in her community would have grown still more untenable, and her isolation rendered near complete. Too, he could relate to the wracking guilt of Reverend Dimmesdale, the lover Hester never betrayed; throughout the novel, Dimmesdale watches helplessly while his lost sweetheart, identified by her illegitimate child and the letter *A*, for adultery, which her cruel neighbors and churchgoers insisted she wear, takes the fall for both of them.

No Cholera Here!

IN OUR SOCIALLY enlightened time, the following story may be categorized as a scandal, though it was business as usual way back when.

In 1849, all across the nation, people were dropping dead from cholera. So pandemic was the disease that within a year U.S. President Zachary Taylor contracted it and died.

No worries on the Vineyard, however. Not according to the editor of the *Gazette,* who had this chirpy comment to make in his paper: "We hardly know of a case of the sickness at the present writing."

In an extremely generous gesture, he invited mainlanders to visit and relax out of harm's way. It clearly hadn't occurred to him that those fugitives from the epidemic might carry the bug with them. Possibly he believed our fresh air and sparkling water warded off even the most virulent diseases. (And perhaps they did. See "Health Care, Colonial Style" in the "Customs of the Country" chapter).

The editor saw no irony in the juxtaposition of this small article only two paragraphs down from his editorial:

CHOLERA!
A MRS. COOPER AT GAY HEAD ATE THE
BEST PART OF A DECAYED WATER MELON,
WAS SEIZED WITH CHOLERA-MORBUS
AND DIED. NO OCCASION FOR ALARM.

Did this downplaying of the situation have anything to do with the fact that Mrs. Cooper was "colored," as the Wampanoag population was classified in those days? If Mrs. Cooper had been an Edgartown debutante with a lineage of whaling captain great-grandfathers, would her death have elicited the same offhand aside, "No occasion for alarm"?

Campground Bad Boys

THE PLACE WAS wholesome to the nth degree.

At the Wesleyan Grove Methodist Campground in Oak Bluffs, the hundreds of white canvas tents that blossomed there during summers from the 1830s through the 1850s gave way to Victorian dollhouses of surpassing beauty to some, and terminal cuteness to others. Many wonder how people could possibly live bunched so close together, sometimes with as little as two feet between neighboring walls. One of the oldest jokes about the Campground was that when someone inside a cottage sneezed, half a dozen neighbors would call out "Gesundheit!"

The fact is, privacy was never an issue. Tourists were invited to come and stare into people's living rooms. They could watch the occupants eat pot roast and potatoes at the dinner table, or read the Bible in a rocking chair, or nap on a daybed just inside the window. The unspoken message was, "Our lives are so pure, we have nothing to hide. This is what salvation looks like."

Frankly, salvation might have looked a little boring.

All the same, the opportunity for voyeurism exerted great appeal. So many tourists flocked to the site, meandering through the lanes and gazing into open windows, they might have thought they had come to a human zoo. A writer in the 1860s joked that P.T. Barnum should buy the Campground—lock, stock, and Methodist—and display it in Central Park.

For the Methodists themselves, the rules were basic and nonnegotiable: No dancing, no swearing, no card playing, no smoking of tobacco—and, absolutely, under pain of banishment, no drinking whatsoever, not even a drop, not even for medicinal purposes. Step away from that bottle!

Of course you'll never get full compliance to rules of personal behavior, not even in a devoutly religious conclave. Every so often someone would be caught with his mouth opened wide and his tongue protruding into a glass of whiskey. When this occurred, there were no warnings, no second chances; the culprit's entire household would be ordered to vacate the holy ground of the Wesleyan Grove forever.

Such banishments were tricky, however. The Camp Meeting Association owned the land, but the congregants held free and clear title to their own dwellings. "So you want us to leave, huh?" a miscreant might sneer, "Very well, I'm going, but I'm taking my cottage with me!"

Moving houses has always been a Vineyard specialty. Hire a squad of brawny men, insert logs beneath the structure, roll that baby onto a wagon roped to sturdy oxen, and away you go.

Nowadays when people ramble through the Campground, they notice that here and there amid the clusters of storybook cottages, they encounter an empty lot with perhaps a single decrepit marble birdbath to commemorate the house that stood on that spot in happier days. A vacant lot means that once a man or woman, or perhaps several men and women, enjoyed an alcoholic beverage on that plot of ground and, for their hour(s) of raging sin, paid a serious consequence.

Liquor Is Quicker

NOWADAYS THE WHOLE hundred square miles of the Vineyard is sought for its vacation possibilities, from the rolling fields and infinite ocean vistas of Aquinnah and Chilmark to the quaint and quirky personalities of the three down-island towns. But rewind back to the latter decades of the nineteenth century, when tourism was a brand new activity in America, and you'll see that only one Vineyard locale was attracting visitors—that was Cottage City, today known as Oak Bluffs.

Perhaps no other town in the United States has so strongly reflected this country's love/hate relationship with alcohol, thanks to its bedrock blending of the holy and not so holy. Starting in August 1835, Methodist camp meetings took place in a splendid oak grove on a sweep of seaside land then known as the Squash Meadow.

In the 1850s the sprawling Wesley Hotel was erected between the harbor and the Campground to allow visitors to ogle the devotions of the camp meeters. At the same time, the tents were giving way to little houses crafted in the trendy new Queen Anne style. In 1872 the tabernacle was built, a three-tiered fantasy of stained glass and iron grillework, open on the sides, and surrounded by central parkland.

From the start the Camp Meeting Association had banned the use of intoxicants within its confines and, by tacit agreement, anywhere within shouting distance of its boundaries. If these founding Methodists could have revised the Ten Commandments, they would surely have inserted "Thou shalt not drink" at the very top of the list.

But it was a boozing age. The post-Civil War years had driven hundreds of thousands of people off the farms and into the cities. Saloons flourished on every street corner, and travelers flocking to Cottage City brought their substantial thirst with them.

A commercial strip called Circuit Avenue reared up three and four stories high along the eastern flank of the Campground. A mini-metropolis flourished on either side of the avenue. Two Japanese stores offered brocades, silks, porcelain, and statuary. The Big Wigwam department store was stocked with furniture, hardware, lawn chairs, and toys overflowing in big bins onto the sidewalk. The post office dispensed one-cent stamps for postcards. For the men, there was a cigar and tobacco shop. The avenue was lined with bootblack stands and numerous ice cream parlors and saltwater taffy vendors.

By the 1880s the town in the summer bulged to a dangerous degree. Men paid to sleep on billiard tables. Many curled up on benches in the tabernacle. The preacher's stand served as a makeshift lodge for women.

Developers arrived with suitcases of cash and plans to reproduce the exquisite dollhouses of the camp meeters in secular neighborhoods, but on larger lots and with more ample dwellings. Before long a community of summer homes dwarfed the twenty-acre Campground. These new cottages speedily filled up with a more "normal" citizenry who, while they may have attended church on Sunday, had no qualms about hoisting a bottle of ale on Saturday, and perhaps every other day in between.

Nonetheless, the Methodists who arrived first on these shores had seen to it that a law of absolute dryness sat like a ten-ton toad on the books. The larger, laxer community of summer visitors took the dry law with a grain of salt. Actually with a whole hill of salt: Boozing went on day and night in a resort known for its gaiety. In effect, the social life of Cottage City during the Victorian Age foretold the later excess of the Roaring Twenties with its Prohibition. Behind closed doors or on back porches or in secluded glades, people drank themselves silly. After a time, when the ministerial forces of the Campground saw what was going on at every compass point around Wesleyan Grove, they ordered an eight-foot wall erected around their holy acres to keep the infidels at bay.

In the summer of 1887 a Methodist minister named E.H. Hatfield decided it wasn't enough to maintain sobriety only within his own ranks. He vowed to wrest every last drink out of every last fist of every last heathen beyond the gate. He organized a posse of the righteous. Clad in tall black hats and black frock coats, his men thundered up porch planks, broke through doors, and tackled the godless holding drinks halfway to their lips. In a series of citizens' arrests, they hauled the miscreants off to the local constabulary.

In this nominally dry town, no public houses existed to dispense liquor, so the Reverend Hatfield and his deputies tracked down the covert suppliers—hotels, private clubs, apothecaries, and even doctors' offices. In his zeal, the man of God believed booze lurked everywhere: under floorboards, in safes behind paintings, inside hollowed-out croquet mallets, beneath ladies' petticoats. And he may have been right.

But as do all obsessive sin busters—Savonarola, grand inquisitor Torquemada, Cotton Mather, the Taliban—the Reverend Hatfield finally went too far.

On a warm afternoon in August, one of the minister's deputies ordered—and was served— a glass of port in a back parlor of the ritzy Sea View Hotel down on the wharf. Rather than collar the waiter, the Hatfield boys broke down the office door of the chief boardmember of the hotel, a rich and influential businessman named Holder M. Brownell. They hoisted him from his posh horsehair executive chair and hauled him off to jail.

In late nineteenth-century America, it was well-nigh impossible for anyone from the upper-middle to the upper-upper classes to receive a prison sentence. This was, you'll recall, the era when a temperamental lass named Lizzie Borden took her famous ax and gave her dad and stepmother a sum total of eighty-one whacks and was later acquitted by a jury. Who could believe a well-brought-up girl from a little Rhode Island town could even think of such a thing? The perpetrator had to have been some itinerant madman, whereabouts unknown.

Mr. Brownell's trial was bumped up to the Superior Court off island. His lawyer read to the court a number of recommendations from other pillars of the Cottage City community, all of whom had assuredly lifted snifters of cognac in the company of the defendant. Indeed a wag at the time hinted that every juror had at one time or another sampled a glass of the Sea View's finest. This first court found the hotelier guilty, but an appeal to the State Supreme Court placed Mr. Brownell back on the streets again.

The elite of Cottage City took action. They leaned on town officials to make sure no more jackbooted religious thugs picked on one of their cronies again. At the next town meeting, the residents of Cottage City voted to remove the ban on intoxicating spirits.

Thus an already wet town, albeit clandestinely so, became flat-out legally sopping wet. Saloons popped up like mushrooms on a moist lawn. And during the Victorian Age, wherever saloons proliferated, bawdy houses could not be far behind.

A Brothel on Every Corner

ALL YOU NEED to do to fan the flames of a favorite vice is to repress it with a vengeance. This is precisely what the Victorians in the second half of the nineteenth century did with sex. No good woman was expected to enjoy it: "Just close your eyes and think of England" (or in our case, New England) was the advice given to brides on their wedding night. Men had animal urges, but the civilized world joined forces to keep men from reminders of their bestial desires. Ladies wore voluminous skirts to conceal their shameful lower regions. Even piano legs, so as not to provide a visual cue for human legs, were flanked with sleeves of lumpy damask.

So what happened? Countless cities in Britain and America exploded with sex em-poria. In New York City alone an estimated six hundred brothels were in operation. Social conditions were perfect for attracting sex workers to the field: After the Civil War, impoverished young widows and orphaned daughters were plucked from their rural roots and drawn to the cities. They could accept factory jobs paying starvation wages of two dollars for sixty hours of work, or they could find relief, however tawdry, by donning low-cut clothes, face powder, and scarlet lipstick to stand beneath a gaslit chandelier and wait for customers.

And customers they had aplenty. Consider the thoughtfulness of the Victorian male: He wasn't about to importune his wife—any more than he had to—for carnal relief. Yet he had to have it, as regularly as possible; the culture had

Victorians Letting Rip

Even though the commercial strip of Cottage City was birthed by an adjacent religious community, this bustling boulevard housed multiple saloons and at least one official bordello.

MARTHA'S VINEYARD HISTORICAL SOCIETY COLLECTIONS (env. 221a)

taught him that his mental and physical health depended on it. Thus, even on vacation, even in the town that had cropped up beside the sacred White City, every red-blooded American male, married and single, was entitled to his habitual nooky on the side.

On Circuit Avenue, the premier cathouse sat on the southeast corner of Lake Street in the very building that today houses Giordano's Restaurant, a popular family pizzeria for the past seventy-plus years.

Because of the building's history, founder Willy Giordano encountered a snag getting a start-up loan in the 1930s. As his son, Buster Giordano, told it to me, the bank president frowned and said, "That was a brothel in 1884."

"So what?" said Mr. Giordano. "After that it was a chicken barn. What does any of that have to do with selling spaghetti?"

The restaurateur got his loan.

Buster also mentioned that when his father first bought the building, "he found a warren of small cubicles upstairs where the prostitutes plied their trade."

Nowadays no shred remains of the antique bordello. All you'll find is a brightly lit restaurant where families gather around platters of fried clams and pepperoni pizza. In fact, the Vineyard has solidified into a stomping ground for family fun. Hardly anyone realizes that once upon a time this sweetie-pie town of Oak Bluffs housed any number of ladies in red satin gowns who, parting lace curtains and peeking out, caught the eyes of many a passing Victorian gentleman.

A more discreet and higher class establishment sat back from the cliffs of Hine's Point, that Shangri-La spit of land glimpsed across the lagoon as you drive between Oak Bluffs and Vineyard Haven. For the discriminating Victorian client, it was well worth the extra time and trouble to journey out to this private location. From Cottage City a gent could climb aboard a horse-drawn hansom cab and head over to the northern shore of the lagoon.

There a silent boatman sat waiting—no questions asked—to row his fare to the tip of Hines Point. From there, a system of weights and pulleys swung the visitor up to the heights.

In the salon, the gentleman selected a lady, accompanied her to a cramped cabana, received his week's allotment of prescribed sex, then hightailed it back to town in time to accompany his wife and kids for a stroll along the boardwalk.

Naturally, more informal venues were available for finding illicit love. The Pawnee Hotel, smack in the center of Circuit Avenue—today the site of Mad Martha's Ice Cream and other assorted souvenir shops—was known for its no-tell hotel ambiance. The word on the Pawnee was that at two a.m. a bell would clang, and everyone in the establishment would scoot back to his or her own room.

The darkest side of Victorian sex was the demand for child prostitutes. No records exist about preteens in brothels on the Vineyard, but the trend nationwide encouraged the practice. Sex with a virgin fetched ten dollars—big bucks in those days when a factory job, for example, paid thirty-five dollars a year. The prospect of receiving that much loot for the surrender of one's virginity was more than a little persuasive. Every whorehouse had its complement of eleven- to fifteen-year-old girls. The shock was that sex with someone this young was legal. In some states, the age of consent was as young as ten, the average around twelve. It wasn't until late in the nineteenth century that reform groups managed to get the age notched up to sixteen, where it remains to this day.

And what did the trustees of the Methodist Campground have to say about all this hanky-panky in the heart of town? Oddly enough, written records are mum on the subject. Prostitution on these shores was so impossible a concept as to fall outside the pale of camp meeters' consciousness. They focused on other, more manageable vices—consumption of intoxicants, smoking, dancing, and card games.

One other surefire infraction was guaranteed to raise Methodist hackles: At the rink, boys and girls skating arm in arm to precious psalms such as "Nearer My God to Thee."

Yes indeed, there were far more young people punished for skating than for selling or buying sex in the whorehouses of Cottage City. It was a most peculiar time.

Hail (Hic!) to the Chief: A Closer Look at Ulysses's Drinking

By NOW WE'RE well aware of the various peccadilloes presidents can commit. For Ulysses S. Grant, who visited the island in August 1874, it was hard to endure a day of pomp and circumstance without a stiff one. In fact, for the general a stiff one was necessary every half hour on the half hour. Chalk it up to bad planning, then, when he accepted an invitation from Bishop Haven to lodge in the clergyman's cottage in the Wesleyan Grove Methodist Campground. Not only was the minister ensconced in a hotbed of anti-alcohol sentiment, but he had also been quoted in the local press as saying, "Great will be the happiness of the nation when no village shall be cursed with a grog shop."

President Grant must have wondered where he could find a grog shop for himself. Perhaps someone cupped a hand over his ear and whispered that a rash of taverns plied their trade just beyond the eight-foot wall of the Campground. But how to arrange a visit, what with all the public assemblies that followed him wherever he roved? Happily for the parched commander in chief, he found distilled spirits in the nearby home of Campground dweller Alderman Collins. It seemed that Grant had so much in common with the alderman that they spent many an hour holed up in the gentleman's study.

Grant attended the Sunday service, and it was the talk of the Campground whether or not the sermon might inspire the crusty old Civil War general to be saved. What a coup that would be for the eager Methodists! All eyes turned to the president where he sat on the ros-trum with his wife and several key cabinet members. He looked serene; could he be stirring with the first inklings of redemption? His eyes began to glaze: Was the Spirit taking hold? Congregants watched with bated breath. The great man's eyes slowly closed. From his flaccid lips and slack jaw a snore zipped loose. When he awakened, he slipped a flask from his pocket and—forgetting where he was—took a swig.

Ulysses S. Grant was asked to find hospitality elsewhere.

Dr. Harrison Tucker (see "Dr. Feel Good" in the "VIPs" chapter), threw a life raft to the disgraced president, who must have sighed with relief to find himself in more compatible company at the doctor's festive house on Ocean Park. From the balcony that evening the president and his host watched a display of fireworks spritzing out over the black waters of the sound. Dr. Tucker arranged for his own indoor lamps to radiate and fade in glissandos of darkness and light. President Grant had all the booze he could possibly wish for, plus a sound and light show. A good time was had by all.

Heat up the Tar, Bring on the Feathers

THE FOLLOWING is the story—duly reported in the *Vineyard Gazette* in the summer of 1874—of a *ménage à quatre* in Cottage City, a town with a law on its books saying that only a family, i.e., blood relatives, could share a house.

And if this tale of a mini orgy is quaint enough, the manner in which it was taken into vigilante hands was even quainter.

A man named Samuel Elliott, a former sewing machine salesman from Rhode Island, moved into an attractive Queen Anne cottage on Tuckernuck Avenue. He threw himself into real estate, and swiftly became a wheeler-dealer in the area. He proceeded to hire two women to keep house for him, both of them married to men away on maritime junkets.

Not much is known about Phebe Dexter's husband (other than that his name was Mr. Dexter), but her sister Lizzie's husband was one Almar Dickson, who served as a cook on a coastal schooner. Lizzie was five months pregnant, an interesting visual considering the scandal about to unfold.

A few weeks into the sisters' sinecure at the house on Tuckernuck, Lizzie wrote to her husband at sea informing him that Phebe would be marrying Samuel Elliott, and he in turn had agreed to support both sisters for the rest of their lives.

Meanwhile, to add to an already questionable living arrangement in a time of extreme prudery, another player was added to the mix: John Vinson, forty-three, a pal of poor rejected Almar Dickson, and a deputy sheriff in town, approached Samuel Elliott about repayment of a debt. The businessman countered by inviting Vinson to move into his house free of charge. That was all it took to get Cottage City's most strident busybodies into a pitch of total outrage over the simple math of two men, single, two women, married, bedded down under the same roof.

Three weeks after John Vinson moved into the cottage, the first tar-and-feather brigade was organized. Eleven men showed up on the night of July 21. They tried to lure the deputy sheriff outside with a story about a disturbance at a nearby hotel, but Vinson must have smelled a rat when nearly a dozen men showed up to relay a simple message. The other thing he may have smelled was the stench of tar heat-ing up in a wagon down the street. And where there is tar, there are chicken feathers.

The lawman very sensibly legged it out the back door.

The next morning Vinson, averse to the idea of being smeared with tar and stuck with feathers—a condition that took weeks for the last of the goo to slough off—resigned his police job and hightailed it off the island.

That left Samuel Elliott to face his punishment.

On the night of August 1, four of the original T & F squad broke into the Tuckernuck den of iniquity. In the pitch-black kitchen, a drunken scuffle ensued, with shots fired. The vigilantes dragged Elliott, kicking and screaming, into the night. Elliott continued to struggle, throughout the whole of his enforced march, through squalls of wind and rain. Down by the beach, the wagon with all the fixings awaited them.

As the melee reached the open fields of Waban Park, the victim broke free, reached for something concealed in his clothes, and brandished a pistol. A single shot spat out in a compressed red blast against the black scrim of the park. One of the men clutched his stomach and bent over.

The injured fellow's name was Caleb Smith, brother of "those no good sluts" (the *Gazette*'s indignant term for Phebe and Lizzie). He'd been drilled through his lung, spine, liver, and spleen. His buddies clustered around him as Elliott raced back to the cottage.

Samuel Elliott was arrested later that night, but three days later was acquitted of murder charges. It was clear that he'd acted in self-defense. He and his two housekeepers packed up all their worldly belongings and fled the island.

That was where the story ended until a few years ago when an intriguing epilogue came to light, duly reported in *Martha's Vineyard Magazine*. Both couples reunited later in New Jersey, although it wasn't apparent that either pair had ever taken the time to legally marry.

Samuel and Phebe lived together, as did John and Lizzie, all in the same small town. Perhaps they thought that all the bother back on the Vineyard had been worth it. Happily-ever-after scenarios eluded them, however, and eventually both couples separated. Phebe outlived the others, dying at the age of ninety-two, in 1936. None of the four, understandably, ever made it back to the Vineyard.

FYI John Vinson was the great-great grandfather of actress Andie MacDowell.

The Serial Fire Starter

LET US PAINT the scene of the last days of splendor in Cottage City—the golden time before it all came tumbling down. Catastrophically down.

In the last quarter of the nineteenth century, Cottage City was considered one of the premier resort towns in America. Visitors sailing into port wrote postcards home about the "towering fantasy by the sea." The jewel in the crown was the brooding, brown five-story Sea View Hotel that spanned the wharf like a palace in a fairy tale: Entering the basement from the steamship, travelers found awaiting them a barbershop, a billiard room, a bakery, and an ice house. Guests at the hotel marveled at the newfangled steam heat, a steam-generated elevator, laundry machines, speaking tubes, and a Walworth gas machine that lit up the whole building inside and out. The public rooms were large and deluxe, with Persian carpets and ornate chandeliers.

To the east of the Sea View was the gazebo-studded nine-acre park surrounded by Victorian manor houses, each one adorned with all the towers, gables, bay windows, and gingerbread glitz that any single foundation could hold. On the northeast arm of the park, facing the sea, the New York Yacht Club was the scene of rich banquets and fancy balls each summer when the club's sailors glided into port.

To the west of the Sea View, a colossal skating rink loomed alongside a gigantic music and dance hall called the Tivoli Building, a two-story bright yellow structure with a red-trimmed tower at each end. A train called the Activ ran from Edgartown to Oak Bluffs, executing a graceful U inside this festive hub of buildings before it headed east again. All that remains of any of these Gilded Age landmarks is the Flying Horses Carousel, its antique calliope organ still tinkling in the summer breeze every day and night of the summer.

But how long could this towering fantasy stay towering and fantastic? Not long, as it turned out.

On the night of September 24, 1892, a little after eleven p.m., fire alarms tolled. People poured from hotels and guest houses to behold a geyser of flame along the wharf. From the brightly painted roof of the Sea View Hotel, volcanic spumes of fire shot a hundred fifty feet into the night sky. Firemen valiantly battled the blaze, but to no effect. By dawn all five stories of the hotel had burned to the ground, taking with them the skating rink and a portion of the wharf and railroad track. The Activ could no longer turn around in Cottage City, so for several more summers it ran backward to Edgartown. It folded in 1896.

Fire was the new Grim Reaper in town. A year after the Sea View collapsed in flame, the second largest hotel on these shores, the Highland House (now the site of the East Chop Beach Club), just across the harbor, was reduced to ashes. Over the course of the following winter, the school and five cottages on Clinton Avenue, plus a sixth in the Highlands, were consumed by fire.

One disastrous fire could be an accident. Perhaps even a second could be viewed with the same equanimity. But by the time the sixth cottage burned to the ground, the citizens of Cottage City realized they had a serial arsonist running amok in their town.

As it inevitably happens when the identity of a perpetrator is unknown in a small town setting, no one feels safe, and trust of anyone disappeared. Neighbor glowered at neighbor. Housewives suspected their grocer, their milkman, their paper delivery boy. The sheriff received long lists of random suspects, and it was said that one or two divorces occurred because a spouse believed he or she was married to the mad firebug.

The worst time for the townsfolk was at night, when they lay in their dark bedrooms afraid to close their eyes for fear that they might wake up engulfed in flames. It was imperative that the culprit be caught before everyone in town went crazy due to fear and sleep deprivation.

One night in the late spring of 1893, a young man who worked on the docks took a shine to a maid from one of the big Ocean Park manor houses, and he invited her out on a date. They dined on oysters and ice cream at a seaside cafe, and strolled back into town by the light of the moon.

The young lady stopped and took a cigarette out of her bag. In a show of gallantry, the young man struck a match for her. She inhaled deeply before exhaling a full plume of smoke. Then with a strange, faraway look in her eyes, she drifted away from her companion until she paused beside a dark cottage. Still strangely distracted, she extended the glowing end of her cigarette to a hydrangea bush growing flush against the house. With a look of pure fascination, and yet uncanny calm, the strange young woman watched as the bush erupted in flames, which in turn fed a line of fire up the cottage shingles.

The young man stared as this drama unfolded, no doubt thinking, "Holy moly! I'm on a date with the fire fiend!"

The next morning the young man reported the act of arson to the police. The girl's name was Julia Danzell, and with evidence collected, the police also arrested her sister, Lulu.

The papers called the sisters "villainesses" and, with a lack of what today we'd call psychological insight, charged them with having a "passion for incendiarism." The Danzell sisters were African American, which, considering the mindless racism of the times, may have drawn down upon them a harsher punishment: An off-island judge

Fancy Pants Hotel

This is the western quadrant of Cottage City's majestic Sea View Hotel, where people thronged to see and be seen, indulge in ice cream and (back room) cocktails, gaze out at Vineyard Sound, and ogle the next crop of visitors to alight from the ferry. This Victorian shrine to luxury was the first building to be torched by the serial arsonist of the early 1890s.

MARTHA'S VINEYARD HISTORICAL SOCIETY COLLECTIONS (env. 272)

sentenced them to a long term in prison; conceivably they died while incarcerated. After their trial, no more information was ever recorded about the young ladies who played with fire.

Today Julia and Lulu Danzell would garner a major book deal and an appearance on *Oprah*, the better for us to understand what, forgive the pun, had inflamed them.

A Spooky Afterword

I MENTIONED IN the story of Julia and Lulu Danzell that no written account remains of their lives, either before or after their arrest. But I have collected a tantalizing piece of oral history, and this takes us down the crooked alleyway of the supernatural.

In the early 1990s when I investigated true ghost stories for my book, *Haunted Island*, I conferred with an Edgartown man named Milton Jeffers. In every small town in New England, each generation yields an individual who becomes the keeper of the stories. For Milton, the torch had been handed to him by a boatbuilder named Manuel Swarz Roberts.

In the first half of the twentieth century, Manuel operated a workshop in Edgartown across from the Chappaquiddick ferry. On stormy nights, when the ferry was shut down, the handful of school kids who lived on Chappy sought refuge in Manuel's workshop. They sat in the flickering lights cast by the boatbuilder's pot-bellied stove, and listened, rapt, as their host regaled them with stories about pirates and witches and damsels in distress and swashbuckling sailors and ghosts.

As a young boy, Milton Jeffers devoured these tales and when, later in life, he grew into the kind of affable and gabby guy who enjoys spinning a good yarn, he passed along Manuel's stories as well as any new ones that made their way to his doorstep.

I met with Mr. Jeffers on a quiet evening in late September 1993 when the symphonies of insect life, lacking all competition from man-made sounds, were very nearly jarring. Milton, then in his sixties, had a welding workshop round back of his house, but we talked in his unassuming front living room, facing each other on brown plaid couches. He possessed all manner of information, but I'd come specifically seeking ghost stories, and he offered me a wealth of them. He told how Manuel Swarz Roberts had helped a couple from New York get rid of a ghost, the spirit of a nineteenth-century farmer, in their house on Dunham Road, by setting out a bottle of whiskey and a shot glass at the bottom of their stairs. He described his own sightings of apparitions of long-deceased Indians in the Tom's Neck area of Chappaquiddick, and Bartholomew Gosnold's phantom ship that appeared once a year, on May 31, off the coast of Cuttyhunk, and many other hair-raisers.

While I had his attention, I sought to fill in holes in some of my other research. Among the questions I asked, "Whatever happened to Julia and Lulu Danzell?"

He shook his head. "That was before my time, but I heard about it. The girls were shipped off island, either straight to the penitentiary or into an old-time funny farm. After that, no islander wanted to hear any more about them."

"The paper said they were maids in one of the Ocean Park mansions. Do you know which one?" I hadn't expected to be enlightened on this score, but Milton knew all right.

"Sure, it was the ugly one. Ugly these days. You know, the one with the red-stained clapboard?

I nodded grimly. Over the years, some of the Victorian cottages of Oak Bluffs had been fabulously restored. Others had suffered the degradation of "modernizing." This particular manor house, located on the eastern arc of Ocean Park, had in the 1980s been treated with aluminum frame windows and clapboard siding daubed an unsightly redwood color with a heavy hand. Once upon a time the house had been truly lovely, when a rich merchant, a Mr. Corbin, built it for his family in the 1880s. Among his staff, according to Mr. Jeffers, he counted two maids—two particular maids, the Danzell sisters. We can bet the Corbins barely noticed them. And that may have smarted, starting a chain of sad events: a cry for attention from two of Cottage City's underclass.

I filed this information away and rarely thought about it, though I felt a certain book-keeper's satisfaction that at least I now knew something concrete about the misguided Danzell girls.

A year or two later, the ugly red clapboard house was purchased by a computer magnate from Los Angeles. In what the buyer termed a favor to the community, his first act of owner-ship was to hire a team to paint the red-stained clapboard white, decreasing its eyesore quota from ten to at least five. And then the major restoration began. This was a project with four walls but no ceiling as far as money was concerned. No effort or expense was spared when it came to recreating the manor house. Nine-teen coats of paint, painstakingly stripped by a forensic architectural archeologist, revealed the original color to have been a drab olive green with greenish black trim. From the razed boards of the red clapboard home, a fairy-tale dwelling rose up like a shimmer from Queen Anne's drawing board—spires and bay win-dow, stained glass, and sublimely lacy molding.

On another occasion, on another byway of research, I held in my hands a bundle of news-paper clippings from the *Vineyard Gazette*, going back the past hundred or so years, all of them devoted to island fires. Weirdly, alarmingly, and per-haps in violation of all compu-tations of the odds, at least ninety percent of these fires occurred in Oak Bluffs. It got so that when I encountered a report of a fire elsewhere, it startled me. A blaze in Vine-yard Haven? A conflagration of a bed and breakfast in Chil-mark? How unusual.

Many of these Oak Bluffs fires during the twentieth cen-tury were declared by whatever fire chief reigned at the time to be of a suspicious nature.

Some of these blazes evoked the 1890's fires in that they gobbled up important sites. In the 1950s a big four-story hotel called the Metro-politan, set smack in the cen-ter of busy Circuit Avenue, went up in flames. In the same year, the extensive Oak Bluffs

Of a Suspicious Nature

Another major fire in Oak Bluffs, this of the four-story Metropolitan Hotel, which went up in smoke in the 1940s. Was it yet another in a long line of conflagrations that may contain a supernatural subtext?
VINEYARD GAZETTE PHOTOGRAPHIC ARCHIVES

wharf burned to cinders on the surface of the sea. The Ocean View Hotel, on the site of the present single-story Oceanview Restaurant on Chapman Avenue, was torched into oblivion.

And then a new, still more significant fire was added to the dreadful catalogue. On a cold February night in 2001, citizens of Oak Bluffs were jangled by the sound of fire alarms. At the time I myself lived about a mile away from town, but glancing at the night sky I could see to the east a ten-story column of fire. I hopped on my bike and followed the volcano-red skies to Ocean Park. The jewel in the crown of Ocean Park—the mansion built by Mr. Corbin in the late nineteenth century and scrubbed and dusted by two future pyromaniacs, later deconstructed and made ugly, then restored to storybook loveliness by a computer billionaire, was busily burning itself to the ground. (Since then it's been perfectly restored, all five thousand square feet of it—at a cost exceeding three million dollars—down to the last turret and panel of stained glass. It is, impossible to believe, even prettier than before.)

The papers reported the findings of the fire chief: The blaze could be attributed to an electrical spark; however, there was nothing wrong with the state-of-the-art wiring. Whatever short may have occurred, it was so insignificant that it failed to trip the breakers. The house also was equipped with excellent smoke alarms. Once again Oak Bluffs had sustained a fire of suspicious origins.

So now the question must be asked:

Can ghosts set fires?

Certainly while the Danzell girls lived and worked in the home, they torched a quantity of buildings. Skeptics will say it's only a coincidence that the home of the pyromaniacs burst into flames more than a hundred years after the young firebugs had been dragged off in chains. Still, as one who tracks down true ghost stories, I can't help wondering if, even from beyond the grave, Julia and Lulu still possess a book of matches.

Milton Jeffers died a few years ago. His wife found him in his favorite armchair, dead from a heart attack—a gentle passing for a man who loved to share Vineyard tales from that very seat.

I've had my eyes open and ear cocked for the next Vineyard Virgil who can extend the stories into the next generation, but so far his or her identify has eluded me. Could it be that in this modern, pepped-up world, with our text messages, faxes, cell phones, and e-mails, there's no more room for a man like Manuel Swarz Roberts, his face half in shadow beside his pot-bellied stove as he offers hot chocolate and ghost tales?

The Final Word on Chappaquiddick?

WHEN YOU MENTION Chappaquiddick to us local yokels, we think simply of the little island off the eastern tip of our larger island, separated from Edgartown by a ninety-five-second ferry ride (yes, I've timed it): There's good fishing at Chappy, and it's quiet, even in summer. Some of the vacation houses are expensive, others about as funky as an old Vineyard cottage can be.

To everyone else in the world, the name Chappaquiddick summons up decades-old headlines of a reckless young senator plowing an Oldsmobile over a decrepit bridge. And the rest of the tale is known down to the smallest detail. After his car plunged into the watery depths, the senator scrambled to shore, but his companion, an attractive young blonde, remained trapped in the vehicle, to die in a slowly decreasing air pocket. The accident went unreported for nine hours while he may have waited to sober up to invent some kind of spin for the disaster.

The date was July 18, 1969, and, of course, the senator was Ted Kennedy, heir apparent to the presidential dynasty. Both his oldest brother John, while president, and his older brother Robert, while running for president, had been assassinated. The psychological twist on the terrible episode at the Chappaquiddick bridge was that Teddy, fearing for his own life should he make a run on the presidency himself—for what nutcake worth his regicidal salt could resist popping the third Kennedy?—was looking for a convenient out.

Though he may have lacked the intelligence and strength of character of his two older brothers, he undoubtedly had no conscious desire to sacrifice a nice young woman like Mary Jo Kopechne in order to bail out of the presidency. But the rumored hard drinking and womanizing that fueled his behavior that summer of 1969 signaled a runaway train where his psyche resided, or as Fonzi used to say, "He was cruisin' for a bruisin'." Unfortunately it was an innocent young woman who got bruised, fatally.

Three probing books provide detailed coverage of the event: *The Bridge at Chappaquiddick* (1970), by Jack Olsen; *Death at Chappaquiddick* (1979), by Thomas T. Tedlow; and *Senatorial Privilege: The Chappaquiddick Cover-up* (1988), by Leo Damone. For readers' edification, I've broken down the data into the following scenario, based on information provided by Olsen, Tedlow, Damone, and eyewitness islanders. The opinions expressed therein are solely mine, not necessarily my publisher's, NPR's, or my Great Aunt Bertha's.

Some of the key players in the law and order business seem so pro-Teddy that I personally can't help picturing suitcases of cash exchanged at crossroads in the dead of night. In reality, there has never been the slightest evidence of payoffs; the favors done the senator may have sprung from nothing more than profound and obsessive sycophancy.

Lieutenant George Killen, of the Massachusetts State Police, was the chief investigator of Mary Jo's drowning. He had just cracked a serial killer case on Cape Cod, and it would be hard to fault his sense of priorities: It was more important for him to bring to justice one Tony Costa—who had hanged from trees, skinned, and partially gutted four women—than to nail America's most famous preppie for a DUI-induced accident.

Killen, however, showed all the signs of "phoning it in." He instructed the medical examiner to skip an autopsy on Mary Jo, even after the D.A. had ordered one. He apparently neglected to ask any pointed questions until August 4, when the looming inquest demanded a few key answers. The Vineyard prosecutor, Walter Steele, ordered Killen to Hyannis Port to interview the senator and his entourage, but somehow the investigator never made it to the legendary Kennedy compound. Neither did he find time to grill the guests from the party preceding the accident, a group made up of six married men and six unmarried women—a recipe for scandal if ever there was one, although by all accounts nothing other than a massive consumption of alcohol went on that night in the modest cottage.

By the way, I've always thought the most amazing feature of the saga is the humble aspect of this particular dwelling. A front door opens directly into the tiny, dark living room and kitchen. Two small bedrooms share a single old-fashioned bath. If they ever make a movie of the infamous event, they'll film the party scenes in a three-thousand-square-foot glam log cabin with tall windows overlooking a brooding bay; in reality, the little Lawrence cottage is miles from water, rendering it even more ironic than Mary Jo should drown that night.

By all reports, Lieutenant Killen dropped the investigative ball.

Bernie Flynn, Killen's chief assistant, also behaved less like a state cop and more like a Teddy team player. He kept an open pipeline of leaks to the Kennedy camp, assuring them that the D.A. had little in the way of meaty material. He even told a couple of the senator's handlers that his cozying up to them could saddle him with a charge of obstructing justice, and that he expected them to help him out if he landed in the deep yogurt: He was afraid of being reassigned to western Massachusetts and, as he later told Mr. Damone, "riding a camel in Pittsfield."

Judge Wilfred Pacquet, who presided over the grand jury, demonstrated the most egregious case of Kennedy kowtowing. The foreman of the jury, Leslie Leland (yes, of Leslie's Pharmacy in Vineyard Haven), had to get right up in Judge Pacquet's face to allow evidence against the senator to be disclosed in court.

The judge then ruled out the jury's access to testimony derived from the inquest. He also barred them from questioning witnesses. Finally, in a flamboyant gesture that changed the proceeding from Grand Jury to Grand Farce, the judge invited a Roman Catholic priest to sit on the bench with him!

Let me repeat that, because it is simply too astounding in today's tougher judicial climate: A Roman Catholic priest rode shotgun with the judge.

The priest led the jurors in prayer. He exhorted them to summon mercy and charity, and to cast out prejudice from their hearts. The only problem with this notion, aside from its gross intermingling of church and state, is that grand jurors are hardly assembled to dispense mercy and charity; they're on hand to hear the facts and, if the facts warrant it, to send the accused to trial.

No indictment was handed down.

The penalty was his fall from political grace; he would never, after the night of July 19, 1969, be considered presidential material. Too, his obvious guilt and disgrace has shown on his ravaged face and bulked up body: Today he looks like a walking effigy of himself. Somewhere in his attic, in a reverse twist of the tale of Dorian Gray, there's a portrait of Teddy getting slimmer and handsomer every day.

So what really happened? What's been left out of the story? What smarmy details were covered up? Juicy theories abound. The most popular is that poor Mary Jo, with one too many rum-and-cokes in her, staggered out from the party and curled up in the backseat of the senator's Oldsmobile, unbeknownst to Ted and some other sexy young government girl who later took the car for a spin and a bit of nooky. The car crashed over the bridge, Teddy and G-girl bailed out, not realizing until way later that they'd left a hapless young tippler in the backseat. On an aesthetic level this is an unappealing version of the tale, reducing it to an act of tragic slapstick. Plus, if this was truly what transpired, why would Teddy and company have failed to latch onto it? While he would still be on the hook for riding around on dark roads with a miniskirted cutie who wasn't his wife, he could at least avoid the charges of cowardice, reckless disregard for human life, and manslaughter, all of which cling to him to this day.

In *Haunted Island*, I addressed the possible element of the supernatural in the play of events. The Oldsmobile went off the rails precisely where, many times beginning in the early 1900s, the inhabitants of Tom's Neck on Chappaquiddick have glimpsed the ghost of one Charles Pease, murdered in the nearby woods (see "Gentleman Farmer Slain by Jealous Lover" in the "Murder Most Foul" chapter). Kennedy, accustomed to being chauffeured almost everywhere, was known by his close associates to be a lousy driver. Add to that any number of gin-and-tonics flooding his veins, a flimsy bridge without guard-rails, and a sudden apparition of a deceased Edwardian age farmer, and anybody could be expected to take a flyer into the high tide of Poucha Pond.

So far no one has pinned an alien abduction on the accident at the Chappy bridge, but that sounds no less reasonable than my own theory coming at you from the extreme fringe.

In the long march of time, two pieces of irrefutable data stand out above all other discussions of the event:

One: Every guest at the party set the time of Ted and Mary Jo's departure at 11:15 to 11:30

p.m. At 12:45 a.m., Sheriff Huck Look, cruising the lonely Chappy roads in his patrol car, observed the dark Oldsmobile back out of the dirt path called, scarily enough, Cemetery Road, and point toward the direction of the Dyke Road, leading to the bridge of the same name. That leaves roughly an hour and a half unaccounted for when it was not entirely out of the question that Ted Kennedy and the otherwise wholesome and idealistic Mary Jo Kopechne may have been involved in an intimate embrace. Or two. Or they may have been sitting in the dark of Cemetery Road waiting for their heads to clear from an excess of spirits while Mary Jo openly mourned the death of her boss and hero, Robert Kennedy, killed earlier in the year, and Teddy waxed eloquent about his pregnant wife, Joan. Then, the heart-to-heart granting them a burst of catharsis, Teddy zipped down the Dyke Road, giving Mary Jo an avuncular pat on the shoulder precisely when he should have had both hands clamped to the wheel.

Two: Ted could have saved Mary Jo if he'd done what all of us pray from the depths of our souls we'd do in a similar crisis—the Right Thing. John Farrar, the scuba diver who recovered Mary Jo's corpse the following morning, reported that her body was contorted in such a way that it was clear she'd been holding on to life in a dwindling air bubble. The diver knew from his own thousands of hours of diving experience that victims trapped in submerged cars have been known to survive for up to twelve hours.

Only fifty yards from shore, a cottage belonging to a family named Malm was occupied that night. At the time of the accident, the lights in the Malm house glowed a radiant yellow-white in the surrounding darkness of Cemetery Road. Inside the cottage sat a working telephone.

Ted himself sustained skull contusions and a serious concussion, validated by island doctors, and this certainly provided a basis for partial amnesia and obvious mental disarray. All the same, this fails to excuse the alleged complicity of his two cohorts, Paul Markham and Joe Gargan, whom he rounded up back at the party cottage to help him deal with the accident. Although virtually no one but perhaps Judge Pacquet has ever believed that Markham and Gargan truly spent a good three-quarters of an hour splashing down for the body themselves, it was taken on faith that the three men hooked up that night and tried to take stock of the situation.

According to Olsen, Tedlow, Damone, et al, the two buddies repeatedly advised Ted to report the incident. Instead, Ted reportedly showed further unsound judgment by diving into the killer currents of Edgartown Bay and swimming for his hotel. Markham and Gargan stayed on Chappy that night, a quiet haven, but nonetheless bursting with summer tenants, most of whom had embraced the twentieth century technology of the telephone.

When the senator woke up the next morning, his first calls were to powerful friends in the Kennedy camp. He never got around to alerting the police. Two surf casters heading over the Dyke Bridge, along with Mrs. Malm of the nearby cottage, a little after eight a.m., discovered the sunken Oldsmobile. Once diver John Farrar and the police appeared at the scene, a scanning of the license plate traced the car to Senator Kennedy.

There may be some Americans who've held against Ted Kennedy the implied adultery of that missing hour-and-a-half between party and accident. Many more compatriots have shuddered at the young man's callousness and dereliction of duty, of honor itself, after the accident occurred. In his place any one of us would hope we'd rise from the cold depths of Poucha Pond, head for the nearby house with the lights on, and ask who opened the door to kindly dial the rescue squad.

Amazing Sea Stories

Storms, Shipwrecks, Sea Serpents, and Other Things
That Go Bump in the Ocean

Lost at Sea

WHENEVER YOU STAND at the site of a light-house on Martha's Vineyard, or indeed anywhere along the New England coast and look out to sea, you are gazing at a maritime graveyard. The purpose of lighthouses, after all, is to warn ships away from treacherous shoals and jagged rocks. Add to these conditions a violent sea or whiteout fog or fatal error in navigation, and no lighthouse beacon can save a sinking vessel.

Down through the centuries, master mariners have sailed with extreme caution across Vineyard Sound from Cape Cod to the ragged shallows of Martha's Vineyard. Churning sands build shoals unmarked on charts. Large vessels give these waters a wide berth—witness the *QE2* in the early 1990s, when it stubbed itself on a sandbar due east of Cuttyhunk. We haven't seen a luxury liner of that girth in these waters since.

So the circumference of the island is lined with wrecks. They lie deep within the roving subterranean sands, or they've been smashed to smithereens by the surf. Many a Vineyarder has installed a pier on his beach only to uncover an ancient skeleton of a vessel lurking only meters offshore.

The whole of the New England coast retains a fearsome catalogue of downed ships. In the 1950s a list was compiled of over seventeen hundred such sinkings, the earliest recorded in 1616. Factor in another fifty-five years, and we can safely assume the sunken vessels have topped the two thousand mark.

English novelist and poet Charles Kingsley could have been describing the lives of past Vineyarders when he wrote, "For men must work and women must weep, tho' storms be sudden and waters deep." Many gravestones in our oldest cemeteries bear the stark inscription LOST AT SEA.

If lighthouses could speak, what a series of tragic tales they could tell. The cliffs below the

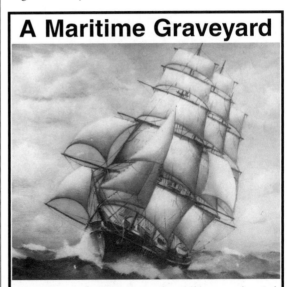

A Maritime Graveyard

The Vineyard's hidden shoals, shifting sands, and occasionally violent seas have sent many schooners to the lower depths of our shoreline.
VINEYARD GAZETTE PHOTOGRAPHIC ARCHIVES, JEFFREY THOMPSON PHOTO

East Chop Lighthouse in Oak Bluffs alone, have presided over a series of catastrophes:

On a calm night in 1884, less than a mile north of the East Chop shore, a three-masted schooner sank a U.S. Navy warship. The collision gave the *Tallapoosa* the regrettable distinction of being the first and only warship to be demolished by a private vessel.

That vessel, the *James S. Lowell,* was en route from Baltimore to Portland with eleven hundred tons of coal in the hold. It glided along at ten knots under a fair wind and tide. Given the clement conditions, both navigators aboard the *James S. Lowell* and the *Tallapoosa* must have been asleep at the wheel to drift so disastrously close to one another. At the last moment, each of the vessels changed course, ostensibly to avoid a collision, but instead, in the ill-judged maneuver, the warship's starboard side was exposed like a bull's-eye to the cargo-laden schooner. The *James S. Lowell* pounded the *Tallapoosa* like a battering ram, slicing her almost in half. Within ten minutes the warship sank below the water, her mast and smokestack waving free like a final call for help. And help was on the way: Nearby fishing vessels scuttled round to rescue the crew, and all but three men were saved.

On November 27, the gale of 1898, still considered the worst storm in New England history, struck these shores. When it was over, forty vessels lay wrecked in Vineyard Haven harbor. The loss was mourned up and down the New England coast, most tragically felt in Maine for, as catastrophic as it proved in these waters, the storm gained momentum and raged still more ferociously as it rampaged farther down east.

Again in East Chop environs, another massive accident occurred in June 1928 when the ocean liner *President Garfield* and a freighter collided two miles east of the lighthouse. Seven crewmen were drowned, and twenty-nine others were rescued from water so turgid with oil that the lifeboats were nearly immobilized.

Then in the horrific hurricane of '44, the Vineyard lightship sank off the west entrance to the Vineyard Haven harbor, taking twelve crewmen with it.

Do all these submerged ships with their lost sailors haunt the jagged edges of the island closest to where they went down? You bet.

The Nutty History of Our Island Lighthouses

IN THE OLD DAYS a bonfire or a cauldron of tar smoldering on a hillside signaled ships at sea. In 1822 a French scientist named Augustin Fresnel invented a lantern with refracting lenses encased in prisms. At the center of the lens was a powerful magnifying glass. Thanks to Fresnel, we now had a working modern lighthouse beacon.

The first lighthouse on the Massachusetts mainland was the Boston Light, erected in 1811. Here on the island, the Gay Head light was built still earlier, in 1799. Its first keeper, a man named Ebenezer Skiff, earned two hundred dollars a year for manning the tower. Most of what we know about Mr. Skiff concerns his attempts to pry more money out of the Federal government. In 1805 he wrote the

Secretary of the Treasury to complain about how the cliffs' red clay begrimed the glass and caused him extra work wiping it clean. He also was required to haul water from a well a full mile away. For his hardship he received a fifty-dollar raise. Ten years later, he complained about the same conditions, presumably to a different Secretary of the Treasury. By this time his comfort level had risen appreciably: He'd become a successful farmer, and he taught the Indians in a nearby school for an additional government salary. All the same, that clay-smeared glass and water portage won him another fifty-dollar bump.

Out on the easternmost end of Chappaquiddick, the Cape Poge Light was built in

1802. The site of many shipwrecks, this spot was isolated in the extreme. Even today you can only reach it by boat or jeep after an hour's bumpy ride over sandy beaches. For the lighthouse keepers on Cape Poge, day after day alone with ululating winds and only the gulls for company, more than a few hardy men succumbed to depression. Periodically a keeper would need to be removed from his post, and some new unlucky recruit would be assigned to this lonely outpost.

From the high bluff of the East Chop lighthouse you can see clearly across the five or so miles of Vineyard Sound to Falmouth. In earlier times, a chap with semaphores bounced up and down on this spot, receiving answers from another eager flag-waver on the Cape. (This worked more efficiently than cell phones, since only a dense fog could interfere with reception.)

In 1869 Captain Silas Daggett, who lived on this site, very graciously put up a lighthouse to guide ships into the harbor. Unfortunately, the tower burned down in 1871, whereupon Captain Daggett stuck a light right on the roof of his house. Later he unloaded the property to the government for the princely sum of five thousand dollars. In 1878, an official lighthouse went up, this one constructed of cast iron and painted a not altogether agreeable shade of brown. Soon people were calling it the Chocolate Lighthouse.

In 1988 the East Chop lighthouse was painted white and, while no one now calls it the Vanilla Lighthouse, it's certainly as pretty as any you'd see along the New England coast.

The first lighthouse on the Edgartown harbor was built in 1828, a Cape-style cottage with a rooftop lantern, slapped together on an artificial island thirteen hundred feet from shore. A couple of years later a wooden pier crossed the water to the lighthouse. Legend has it that this walkway was called the Bridge of Sighs because whalers rendezvoused there with their wives or girlfriends to bid them good-bye. Seeing as how nineteenth-century seamen were known for their utter want of romance or sentimentality, and that New Englanders overall have never been fond of public displays of affection, this smacks of fiction, if not outright fairy tale.

The current tower was built in 1875 and barged over to Edgartown from Ipswich, Massachusetts. The original lens was replaced in 1988 with a solar-powered two-hundred-fifty-millimeter optic. Over time, sands washed ashore and built up a beach around the lighthouse, rendering it a peninsula rather than an island.

Two thousand cobblestones surround the tower, each dedicated to the name of a deceased child.

On a happier note, whether or not nineteenth-century seamen ever kissed their sweethearts good-bye on this site, the spot has turned into a love magnet in the past few decades. Many a wedding ceremony is performed on this hallowed land with water stretching away on all three sides, only a short walk from the fabled village of whaling captains' houses. Too, the beauty and isolation of the peninsula has inspired many an ardent lover, under the red beacon winking on and off, to propose marriage. Perhaps, knowing this, amorous couples should steer clear of the Edgartown Harbor Light unless they're good to go.

In Vineyard Haven the first West Chop Light, constructed in 1817, was a twenty-five-foot rubblestone tower, set back a thousand feet

Day after day alone with ululating winds and only the gulls for company, more than a few hardy men succumbed to depression.

from the current site. Trophy homes of the late nineteenth century hemmed in the lighthouse as rich Bostonians built behemoth-sized summer houses along the cliffs of West Chop—perhaps in imitation of the still more ostentatious New Yorkers building their massive chateaus in Newport. Eventually these bulky homes obscured the view of the lighthouse, and in 1891 a new, forty-five-foot brick tower was erected on a more advantageous point.

The last lighthouse to go automatic, in 1976, the West Chop complex still houses all the ancillary buildings, including the keeper's cottage, plus the fog signal and oil houses. All of this makes it possible to daydream about what life was like for a lighthouse keeper's family—arguably one of the sweetest jobs going, back in the day.

Baby, It's Cold Outside

FOR THE FIRST many decades of the whaling industry, sailors believed that anybody venturing into Arctic realms had to be out of his mind. The extreme northern hemisphere was the most dangerous part of the planet, with treacherous currents and roving ice packs that could crush a ship the way a man's hand could collapse a tin can. But then in the summer of 1848 two New England vessels stumbled onto a new kind of ice fishing. The bark *Superior* of Sag Harbor, helmed by Captain Royce, and the ship *Ocmulgee,* under the watch of Captain Frederick Manter of Vineyard Haven, drifted through the Bering Strait engulfed in a pea soup fog. Unwittingly the two ships straggled into the Arctic Ocean. When the fog lifted, the sailors found themselves surrounded by the fattest whales they'd ever seen—bowhead whales, as it turned out. They set to harpooning like a band of men possessed, and soon enough they sailed for home with a cargo beyond all expectations.

The *Superior* and *Ocmulgee* adventure launched the gold rush of whaling. Before long, word of Arctic plenty spread far and wide. San Francisco became the embarkation point, luring many Vineyard captains, ships, and crews to that coast. The plan was to spend a short summer season in the lower netherworld of the ice pack zone. Initially none

pushed far into the Arctic. Whaling was already a perilous sport; to sojourn ever farther northward was to court certain death.

Then a handful of younger officers began to hatch a plan for extending the all too short Arctic whaling season: How about wintering-over in that cold region, so as to be on hand when the ice first broke up in the spring? That way they could push the hunt into the shoulder seasons of spring and fall, whaling away before vessels sailing up from San Francisco made it past Point Barrow.

One of these whaling cowboys was Hartson Bodfish of Vineyard Haven. Some men are born with unusual passions, and Bodfish, from an early age, longed to devote his life to Arctic whaling. In his early teens he shipped out on the *Belvedere,* only the second steam whaler to be built in the states. Bodfish returned year after year, fascinated by the cold north, all the while climbing the maritime career ladder in order to take further charge of Arctic operations.

Finally in 1889, he achieved the level of second mate to Captain Henry Dexter of Vineyard Haven aboard the *Grumpus.* At anchor in Harrison Bay, Dexter, counseled by Bodfish, learned of a stretch of open water up in the forbidden zone. Other whalers felt equally spunky, and the *Grumpus,* with seven other steamers, headed north four hundred miles to the mouth of the Mackenzie River, east of Hershel Island. They arrived in the frozen hinterlands on August 11.

A few of the ships encountered fearsome shoals. Their captains, spooked by the situation and weary of the extreme cold, hauled up anchor and turned back. At last the remaining vessels, the *Grumpus* included, retreated south, but the idea of penetrating deep into this frozen territory, and consequently wintering over, was born.

Over the next twenty years, a number of Vineyard vessels ventured into the Arctic Ocean. One could almost say Vineyarders had a libido for the frigid. The going was never easy. The ice was unimaginably thick and constantly splintering, shifting, reformulating. It was the work of a moment for a whaling vessel caught in an ice pack to cave in, crushed by the relentless pressure. The August 1971 issue of the *Dukes County Intelligencer* tells how Vineyard Captain Fred Tilton, marveling at the risks the whalers were taking, recalled that when he first explored the Arctic in 1882, "Any captain who took the vessel as far as Franklin's Return Reef was considered stark raving crazy."

And yet by 1897 ships were traveling seven hundred miles farther north than that.

In the winter of that same year, four boats with one hundred forty-seven men all told were stranded in the ice near Point Barrow. A few of the men inventoried the supplies: They had enough for two meals a day through the first of July. Beyond that, the stores would grow increasingly scarce and men would surely die. A Vineyarder named George Tilton volunteered to trudge south for relief in the company of two Siberian natives—a three-thousand-mile trek. After encountering hurricanes and blizzards and being deserted by his two guides, Tilton arrived in San Francisco on April 17, a full five months after setting off from Point

Barrow. His news mobilized the cutter *Bear* to head north after the stranded seamen, who were rescued at last on July 22.

Just as Vineyard whalers were among the first to penetrate the Arctic, they were also among the last to leave. Arctic maniac Hartson Bodfish spent twenty-three summers and eight winters in the far north. He permitted himself one year off for rest and recuperation on the Vineyard, before he returned to his beloved ice. As master mariner of the *William Baylies,* he landed thirty-five thousand pounds of whalebone and fourteen hundred white fox skins.

Bodfish indulged in three more voyages on the *Baylies*. On the third trip out, in Anadir Bay, Siberia, the vessel was crushed by ice. Captain Bodfish assembled his men on the nearest floe and they watched glumly as, inside of twelve minutes, the *Baylies* sank. They had no shelter and no supplies. By nighttime a gale descended. For many hours the men huddled in the blinding snow, as ice cracked all around them. By daylight the storm dissipated, and through the clearing air, the men could see the steamer *Bowhead* two miles away in open water. With Bodfish leading the way, the men marched nine and a half hours and at last reached the *Bowhead*.

Even this failed to rattle Hartson Bodfish, however. He kept on whaling for a few more years, making his last trip in 1914. The whale oil business petered out before Bodfish did: Petroleum had replaced whale oil, and whalebone had been trumped by steel. Furthermore, the so-called golden age of whaling had depleted most of the ocean's stock. It was time for men like Captain Bodfish to hang up their harpoons.

In 1915, the *Bowhead* was sold to a motion picture company and promptly set on fire for the camera—a fitting metaphor for the end of an era.

Our Own Nessie (as in Loch Ness Monster)

FORGET ABOUT *Jaws*—the only great white shark that has ever menaced our waters was made out of metal and Plexiglas and responded to the direction of Steven Spielberg.

But we've got a bigger creature in our ocean, and maybe even badder. For more than two hundred fifty years, there've been sightings of a Vineyard sea serpent, and everyone who has lived to tell the tale has been haunted by it.

Circa 1700, a British man-of-war, gliding through Vineyard waters, came abreast of a sea monster. The sight was duly noted in the ship's log: *beastly head, unus'ly large, genus unknown.*

Sometime in the 1860s, an Edgartown packet captain whose "truthfulness and aversion to exaggeration" were vouched for by the editor of the *Vineyard Gazette*, reported sighting a marine beast in the stretch of water between Gay Head and Newport. The captain described the creature as measuring about seventy feet in length, with a head shaped like a horse's, eyes the size of dinner plates, and with fore flippers extending from its chest to perform a paddling motion.

The newspaper editor reported that the captain was clearly unnerved by the episode, worried that his veracity, and even sanity, would be called into question. Yet he felt he needed to divulge the existence of this creature.

In 1890 the grandfather of island author Everett S. Allen—who according to Allen, had no imagination and no story-telling ability, none whatsoever—swore he once saw a sea serpent frolicking in the surf of South Beach. The man was mowing salt hay when he looked up to see a gigantic lizard-like specimen splashing in and out of the waves. The man froze in his work, then turned his back and headed for home. He spent the remainder of the day in bed, staring off into space, trying to make sense of what in God's kingdom he'd witnessed gamboling offshore.

In the 1930s, Captain Fred Caldwell of Fairhaven and his mate George Roche were out trawling in Menemsha Creek. It was a sunny day in early July as they steamed west from Gay Head. They passed the bell buoy in the Devil's Bridge area and noticed something thrashing in the water. Just like in those old horror movies when the audience screams at the doomed characters, "NO! Don't go that way," Captain Caldwell and Mate Roche steered over to the roiling water to investigate. As they drew closer, the waters parted and a sea serpent reared up alongside them. It was longer than their fifty-two-foot boat. They stared in shock at the plate-sized black eyes in the horse-shaped head. Then with a flick of its immense fin, the creature sent the boat sprawling away from it before it plunged back into the depths. Later, everyone who heard the story remarked that Caldwell and Roche were severely rattled by the encounter. For a number of days they continued to display enormous stress.

Many wondered whether their tale shed light on a mysterious event that had taken place a few days earlier. Near Wood's Hole a boat had been found motoring along, absent its owner, a Cape fisherman. A lobster buoy had been jammed between two bait barrels on board, and its line trailed in the water, broken off and frayed as if from some violent tug. The man's body was never recovered.

No new sightings have come to light, but it's possible that something still lurks out there ... the American cousin of the elusive beast of Loch Ness.

This Just in From Nantucket

THE FOLLOWING IS such a choice maritime yarn that Nantucketers will, I hope, forgive me for including it in our sea stories section. Old-timers swear this is true, but you be the judge:

There once was a man from Nantucket...

Sorry. Let's try again:

There was once a Nantucket sea captain who sailed the banks of Brazil and the frigid fringes of the Arctic and the west coast of Africa, all the while without once consulting his ship's sextant or chronometer. Didn't need 'em. A glance at the sky and water, a sniff of the breeze, and a taste of particles from the sea bottom picked up on his sounding lead—these were all he needed, especially the latter, to know precisely where they were: latitude, longitude, and every last crosshair in between.

One day the cook on this vessel decided to play a prank on the captain. He'd brought along a box of soil for growing such herbs as thyme and rosemary to perk up the cuisine. The cook, cackling demonically, smeared a quantity of potting soil over the captain's sounding lead.

Minutes later, with a number of crewmen standing by, the captain touched his tongue to the lead. His eyes popped open:

"Shiver me timbers! Nantucket's sunk, and here we are, right over old Marm Hackett's garden!"

Dog Overboard

THIS IS AN amazing sea story that would have made the national news had not an even bigger ocean disaster burned up the international wires.

On July 26, 1956, the far more significant story was the sinking of the *Andrea Doria* off the southwest coast of Nantucket. Dense fog had hung over the wine dark sea, and in spite of modern navigational systems, two enormous luxury liners steamed along on a collision course. Sometime after midnight, the mists cleared. The late night revelers in the *Andrea Doria*'s plush salons stared out the large windows to behold a towering vessel of lights bearing down on them.

The *Stockholm* rammed the *Andrea Doria* amidship, and then plowed backward as the breached vessel took on water. Hours later,

most of the 1250 passengers were off-loaded to other vessels, but 125 unlucky passengers descended with the ship. Mariners speculated that these doomed souls may have survived for several hours inside air bubbles trapped in their cabins—alive, alone, at the bottom of the ocean.

The glamorous tragedy attracted deep-sea divers the very next day! Over the years, the ruined ship, resting hundreds of feet below the ocean surface, has proven to be the Mt. Everest of the water world. With diving conditions so extreme, a disproportionate number of scuba freaks die while swimming through the wrecked hull and have joined the remains of the original lost passengers.

Anything else occurring on that same date, especially another maritime incident, was bound to be overshadowed, and in fact only the *Vineyard Gazette* picked up the smaller story: From a fishing vessel trawling due west of the Aquinnah cliffs, a wire-haired fox terrier named Shakespeare fell overboard without anybody noticing until he was long out of sight.

Imagine the small pup's misery and disorientation. Within moments he could have seen nothing around him but rough swells of water. He was lost from the boat he knew as home, lost from the man he knew as his master. What's more, if the dog's fear got the better of him and he let out a yelp, his throat and nostrils would have burned with saltwater. And yet his stout little terrier body kept paddling for more than two hours.

At last a white hull reared up alongside the sodden pooch. Had the *Seer*'s sportfishing crew been engaged with a swordfish on the far side of the boat, poor Shakespeare would have missed his single chance. But one of the sailors spotted the dog and set up the alarm. The terrier was scooped from the water, wrapped in a towel, cuddled, stroked, fed, and given water during the long ride to shore.

To tinker only slightly with the human Shakespeare's words: *That island [in New] England breeds very valiant creatures: Their mastiffs [and fox terriers] are of unmatchable*

Love, Vineyard Style

The Special Mating Rituals Among Men and
Women on a Cold New England Island

Inbreeding, Anyone?

WHO KNOWS WHEN it was that marriage between first cousins began to be frowned upon in this country. Up until the twentieth century, Vineyarders found nothing wrong with it. Like rural New Englanders everywhere, they drew the line at nuptials between half-siblings, or nieces and uncles, or nephews and aunts. But for two hundred years on the ultra-insulated island, first, second, and third cousins married routinely, because to wait for an unrelated partner to come along would have made lifelong bachelors and spinsters of everyone.

By the end of the 1700s on Martha's Vineyard, over ninety-six percent of married couples were related to each other many times over. Husbands and wives shared ancestors—mostly from Kent, England—the way kids today download music from one another. Mostly islanders stayed close to home in those days when a trip from Edgartown to Aquinnah was a two-day operation. Unless some kind of social function inspired Vineyarders to hitch up the oxen or don their hiking boots, they stayed within a one- or two-mile radius of their homesteads. As an old-timer put it in an interview with historian Nora Ellen Groce for her book *Everyone Here Spoke Sign Language* (2005), "You know, the North Roaders stayed on the North Road, and the South Roaders stayed on the South Road. There was a lot of feelings, bad feelings, between these parts of town, too." (Well, that makes sense; if you're looking for excuses not to walk an extra four or five miles to socialize, you're going to tell yourself that other folk, those geographical undesirables, are braggarts, slackers, rascals, shiftless sons of sod—take your pick.)

The same old-timer disclosed in his interview, "I was a creeker [of Menemsha Creek] and my wife, she come from the South Road, and God, her father was mad! 'Marrying one of them damn creekers!' he said. 'I never knew a creeker that amounted to anything!'"

So we can see how it was easier to marry your first cousin next door than to incur the wrath of an alien family on the far side of the sheep meadow. (In the case of the creeker/South Road match; the couple probably shared only forty-nine Kentish ancestors compared to the usual one hundred seventy-six.)

The upshot of all this overlapping DNA was that a deafness gene blazed through the island's human stock, particularly in the upcountry towns of West Tisbury and Chilmark by way of a single earlier settler—another shiftless son of a sod from Kent, presumably—who carried the recessive gene for deafness. For 250 years on the Vineyard, one in 125 islanders was born deaf, compared to the mainland average of one person in every 5728.

It wasn't until the early 1900s that increasing scientific understanding of heredity explained various medical conditions. Up until that time, the cause of massive island deafness was blamed on the usual culprits: God's displeasure, sins of the father, a good scare delivered during pregnancy. In the late nineteenth century, Alexander Graham Bell paid a trip to the Vineyard to satisfy his fascination with all things pertaining to sound—or lack thereof.

His conclusion? Island deafness may have derived from the thick layer of clay beneath the Chilmark soil. Hmmm . . . Just shows you can be brilliant enough to invent the telephone and still not have all brain fuses switched on.

A lovely result of island deafness was that everyone—and I do mean everyone—knew sign language. No one thought twice about it; you picked up hand signals from earliest childhood. Vineyarders were bilingual in this way. And because it was easy as pie to communicate, people barely noticed when a friend or neighbor or family member (well, now, that's redundant) was hearing impaired. A typical description of a fellow islander might sound something like this: "Yeah, old Horace Norton, he was a great fisherman, loved trawlin' the bight in foul weather. Could chop wood like a bastard, even though he was missin' three fingers. Wife's name was Mary Jane. Had eleven kids. Some of 'em married into my family. What's that you say? Was he deaf? Oh, right—I do believe he was."

The last of the hereditary Vineyard deaf died in 1956. Clearly, enough fresh blood has entered the community to dilute the ancient gene for hearing impairment. In some ways we've lost a lot that was special in smalltown communities when a given child could take for granted that all four of his or her grandparents lived a stone's throw away. But even if we could return to that simpler, carefree way of life, it still might pay to saddle up the horses to go out and find a date a good hour's ride away.

"Sheer Off!"

NOTHING COMES BETWEEN loving partners more quickly than a nasty germ.

In the early 1800s, Jacob West of Edgartown, at seventy-two years of age, had spent a lifetime in the ruddiest of health; not a single cold had interrupted his daytime farming and his nighttime . . . well, boozing. He was shocked, therefore, when one winter morning he woke up feeling rotten. What was this? Unfamiliar with the giddiness that filled his head and the nausea roiling up from his stomach, he recalled rumors of smallpox afflicting a few poor souls on the island.

But Jacob West wasn't about to let a little case of imminent mortality cause him to stumble. He knew what he needed to combat the symptoms. It was his answer to everything that ailed him: liquor—and the quicker, the slicker. He pushed himself from bed and set off on foot for the six-mile trek to the nearest distillery.

He purchased a quart of rum, then immediately set about imbibing it on his long march home. At last he saw in the distance the whale-oil lamplight of his farmhouse kitchen. He raised the jug once more as the last trickle rolled down his throat. To his dismay, he realized he still felt sick, in fact, sicker than before. He was also staggeringly drunk, so somehow the wisest course of action seemed to be to galumph back to the distillery for another bottle of rum.

On the rebound from his second round-trip, his wife met him at the kitchen door, a loaded musket leveled at his chest.

Local lore has it that she shrieked at him, "Sheer off! You've got smallpox and you're all ready to break out!"

Jacob had no choice but to sleep in the barn, nestled between his oxen. Before the week was over, he'd recovered from the dreaded disease (perhaps there is some virtue in the Rum Cure), and Jacob West's wife permitted him to return to their home of wedded bliss.

The Case of the Missing Wife

ON FEBRUARY 22, 1867, the following boxed item was printed in the *Vineyard Gazette*:

NOTICE

WHEREAS MY WIFE, MARY J. CLARK, HAS LEFT MY HOME AND NOW IS ABSENT FROM ME AGAINST MY CONSENT, ALL PERSONS ARE FORBIDDEN TO HARBOR HER OR TRUST HER ON MY ACCOUNT, AS I SHALL PAY NO BILLS OF HER CONTRACTING.

The twenty-nine-year-old Frank D. Clark, a grocery clerk in Holmes Hole, was miffed at his twenty-year-old runaway wife. But did this constitute the whole story?

A month later, the absconding Mary Clark sent a letter to the same newspaper outlining her version of the matter. Mary maintained that Frank D. had, in fact, consented to her visiting her mother in Monticello, Florida, and had actually escorted her to Boston on the first leg of her journey. He'd dutifully handed her money for the trip south but had, curiously, neglected to pay for her return fare.

Frank D. apparently woke up one day in full realization of what a jerk he'd been (or in language more appropriate to the period, a bounder or a cad). He journeyed to Monticello, Florida, to beg for Mary's forgiveness. She granted it, and together they returned to Martha's Vineyard.

The reconciliation endured, as they later conceived a child: Frank E. Clark was born in 1870. (We have to wonder whether future sons of Frank D. would have been named Frank F., Frank G., and so on.)

The rest of the family history is meager, indeed only two further scraps of information remain: 1) The Clarks did not prosper, and 2) Frank D. died in 1887 at the age of fifty-four, an embittered man. Perhaps his life would have taken a more salutary direction if he'd remembered to give Mary her return fare from Florida.

A Summing Up

IT ISN'T OFTEN that a tombstone tells a love story, but here's one in a nutshell, long admired on a slab of slate in the Oak Bluffs cemetery, marking the grave of Lydia Claghorn, who died in 1799:

JOHN AND LYDIA
THAT LOVELY PAIR
A WHALE KILLED HIM
HER BODY LIES HERE

The Captain's Wife

SAILORS IN THE old days had a superstitious dread of having a woman onboard their vessel. But on the Vineyard where women are, and always have been, strong (plus, the men are beautiful, and the children are above average), some of our sea captains saw fit to take their wives to sea. Of these, the most notable was Joshua Slocum, the man who later in life sailed a thirty-seven-foot sloop single-handedly around the world (see "Solo Sailor" in the "VIPs" chapter).

In 1869, when he was twenty-five and had command of his second ship, the *Washington*, running cargo from San Francisco to Sydney, he met and almost instantaneously married the bewitching young Virginia Alberta Walker on one of his trips Down Under. Virginia had been born in New York in 1849 and reared in the California gold rush camps, and somewhere along the line her DNA heritage had picked up some Native American fibers. A skilled horsewoman and shooter, she loved the outdoor life and, as such, was a boon companion for the adventurous sea captain.

You know how they say when people fall in love, "the earth moved"? Well the moment Virginia first set eyes on Joshua Slocum, something moved under her feet, but it was the ocean, and she would rarely set foot on land again for the remainder of her days.

The deck cabin aboard the *Washington* became the Slocum's "mobile home," and for their honeymoon they sallied forth to Alaska in search of schools of salmon. In a gale off the coast of Canada, the *Washington* ran aground on a sandbar and proceeded to break up. Virginia was rescued, and Joshua, who returned to his grounded vessel to transfer his catch to a craft he'd hurriedly improvised, rowed away in the nick of time.

The boat owners rewarded Captain Slocum with the command of the barkentine *Constitution,* which ran a packet route between San Francisco and Honolulu. Virginia and Joshua's first child, a son, was born while they were moored in San Francisco harbor in 1872. Virginia gave birth in 1873 to their second child, another boy, aboard a square-rigger called the *B. Aymar.* A girl was born in 1875 when they were anchored in waters off the Philippines.

After a year spent on unfamiliar *terra firma* in a thatched hut on Subic Bay, Joshua refurbished a forty-five-ton schooner, the *Pato,* and brought his family aboard. They sailed across the South China Sea on a path to the codfish grounds in the North Pacific. Virginia gave birth to twins just as Joshua was hauling in a prize catch. While they were in transit to Portland, Oregon, the twins died—a not uncommon tragedy for large families in those times.

Joshua sold the *Pato,* bought the 350-ton full-rigger *Amethyst,* and proceeded to ship freight throughout the Pacific. Meanwhile Virginia gave birth to another daughter who also died. In 1881, their seventh child, James Garfield, was born while they were in Hong Kong harbor.

His fortunes rising, Joshua bought his biggest ship of all, the *Northern Light,* fully five times larger than the *Amethyst.* The proud husband and father brought his family aboard to spacious quarters consisting of several spacious cabins and a library housing more than five hundred books.

They sailed from Manila around the Cape of Good Hope and across the Atlantic to New York, where they had to trim the highest pinnacles of the rigging to enable *Northern Light* to fit beneath the Brooklyn Bridge. They went on to New London for needed repairs on the rudder. For the crew, paid in advance as was the custom, this stop in their own country offered a rare temptation to jump ship. Virginia held the crew onboard with a pistol pointed at their heads, while Joshua gave them a tongue lashing before confining them to their cabins until the ship again cast off.

On one return run from Manila, the Slocums passed within miles of the volcano Krakatau just as it was blowing its stack so high that the island itself was blasted clean out of existence.

In 1884, in Baltimore, Joshua stowed his family aboard a beautiful bark called *Aquidneck.* Carrying a cargo of flour, they headed south to Buenos Aires, Brazil. On a trip ashore one day, Joshua looked back at the *Aquidneck* to see a signal requesting his return: a pennant with the letter J (for his name) waved in the breeze. Virginia had developed a fever. On July 25, 1884, Virginia died at sea. She was thirty-four years old, Joshua forty. He buried her in the English cemetery in Buenos Aires. Although two years later he took a second wife, twenty-four-year-old Hettie Elliott, marital happiness post-Virginia eluded him. Unlike her predecessor, Hettie was unwilling to spend a life on the high seas, and consequently she rarely saw him. Joshua parked her with the children on Martha's Vineyard.

After Virginia, the only other soul mate he would ever know was his beloved sloop *Spray,* which he sailed solo around the world, beginning in 1895. Actually if Virginia had survived, she most likely would have found keen competition in the *Spray* for Joshua's affections. Most sea captains' ladies took second place to their husbands' vessels, or third and fourth place if their men owned more than one boat.

When You Have a Prince for a House Guest

BACK IN 1983 my buddy Marcia Smilack, who summered in Menemsha, happened to be dating a Spanish royal. Prince Carlos was his name. Actually his official name was Carlos followed by a string of Spanish surnames ending in de Bourbon. Pretty posh, huh? He was handsome and charming and also *muy intelligente,* as evidenced by the fact that that he taught political science at Harvard's Kennedy School of Government.

Marcia would bring Carlos along to parties and picnics on Chappy (he loved to drive Marcia's jeep across the sands) as if he were just any old boyfriend. He blended in beautifully, never for a moment revealing any hint of royal arrogance. As a matter of fact, he was just about the most perfect prince I'd ever met. He was also the only prince I'd ever met.

Once I asked Prince Carlos if he had know Franco, Spain's Fascist dictator from WWII, and the man responsible for the country's royals living in exile. Carlos chuckled, "I met him any number of times. He was always charming whenever he wasn't trying to kill me."

Now that's primo cocktail party patter.

Prince Carlos was divorced from Princess Irene of the Netherlands. He had four kids, two boys and two girls, their ages running from eight to twelve, all of them nieces and nephews of Queen Beatrice of the Netherlands. Like any bachelor dad, Carlos had custody of his progeny for part of the summer. One weekend he phoned Marcia to ask if he could bring the tykes down to stay with her for the weekend. Marcia said she would be delighted.

Her only problem was that her summer rental, tucked into the woods off Menemsha Cross Road, was a tad under code for European nobility. It was a notch up from the old-style Vineyard camp because it had working electricity and indoor plumbing. But the exposed beams and single-ply walls were weathered, the furniture had been salvaged from the West Tisbury "dumptique," and the entire living room, kitchen, single bathroom, and two bedrooms occupied all of eight hundred square feet.

But Marcia needn't have worried about the accommodations. The kids were delighted with what must have felt to them like a playhouse. When they bedded down for the night, they gleefully called out to their dad through the open door of their bedroom, thrilled to be able to communicate with him across a simple hallway rather than via intercom across wings of a palace the size of a shopping mall. They also told Marcia what a treat it was to have free and easy access to the kitchen. "At the palace, if we want a snack we have to ask our governess to accompany us. And once we arrive at the kitchen we have to say 'please' and 'thank-you' to everyone!"

At the end of the weekend, the mini-sized royals bid "Marcialita" a tearful good-bye, and she promised them that if they returned the following summer, she would find a rental still smaller and more rustic.

The Start of a Beautiful Friendship

IT WAS A SCENE straight out of a horror movie.

One dark and stormy night in November, a Milton woman spending the weekend in her antique cottage near Owen Park in Vineyard Haven was awakened by a thumping sound downstairs. She sat up in bed, her heart beating double-time. Winds blew like a gang of banshees around the eaves, and rain pelted the windows. She reasoned that the noise from below had been a shutter come loose from its hinges, but still she felt moved to investigate.

She padded softly down the corridor until she stood at the top of the stairs. The living room and foyer below were a jumble of shadows, black upon still deeper shades of black. But then, as her eyes adjusted, her heart flipped back into overdrive.

Inside the front door, the silhouette of a man lurked beneath the lintel.

The woman gave a shout and reached for the light switch at the top of the stairs. The hallway light beamed down on the intruder. His clothes—gray sweats, sneakers, windbreaker—were drenched with rain dripping down on the indoor welcome mat. Under a baseball cap, his lean, tanned forty-something face looked as shocked and as scared as did the woman's.

According to my source (a good friend of the homeowner), his words spilled out something like this: "Omigod! I'm so sorry! I came in on the late ferry. My house is off Hatch Road, but this storm—this storm caught me by surprise! I took shelter under the gazebo—" gesturing in the direction of the bandstand in Owen Park, "but the rain was coming in every which way. I thought no one would be home this time of year, and I was hoping, quite honestly, for an unlocked front door. Turned out to be yours!"

They simply stared at one another while the woman's fears decompressed. She realized she believed him. He sounded truly embarrassed, and besides, he looked so forlorn in his soaking garb. It occurred to her that she had given him a scare, too.

"Well!" she said at last. "Can I make you a cup of tea?"

They had tea and scones in her kitchen, and yakked for an hour or so until the storm abated, and the man could walk home. It wasn't the start of a torrid romance, even though the scene would have played out that way in a movie—maybe starring Kevin Klein and Goldie Hawn? But since then, whenever the two meet in town, they greet one another fondly, exchanging news like old friends.

From Russia, With or Without Love

A COUPLE OF years back I ran into a captain on the steamship line who had recently attended a friend's wedding. Not your normal American wedding. The friend, a businessman in Edgartown, was taking for his wife a mail-order bride from Russia.

The captain told me the groom's earlier attempt to marry a Russian girl had failed miserably. Contrary to the way these matters are depicted in fiction or the way they were conducted back in the old days, the unknown woman was not obliged to arrive and marry on the spot. Instead time was allotted for the semi-betrothed to get to know each other and see whether they were compatible.

The pair was hampered by the young lady's inability to speak a word of English, and, not surprisingly, the man knew no Russian whatsoever other than *borscht* and *perestroika*. The young lady managed to convey to him that as a wedding settlement she expected him to buy her folks in Russia a dacha outside Moscow. He signed over a check, and soon the all-clear arrived from the mother country that the parents were now ensconced in their new home.

And yet the would-be bride never cottoned to this man. Every time he came too close, she slapped him. Ouch. The bride-manqué returned to Russia.

The businessman's second attempt, however, had apparently succeeded, for now he stood in a dapper dark suit, a goofy smile on his face, as his bride approached in a lacy, flowing white gown and veil.

The ferry captain gushed to me, "She was so beautiful! Long blond hair, perfect makeup, tall and thin. Do all Russian babes look that good?"

Actually from what I've heard, they do. They've come a long way from the farm commune days when marriageable Russian girls wore babushkas over doughy faces and recommended themselves to matchmakers as being wide as barn doors, the better to haul tractors. One thing you can say about capitalism is that it frees up money for manicures, hair highlights, luscious lipsticks, tight jeans, and silk blouses.

The ferry captain was entranced with the sight of the storybook bride. Later at the reception, he approached the woman who ran the agency for foreign brides. "How much did it cost to hook this girl up with my friend?" he asked her.

"The fee is twenty-five hundred dollars," she said.

"Damn! I'm gonna order one!" he declared.

The last I heard, he was still dating Vineyard women, but he may secretly be stashing extra dollars in a jar marked "Russian Wife."

Why Some Men and Women Look Better in February

AMONG THE MORE freewheeling of the single population on the island, two separate seasons pertain to romance: In the winter you want one person to snuggle with, someone with whom to share pizza straight from the box, and with whom to hunker down evenings to watch the latest batch of DVDs from Netflix. And it pays to remain on good terms with this significant winter other because to split up mid-season puts you in the bind of having to meet someone new when a blizzard is raging outside, or your dirt road is too slushy to allow you to get out and hit the bars.

Come June, however, island heads are turned by the influx of summer cuties: girls with silken hair down their backs, taut, pierced tummies, and platform sandals; guys with good haircuts, bronze flesh tones (all over arms and torsos rather than ending at the tee shirt line), and muscles trained with strategic precision in a gym rather than from the random push and pull of operating heavy machinery.

This is the time when Vineyard couples pick fights with the idea in mind that they can always make up again in the fall. And who can blame them? If you've been eating hamburger all winter, a smorgasbord offered by a roster of cosmopolitan chefs is bound to appeal. And it isn't as if Vineyarders are intrinsically less attractive. It's just that island living makes you lazy as far as your grooming is concerned.

Women favor helmet-shaped haircuts or long hair pulled back in a frizzy braid so it won't get in the way when they're hauling scallops up from the ocean floor. Letting hair go gray is big. Way big. Women with gray hair have lots of sisters in grayness here, and they convince themselves it doesn't add an extra twenty years to their looks. Clairol long ago recalled its sales rep from Martha's Vineyard.

As far as local men are concerned, they get sloppy. They have a collection of work clothes—holey sweatshirts, torn jeans, paint-splattered tees—that they forget to change out of when they dine out. And dining out means forty-five minutes spent at the local coffee shop, so no one's going to really care that these guys are still wearing their waders.

On waking up in the morning, an island man's first bit of business is to don his baseball cap, brim shading his eyes; he'll refuse to remove it until his head hits the pillow again. Island men, in other words, do not "clean up good." They may have defined biceps from hauling lumber, but winter bellies encroach over the top of their jeans, and they've never heard of Dr. Atkins or how French people, women and men, don't get fat.

Come summer, Vineyarders spruce up enough to have some hope of attracting a seasonal honey. I've heard it said that a percentage of island couples actually agree to split in June and reconvene in September—mid-September, that is. But frankly, I've never met anyone up close and personal who was open-minded enough to entertain so wild and wacky an arrangement.

Still, whatever transpires in the balmy months of July and August, come October or, at the very latest, January or February, fellow and sister islanders begin to look just fine. After all, her hair may be gray, but consider her porcelain complexion and twinkly hazel eyes. And how about that guy with the cute dimple in his chin? Word is out that he's been good as gold about attending AA meetings.

And of course some of these winter couples marry, or else they meet a summer sweetie who agrees to stay on island and make a go of year-round living. Whatever, people meet and marry and raise kids on the island, though most of these kids, when they grow up, vroom off to sample the pleasures of the larger world. Some of them return eventually to begin the Vineyard mating dance all over again.

Hurricane Love

IT WAS AUGUST of 1991 and Hurricane Bob was bearing down on New England. The storm had been predicted for a couple of days, and we waited and watched as it slammed into Long Island. On August 19, it shrieked up the south side of the Vineyard. It shed its rain back in New York, but its winds galvanized at 115 miles per hour, kicking up deadly mini-tornados. It was as dark and brutal and loud as a freight train hurtling past your front yard, and it raged from nine a.m. until three p.m. Gales laced with sea salt nuked fields and forests and laid bare our gardens. Afterward piles of leafless trees with twisted, blackened boughs, lay everywhere like dead soldiers. Not a single blossom remained in a single yard.

At midafternoon, Susan Phillips of Oak Bluffs wondered what might have happened to

It took the big blow of '91 to convince Susan Phillips to accept Jim Cage's proposal of marriage.
PHOTO BY ANONYMOUS WEDDING GUEST

her boyfriend. Jim Cage was a police officer on the Oak Bluffs squad, and he was due at Susan's house at four p.m. when his shift was normally over.

The phones were down all over the island, so there was no way Jim could let Susan know he still had to protect and serve. Not a single cop could go home until the wreckage from Bob was brought under control. Trees lay across roads, Five Corners was flooded, and in all the towns the darkened businesses with smashed windows were vulnerable to any passing marauder. To make matters worse, the deadened telephones made it impossible for a single emergency to pass through the dispatchers at Communications. All the police could do was patrol the towns, patrol the neighborhoods, patrol the beaches, watch out for looters, storm victims, and injured animals, and radio the other island first responders about downed telephone wires and obstructive fallen trees.

Meanwhile Susan began to worry as each hour ticked by and no Jim appeared at her door. Up until that time, the company they'd kept had been a casual matter to her. Jim himself had given away his heart, had even asked her to marry him, but she'd replied, "I'll marry you when Hell freezes over." It bothered her that he was seventeen years her senior. No way did she think their little fling would last. But as the night grew darker and positively sinister with silence, Susan's anxiety increased until, past midnight, she was beside herself.

A little after two a.m. Jim tromped through the kitchen door, haggard from his hours of combat duty. Susan threw herself into his arms.

She cried, "I think I love you!"

He stayed the night and became her live-in love. They married three years later. On their wedding day, Jim gave Susan a necklace, a gold heart with an engraved message on its back: "Hell froze over, September 18, 1994."

Loopy Legends and Lore

In Which We Learn That We Are an Odd and Superstitious Bunch . . .

What's in a Name?

Q: WHAT'S THE most frequently asked tourist question?

A: "Where did the name Martha's Vineyard come from?"

First let it be said that any islander who supplies an emphatic answer is blowing smoke rings. No one knows for certain just how our rock got its name. The most cited account is the old chestnut about Bartholomew Gosnold. In 1602 the English explorer fiddled and faddled about these shores. There is no qualitative proof that he actually trod upon the Vineyard, but he definitely landed on nearby Cuttyhunk, put down a few basic fortifications, and left when his men grew justifiably bored with the tiny outcropping of soil. (If Peggy Lee had recorded "Is That All There Is?" more than four hundred years ago, the men would have been crooning it all the way back to England.) In any event, it is often noted that Captain Gosnold had a daughter named Martha who died in early childhood, and upon the Vineyard he conferred her name.

Serious scholars will tell you that only royal names were dusted off to designate new locales, so baby Martha Gosnold would not have made the cut. Too, in the earliest written record of this part of the world, the island was referred to as Martin's Vineyard, leaving any early seventeenth-century Martha out in the cold.

But if there's one thing you could say about early explorers, they were obsessive namers. Around 1000 A.D. Norsemen may have touched down on these shores and named the island Vinland. It's known for a fact they dubbed something in these waters Vinland, and it's a sound phonetically close enough to Vineyard for the connection to be made.

In 1524, globe-trotting Giovanni de Verrazzano sailed by the island and christened it Luisa. Adrian Block, who had already donated his name to Block Island, had to come up with something fresh, so he called this rock Texel (sounds like a gas station). The French explorer Samuel de Champlain passed this way and named the future Vineyard *La Soupconneuse* which, roughly translated, means the Doubtful Island. Did he mean it was questionable this land was an island or did he suppose it hooked up by a long twisting peninsula to the Cape? Was it shrouded in mists and thereby deemed not entirely real, like Bali Hai? Or had Champlain perhaps been at sea too long and was feeling too dyspeptic to come up with a snappier moniker? We will never know.

So Martin, whoever he was, ceded his name over to Martha, whoever she was, and in this transgender change we count ourselves lucky that Vinland, Luisa, Texel, and *La Soupconneuse* never took hold. Especially Texel.

The Liberty Pole

ON MARTHA'S VINEYARD the three great heroes of the American Revolution were three teenaged girls.

The date was April 1778, three years since the first shots had been fired—the ones heard round the world. In the previous year, the Massachusetts Bay Colony had abandoned the islands off its coast to neutrality, meaning it would cost too much to garrison troops here. Wishing to help without spending money, the colony's officials suggested islanders send their livestock to the mainland for safekeeping. Vineyarders ignored this advice, no doubt wondering who was helping whom.

The neutral designation didn't stop Vineyard men from signing up on the side of the good guys. A number of islanders went ashore to enlist with the Massachusetts militia. Others with sea experience hired on with privateers. Still others stayed and formed local defense units. However, the Vineyard was still at the mercy of English troops, should they decide to tussle with the island. Neutrality was their only protection.

In 1775, Holmes Hole (now Vineyard Haven) raised a liberty pole bearing the new standard of the American colonies; thirteen stars against a blue background with red and white stripes. The flagpole stood tall on Manter's Hill overlooking the harbor. When the original hole was dug, local women had poured supplies of tea down the chute to protest the Boston Port Bill, one of the "Intolerable Acts" passed by the British Parliament in 1774 in retaliation for the mainlanders' rowdy Boston Tea Party the year before. (In Chilmark the townsfolk were more prudent: They consumed the tea, at the same time refusing to pay the tax, thereby having their tea and drinking it too).

Between forty and fifty houses dotted the shores of Vineyard Haven in those days. The two hundred twenty-five residents were mostly

In Chilmark they consumed the tea, at the same time refusing to pay the tax, thereby having their tea and drinking it too.

descended from the original settler families. Three of these families had produced the three daughters that figure in our story: Maria Allen, Polly Daggett, and Parnell Manter.

On a mild evening on April 19, 1778, Polly scurried from her family's dinner table to join her two friends, Parnell and Maria. Earlier in the day His Majesty's ship *Unicorn* had appeared like an evil genie in the harbor. A delegation sent ashore informed the townsfolk that the *Unicorn*'s mast had broken. The provocative flagpole on the nearby hill suggested itself as the perfect hunk of wood to replace the downed mast.

The town's selectmen met with the sailors but refused to sell their symbol of liberty. The Britishers left in a huff, vowing to take the pole by force. In effect war had been declared on Martha's Vineyard.

It was the talk of the town throughout the evening. Polly, Maria, and Parnell decided to take action: They would blow up the flagpole rather than surrender it to the English.

The girls dispersed to gather materials. Maria collected her father's ship's auger to drill holes in the wood. Parnell requisitioned some of her own dad's powder horn. As darkness fell, the girls met on the hill named for Parnell's father. The three of them took turns drilling holes and stuffing them with gunpowder. Parnell got the bright idea of ripping the hem of her woolen petticoat and cramming the pieces into the holes to pack the powder.

Suddenly they were faced with a new dilemma: How would they light the powder? Matches were not readily available in those times. Fire could only be obtained from fire. Very well, Polly hurried home to grab a pan of coals.

When Polly reappeared with her red-hot chafing dish, Parnell tore new strips of cloth from her petticoat. One of the girls plucked a beanpole from a field, and they used this as a rod around which they wrapped the fabric. Then they shoved their makeshift fuse into one of the holes. After several tries, the girls got the pole to burn and ran for cover. (In the movie version we'd see the flagpole exploding behind them, hurtling the girls through the air.)

The first explosion lit up the night sky for miles around. It boomed over the water like a thunderbolt detonating close to shore. The second explosion toppled the pole where it lay splintered, blackened, thoroughly useless.

The girls sneaked home undetected. It would be many years before their identities were revealed.

The *Unicorn*'s captain was outraged. He dispatched soldiers into town to interrogate the citizenry. No one could help him nail the culprits. Mercifully, no revenge was wreaked on the town; perhaps in some rarely used recess of the captain's unconscious he could relate to the act of defiance. The *Unicorn* sailed away still in search of a new mast.

Sadly, Parnell Manter died a scant three months later of a fever. She is buried in the Crossways cemetery of Vineyard Haven. After her death, her mother gave birth to a baby girl whom she named Parnell. (It was a common Colonial practice to keep on stamping kids with the same name until one of them survived past childhood.)

In 1788 Maria Allen married a widower with four kids, thus acquiring an instant family. She and her husband then had two children of their own. Maria died in 1820 at the age of sixty-two. She is buried in the old graveyard behind the Vineyard Haven town hall.

Polly married in 1779 and moved off island. Years later she divorced her husband, and returned to the Vineyard. She had no children, but was a beloved Aunt Hillman to her nieces and nephews. She lived a long life, and is also buried in the cemetery behind the town hall.

In 1898 the Martha's Vineyard Daughters of the American Revolution placed a brass plaque on a flagpole near the spot where the three brave teens set their petticoats ablaze and lit up the night.

A Noble Tradition of Bumboating

No, THE BUMBOAT wasn't a barge bearing hobos out to the island. Back in the day of the tall ships, the harbor of Holmes Hole hosted a fleet of hefty, tugboat-sized vessels. These so-called bumboats would ferry supplies out to the vessels at anchor: fresh milk, butter, eggs, vegetables, barrels of salt beef, fresh water, and—best of all from the mariners' point of view—home-brewed liquor.

Many a native son got his first job staffing a bumboat before pursuing a more challenging role at sea on high-riding whalers. (And were there just as many who served their time as bumboat deckhands and then decided, enough with the seasickness and saltwater, how about a nice job in an office?)

The bumboats died away when in the early 1900s the Cape Cod Canal opened for business, and all the two- and three-masted schooners could scoot in and out of Boston without sailing through Vineyard Sound. And by this time, of course, the big commercial ships were a thing of the past, so bumboat service was no longer required.

But times change, and I can't help wondering whether today someone should think about outfitting a new half-dozen or so bumboats to bring fresh milk, eggs, and produce to the Donald Trumps and assorted Arabian sheiks who sail their yachts into these waters every summer.

After all, the rich have to eat too.

Panic Rooms, Then and Now

EVERY SO OFTEN we'll hear about a Vineyarder renovating an antique dwelling and discovering a secret passageway. If a tunnel leads to the beach, it's a sure bet the original owner had engaged in smuggling. From the earliest days of recorded history, ships brought contraband to the darker coves of the Vineyard, where willing islanders off-loaded the goods and brought them to illicit buyers. In the seventeenth and eighteenth centuries, the chief product was jewels and coins stolen by pirates, in the nineteenth century, it was runaway slaves seeking refuge up north. In the infamous Prohibition era of the twentieth century, countless rum, gin, and whiskey runners made their fortunes around the midnight waters of Martha's Vineyard. As the late island legend and former smuggler Craig Kingsbury said in *Craig Kingsbury Talkin'* (2005), "When Prohibition was repealed, it ruined many a good man and a lot of local enterprises."

Another purpose for the age-old secret room was the ever-popular desire to avoid paying taxes. In the old days the Feds often seized a person's hard-earned dollars face to face. If the tax man called, but the master of the manor happened to be away (a.k.a. cowering inside the windowless walls of a hidden chamber), the government gent would be forced to leave empty-handed.

The best-known secret room on the island was, until very recently, located in the Daggett House on North Water Street in Edgartown. The oldest part of the inn had been built as a tavern in the 1750s. In those days Vineyard Sound was the second busiest waterway in the western world, after the English Channel. Accordingly, sailors in the hundreds thronged the seaport towns of Holmes Hole, Eastville Beach, and Edgartown.

In the pub built by Captain Thomas Pease and later owned by Captain Timothy Daggett, sailors smoked corncob pipes, played cards, and swilled local spirits, singing "Yo ho ho and a bottle of rum," or so we can well imagine. What they didn't know was that, just to the left of the beehive-shaped brick fireplace crackling with burning logs, a built-in bookshelf held a hidden lock that popped open a secret doorway. The doorway disclosed a narrow staircase which in turn led to a mysterious chamber. In more recent times this chamber was converted to another of the inn's many guest rooms.

Legends abound to explain this clandestine passageway. Some maintained that the original Peases, and then the Daggetts, kept hidden a sadly deformed or mentally disoriented child. Others cited the above-mentioned need for a lickety-split tax dodge. In addition, ghost tales have for decades shrouded the Daggett House, with the secret staircase and chamber part of the Edgar Allan Poe atmospherics.

Sadly, the shivery features of the Daggett House are no more (though you can read all about them in a full chapter devoted to the inn in my book *Haunted Island*). In the spring of 2004, the property was purchased by off-islanders for conversion into a single-family home. The first order of business was demolishing the old house and putting up a new one that, while outwardly evoking the old manor, is a *tabula rasa* inside. Gone is the eighteenth-century tavern with its venerable beams, antique beehive fireplace, and secret staircase. (In good conscience, how could they do that?) If the new owners believe they're putting the ghosts to rest by starting over, they're in for a rude awakening. Take it from this island ghost hunter: The spirit world detests remodeling, cannot abide it—a big renovation job is perceived as *the* Insult Direct. Once the new house is up and running, the supernatural component of the property may very well decree, "No more Mr. Nice Ghost!"

Out on a westerly part of the island, another secret room of twentieth-century provenance exists. Back in the 1980s, actress Mia Farrow and then-husband conductor André Previn, bought a five-bedroom house on the shores of Lake Tashmoo. Ms. Farrow, you'll recall, was the adoptive mother of umpteen children of various ethnicities. The pixie-haired movie star could sometimes be glimpsed leading her brood on a beachcombing jaunt, all linked by held hands like paper-doll cutouts. Back home, however, Mama Mia needed to know her kiddies were safe and sound. She had a panic room constructed: a windowless chamber undetectable from either inside or outside the home, and entered through a fake slab of wall panel.

Ms. Farrow has long since sold the house, and many other families have availed themselves of the property as a vacation rental. The subsequent owner, a dentist turned builder, believed that not a single tenant had ever hit upon the secret latch that triggers the hidden door. One thing is certain: It's a good guess Mia Farrow now wishes she'd locked young Song-Yi in the panic room when she'd had the chance.

Ghost Ship

ON MAY 25, 1902, a Vineyard fisherman anchored at Cuttyhunk observed a thunderstorm swirling up out of the northwestern sky. Through the murky mists, he beheld an old bark with a crew of transparent sailors and a transparent captain. The fisherman hauled up his anchor and fled for home.

The next morning when the man docked in Edgartown, he practically ran to his favorite pub and ordered a shot of whiskey to calm his nerves. He turned to his fellow bar mates and regaled them with his tale of the previous night's unholy sighting.

They guffawed at his story, but legend has it that one grizzled sea salt, a veteran of whaling days, wasn't laughing. He pointed a bony finger at the fisherman. "What you saw, son, was none other than the phantom ship of Bartholomew Gosnold."

The old guy's manner caused the others to grow silent. One and all, they stared at him, awaiting explanation.

"You all know who Bartholomew Gosnold was?" he asked with a sneer, as if none of them had been amply schooled in their local history. Someone at the back of the bar finally mumbled something about Gosnold being the English explorer who touched down at Cuttyhunk in 1602.

"Sixteen hundred and two it was, boys. Now, look at yon calendar hangin' over the bar."

Dutifully all eyes swept up to the dog-eared calendar. They saw for themselves that that day's date was May 25.

The old salt proclaimed, "It was on May 24, 1602, when Bartholomew Gosnold anchored in Cuttyhunk bay. Four hundred years ago to the day last night when our fisherman friend here saw the phantom ship. I saw it myself on May 24, 1864. There've been other sightings over the years—lots of 'em!

"My advice to everyone in this room is to stay away from Cuttyhunk on the night of May 24. It's too terrible a sight for human eye and heart."

Yes, We Had Our Witches

ONE THING WAS for certain: It was easier to be a witch on Martha's Vineyard than almost anywhere else in Colonial New England.

Witches were on everyone's mind in those days, but no other region in America could match New England's obsession with witchcraft. Witches made handy scapegoats. Every last thing that went wrong in a typical village, from an overturned wagon to an infected blister, could be blamed on witchcraft. People believed that a bad-tempered witch could put a curse on people, crops, and livestock. Midwives swore they'd seen witches give birth to demons. And townsfolk truly believed that on a starry night you could look up in the sky and see the silhouette of a devil's handmaiden astride her broomstick as she flew across the moon.

Healers were particularly susceptible to accusations of sorcery. If a woman in a small New England town had learned how to use elder blossoms to cure kidney infections or burdock root to quell seizures, townsfolk relied on her skills until something went wrong. (Come to think of it, this blaming was nothing short of a Colonial malpractice suit.) If a patient died, and that was bound to happen in any medical practitioner's career, suddenly treatment looked more like black magic.

But how to identify a witch in order to put a stop to, say, a bad potato harvest? Well, you could look for devil's marks on the subject's body—anything from a simple mole impervious to pain when pricked by a pin to an odd-colored birthmark. Obviously all of us harbor any number of these blemishes on our bodies, and only the most vicious and idiotic of witch-hunters would cite a freckle as a sign of the Devil. Unfortunately a great number of vicious and idiotic people lived in those days.

Many stupid methods were adopted to determine whether or not the subject was a witch. A favorite stupid method was to throw the suspect into a dangerous current. If she drowned, she was perforce a witch. If she lived she was a good person having a bad day. You have to wonder why her prosecutors failed to take into account a true witch's scary powers: Wouldn't any self-respecting she demon be able to fly above the water, wag her hands against her ears, and sneer, "Naah, naah, naah, naah, naah!" to the troops below? And wouldn't the nice person, with no supernatural abilities to call upon, be the one to perish? Clearly some part of the witch-hunter's rationale knew that a Witch Survives/Good Person Dies policy would be potentially embarrassing. Every time an innocent person drowned there'd come that "Oops! I goofed" feeling.

(Recently I interviewed a modern historian on witchcraft, author Judika Illes, who told me, "Basically with the water test, everyone drowned. Since the authorities only imposed it on people

The Spooky Side of Island Living

The old-timers used to say that ghosts can't cross over water, and perhaps that's why so many spirits appear to be trapped on Martha's Vineyard, sharing "living" quarters with the rest of us. Vineyard artist Marcia Smilack's reflectionist style of photography (images captured on the rippling surface of water) hints at the supernatural shimmering just beneath the surface of our daily lives here.

COURTESY OF MARCIA SMILACK

they strongly suspected, they believed each time that they'd proved their case.")

Although New England bore the stigma of witch hunts in the late 1600s, most famously in Salem in 1692 when nineteen putative witches and one putative warlock were executed, in actuality the witch phobias of New Worlders were far milder than those of seventeenth-century Europeans, who massacred so-called witches by the thousands. In England, just to provide an example of how commonplace was the belief in witchcraft, Oliver Cromwell appointed a Witch Finder General to his cabinet.

Here on the Vineyard, no one was ever brought up on witchcraft charges. That's not to say we didn't have our share of self-professed witches. But those who practiced the dark arts were left in peace, as eccentric folks tended—and still tend—to be on the island. The following accounts of Vineyard witches were passed along to me in the oral tradition by island folklorist and psychic Karen Coffey, with whom I've collaborated on various ghost-hunting adventures.

In the early 1700s, a practicing witch lived in the Scrubby Neck area of West Tisbury, out on one of those winding roads that eventually lead to the white sands of South Beach. Rather than reviling this wise woman, Vineyarders sought her services, saddling horses or hitching up wagons to hear their fortunes told by the Scrubby Neck Witch.

Sailors, a superstitious breed in a superstitious age, would often visit the fortune-teller before a three- or four-year whaling voyage to get an idea of whether or not they'd be making it back alive. One day, a first mate of an Edgartown whaling bark consulted the witch, who foresaw trouble for him in the seas off South America. Annoyed at this ill omen, he refused to pay her fee and stomped off in a high dudgeon. A few days later, his ship was preparing to cast off from the Edgartown wharves when suddenly cries rang out from the pier. All men

on deck beheld an elderly woman in a black ragged gown, swearing oaths and raising a fist at the departing ship.

"A curse on this voyage and on the first mate!" she shrieked. It was, of course, the Witch of Scrubby Neck.

The first mate guffawed and turned his back on her, but later something happened—and kept on happening—that caused him grave concern: At every port of call his ship sailed into, an angry black crow swooped in around the first mate's head, cawing and swiping at his forehead with its talons. His fellow sailors began to rib him, for it was clear to all that the enraged black crow was the "familiar," in black magic speak, of the witch, sent to harass the man for his stinginess.

The first mate became increasingly afraid of the black crow and its obvious intent to harm him. One afternoon, as the ship rounded the bay into a port in Ecuador, the man stood ready to defend himself. From out of the skies the black crow swooped low, streaking for the sailor's head. The first mate raised a bow and arrow and shot the bird through its shiny black breast. It dropped to the deck, dead with the arrow in its heart.

Those who practiced the dark arts were left in peace, as eccentric folks tended—and still tend—to be on the island.

Two years later, the whaling ship returned to Edgartown. When the first mate debarked, he learned that the Scrubby Neck Witch had dropped dead, clutching her chest, on the very day and hour and minute that the man had shot the bird along the Ecuadorian coast.

Maybe in the sailor's next life he came back as a crow, or a crow's favorite snack.

Here's another tale, also reputed to be true: In the late 1700s, in a sheltered valley just north of Tisbury, a farmer built a home for his family. Nearing the end of construction, he incurred the wrath of a neighbor because he'd encroached on her property and refused to do right by her. She happened to be a witch, and leveled a curse on him:

"The fruits of your ambition, all that you possess, shall turn to dust in your mouth. This dust shall choke and smother you and yours and all who shall come after you."

When the house was ready for occupancy, a fine, grimy sand began to drift down from the ceiling. Carpenters pored over the rooftop, but no one could determine where the dust was coming from. Soon the plaster browned and stained from the steady rain of dust. Eventually the family moved out of the house, and over the years it lay derelict. Eventually forest and swamp reclaimed the property. Sheep came and grazed in the grass, and sometimes wandered into the abandoned house for shelter. Occasionally humans rambled onto the property, stooping to pick blueberries. When they returned home with their pails, they found the freshly harvested fruit was inedible, coated with a soft, grimy dust.

No traces are left of the sad house, and with the current rate of growth, someone is certain to build over the old foundation. It will be interesting to see if the supernatural dust continues to waft down. With any luck, it'll be one of those ten-thousand-square-foot trophy homes.

Old-Timey Superstitions

YOU STILL SEE red front doors on Vineyard houses, though nowadays this is more of an aesthetic choice than an occult one. In the old days, however, meaning up until the twentieth century, a goodly number of islanders painted their front doors red to protect their homes from evil spirits.

Here are some other superstitions culled from New England communities and disseminated into Vineyard lives:

- Walk in the rain to attract good luck.
- When visiting, always leave by the same door through which you originaly entered so you don't take that family's luck with you.

- Sleep with your head facing north.
- Place your shoes side by side at the foot of the bed, toes facing away from the bed, to avoid nightmares.
- To ward off vampires, scatter handfuls of rice, barley, or corn kernels; vampires are obsessed with counting things, and if they're distracted by these nuggets, chances are they'll be thus occupied until dawn, at which time they need to betake themselves back to their coffins.
- To keep witches from the house, place a broom outside the door.

And there you have it. There's no reason why today we shouldn't continue these customs, just to be on the safe side.

Celebrity Dish

In Bite-Sized Morsels

More Jackie O

ODDLY, ALL THE bite-sized gossip I've managed to collect locally about Jackie O revolves around her urinary tract. Well, you know what they say—even the most exalted among us have to use the toilet.

Some years back, Mrs. Onassis and two friends showed up for a performance at the Vineyard Playhouse. A buzz developed backstage; the performers were elated to have the most famous woman in the world in the audience. To make matters still more exciting, Mrs. O and her friends took seats in the front row, causing the cast to feel doubly stimulated to have them there, in their faces practically.

After Intermission, as the lights flared on for the second act, the performers were shocked to behold those three seats empty. Starkly empty. A pall fell over the cast and crew, though they proceeded gamely to the end of the play. It was clear to everyone that Mrs. O had *not* enjoyed the evening's theatricals.

The next morning around ten a.m., Sally Cohn, working in the Playhouse box office answered the phone. She recounted to me how she heard a most familiar voice over the line:

"Hello, this is Mrs. Onassis. I took your program home last night, and didn't get a chance to peruse it until I read it this morning in the bathroom. I had no idea there was a second act! The drama seemed so complete at the end of the first act, we thought the play was over. Will you apologize to the cast for me? I wouldn't want them to think I didn't appreciate their efforts."

Jackie Unveiled

Normally Vineyarders were accustomed to glimpses of Mrs. Onassis wearing a paisley head-scarf, jeans, tee-shirt, and sunglasses. Here, during a book signing for her friend Carly Simon, Jackie O. proved she could, in island parlance, "Clean up good."

One summer back in the late 1980s, Sharon Kelly, owner of The Secret Garden, a Victorian-accented gift store in Oak Bluffs, was fed up with her staff allowing the public to use the shop's elderly bathroom.

"We're on a very shaky cesspool system, and we can't have people using our toilet. You've got to direct them to the public facilities. No exceptions, do you understand?" announced the normally gracious Ms. Kelly. Her staff nodded, silenced by her uncharacteristic outburst.

Some minutes later, Ms. Kelly noticed that a store patron had dropped some cards on the floor. She stooped to pick them up and handed them back to the customer.

"Oh thank you!" said the lady in that legendary half-whisper, half-lisp. It was, of course, Jackie O, clad in her island uniform of jeans, a white tee shirt, and a blue-and-white paisley bandana over her head.

A few minutes later, Mrs. Onassis paid for the cards at the counter. The transaction finished, Mrs. O asked the awestruck Ms. Kelly,

"Do you by any chance have a bathroom I could use?"

"Right this way!" chirped Ms. Kelly.

Her staff ribbed her about this for many days thereafter.

At the Vineyard airport one afternoon in the mid-1980s, my (now-ex) husband, Marty was on hand to notice two stars of this earthly firmament waiting for the shuttle to New York: Jacqueline Kennedy Onassis and Joe DiMaggio.

Marty told me later, "All the guys had their attention on Joe DiMaggio, and all the women were ogling Jackie O. When Jackie got up to use the ladies room, every female in the joint trooped in after her. I felt sorry for her. How many years has it been since she's been able to take a leak in private?"

Woody Allen and Mia Farrow

MS. FARROW ALREADY had her home on the shores of Lake Tashmoo to which she brought her busload of kids, both biological and adopted from a rich mix of Third World countries. Now that she was the boon companion of Woody Allen, the two decided it was time for him to acquire his own house on the island. Don't forget that, as much time as they spent together, even in Manhattan they maintained separate apartments, his on Fifth Avenue facing Central Park, hers on Central Park West, across from Woody's place. They often signaled one another by waving towels from their balconies.

Perhaps their plan was to reproduce this arrangement on the Vineyard. Woody's secretary phoned a real estate agent in Vineyard Haven, saying the maestro of American comedy wished to view property on the island. Maybe in towel-waving distance from Ms. Farrow's house?

If the real estate agent, a young man in his mid-twenties, had any sense of anticipation about escorting the movie stars around the island, he was brought up short by a memo faxed to him from Woody Allen's office. On it were Rules of Engagement for spending time in the not-always-so-funny man's company. The most distressing part was the requirement that the agent remain silent unless spoken to.

"I felt like the Deborah Kerr character in *The King and I!*" he confided to me years later.

The afternoon bore no fruit from a real estate perspective. The agent had the impression that the comedy writer and director, known for his various neuroses, was cadging a free drive around the island. At the end of the tour, Woody and Mia asked their "chauffeur" to take them to an ice cream parlor, and they slurped their melting cones in the back seat of his car.

The perks of fame are many.

Diane Sawyer

THIS FROM AN anonymous source at the Vineyard airport, where an electric cart is available to collect bags from private planes and hustle them over to the terminal while passengers deplane and walk to the building. The length of tarmac that the passengers must cross is perhaps thirty yards.

"Diane Sawyer is the most demanding of all our VIPs," said my source. "She insists on being driven to the door, rain or shine, even though it's a nine-second walk." Roughly the time it takes for the lady to traverse her Vineyard living room.

Carly Simon

LET ME GO ON record to say that Ms. Simon is our most adored celebrity. She has summered—and off-seasoned—here for years, in various domiciles. If you're lucky enough to meet her socially she's the image of Your Favorite Friend—witty, warm, funny, and wise. She always appears to be pondering some new point of interest that has piped her way. Once I heard her discussing the newly discovered Tourette's syndrome wherein people blurt out involuntary profanities; she mused aloud that many writers and artists must have at least a bit of that. Another time I told her I'd recently met a man she'd once composed a song around, a comedian named Jack Burns who, when he heard about a hurricane brewing somewhere, jetted off to place himself at the center of it. She nodded and reminisced about the song she wrote about the Man Who Chased Storms.

Recently I interviewed Carly for the *Gazette,* following her debut of a collection of Gershwin interpretations set to dance by The Yard. She wore a form-fitting dress, black with little white buttons. I asked her if the design was polka dot or dotted Swiss. "Polka dots!" she exclaimed as if there could only be one choice in the matter. We shared a giggle like two girls comparing lipsticks in a high school john.

The coolest thing about Carly is her island philanthropy. You cannot be a part of a local fund-raiser without noticing that the singer has contributed time or money. Her most famous contribution is her yearly offering of herself as a biddable item in the Possible Dreams Auction, held every first Monday in August, outdoors at the Harborside Inn in Edgartown and presided by Art Buchwald as auctioneer. Some of the island celebs offer their favors each year: Walter Cronkite throws in a sail on his sloop, the *Wynje*; Mike Wallace provides a tour of the set of *60 Minutes.* When Katharine Graham of the *Washington Post* was still alive, you could bid for lunch with the grande dame on her estate in the Makoniky area off Lambert's Cove. The auction profits go to the island's Community Services program.

> *We shared a giggle like two girls comparing lipsticks in a high school john.*

But consistently the star earner of the auction is Carly Simon's company, in your home. Every year, for sums in excess of forty thousand dollars, the lady with the big lips and even bigger voice will appear at your party and sing for your guests. One time two separate fans kept on outbidding each other. When each of them topped fifty thousand, Ms. Simon, who invariably stands beside Mr. Buchwald to assist in her own price-fixing, gamely offered to accept both bids and sing at both parties. The lady's take for the auction? One hundred thousand dollars.

One year Carly raised the excitement level: Whoever won her presence at this time would be vouchsafed the identity of the mystery man in her breakaway hit, "You're So Vain" (I Bet You Think This Song Is About You). When the song broke through the pop charts back in the 70s, speculation was rife that the conceited subject of the song was Mick Jagger or Carly's ex-husband, singer James Taylor. Carly herself has said in interviews that the secret behind the song made it a bigger hit than it would have been had she simply provided the identity of the vain Mr. X.

But now at the Possible Dream Auction, she announced that she would whisper The Name in the ear of the high bidder. Of course, he or she would be sworn to secrecy.

The lucky and (temporarily) financially cleaned-out bidder was Dick Ebersole, NBC Sports president and husband of actress Susan St. James. Both of them are long-time vacationers on the Vineyard. The sum Mr. Ebersole forked over? Fifty thousand dollars. We have to wonder whether he asked permission to share the identity of Mr. Conceited with Susan. Knowing Carly Simon's generosity, she probably said okay.

And Speaking of Art Buchwald . . .

THE ROLY-POLY faced Washington D.C.–based columnist, and author of many trenchant political books such as *While Reagan Slept* and, just out, *Beating Around the Bush* has for decades summered in his West Chop house in Vineyard Haven. The pleasure of having this witty man on island is that when you run into him he'll often treat you to his most recent bon mot. Perhaps he's trying it out for his column, but he's happy to give you an advance peek.

Back in the early 1980s, Marty and I were seated at the outdoor tables below Le Grenier in Vineyard Haven when Art strolled by. He leaned over the rail for some neighborly chit-

chat. We discussed the recent flap in the news: President Reagan was visiting Normandy in honor of D-Day, and he'd scheduled a wreath-bearing ceremony at what turned out to be a Nazi graveyard. In the meantime, Art, who never missed even the smallest piece of news, was aware that down in South America the relics of what was speculated to be the remains of the Nazi regime's evil Dr. Mengele were being inspected by forensic experts.

Art said, "Ronald Reagan is waiting for confirmation that the bones are Mengele's, so he can lay a wreath."

And Speaking of Graves . . .

OUR MOST FAMOUS Dead Person on the Vineyard is John Belushi, crazedly funny actor, star of hit films *Animal House* and *The Blues Brothers*, and the TV show *Saturday Night Live*. He died of a drug overdose in L.A. back in the '70s and was buried at the charming hillside cemetery in Chilmark.

Following the interment an uncustomary late-night racket erupted from the graveyard and alarmed the neighbors. No, it was not the ghost of John Belushi waging food fights with departed frat brothers. What the neighbors

were hearing were the gleeful shouts of die-hard Belushi fans who'd made a pilgrimage to his grave to do what they felt their idol would have wanted them to do: Party hearty.

In the gimlet light of early morning, disgusted Chilmarkers found the detritus from the noisy night scattered around the late comic's grave: empty beer bottles, half-eaten chips and dip, sandwich wrappers, and, from the more generous of the worshippers, lovingly rolled marijuana cigarettes, untouched by human lips, carefully placed at the base of Belushi's headstone, along with a book of matches, for the comic's toking pleasure on The Other Side.

The rowdy visits continued, and neither the deceased movie star nor the living neighbors were being allowed to rest in peace. A plan was put forward, approved by John's widow, Judy, to transfer Belushi's remains to a remote site in the cemetery.

Now here's where the story gets interesting, albeit morbid.

The move was scheduled for five months after the original burial had taken place. My then husband, Marty, was rambling along New York Avenue in Oak Bluffs when a guy he knew gave him a lift into town. Now Marty,

who claims he knows one of every three people in the world, quite naturally knows everyone, and I mean *everyone*, on Martha's Vineyard. This particular local worked for Chapman & Cole, the island's mortuary.

"Hey, Mahdy," the man said, "We just transferred your buddy, Belushi, to his new hole up in Chilmahk. Funny thing—while we were haulin' out the coffin, the lid cracked open, and the body rolled out. He looked good, Mahdy. Lost some weight."

'Mahdy' had a flash about what the tabloids would do with this information: EXCLUSIVE: THE BELUSHI DEATH DIET. Fortunately no one thought to phone it in to the *Enquirer*.

Young Teddy Kennedy

(THIS ONE WAS related to me by an elderly member of the Edgartown Yacht club who wished to be placed in the Witness Protection Program.)

It was back in July of 1962 when Ted Kennedy was the cute, cuddly younger brother of big boys, John and Robert. It was regatta weekend in Edgartown and, in pre-start maneuvers, a young deb named Nini Tappen sailed her boat, a small Smyra, too close for comfort alongside Teddy's craft. He yelled at her to get out of the way, but then, reading the name of her boat, *Inshallah*, he asked what the heck that meant.

"God willing!" she called back. "It's Arabic."

He wanted to know when and where she'd learned Arabic.

"When my father was ambassador to Libya." She added with a coy smile, seeing her chance to get back at him for his earlier rudeness, "He was appointed by President Eisenhower."

Frank Sinatra Proposes—or Doesn't

WE TEND TO THINK of media overkill as a fairly recent phenomenon, but the island has hosted its share of this nonsense at least since the summer of '65. That was when Frank Sinatra's 168-foot yacht *Southern Breeze* sailed into Edgartown harbor and parked for a spell. In years to come, Mr. Sinatra's boat of choice, whether the *Southern Breeze* or another still bigger and sleeker model, deigned to enter our ports of call, but this particular voyage had some extra sudsy soap-opera-spewing bubbles.

On board with Old Blue Eyes was nineteen-year-old starlet Mia Farrow, the gamine from the TV series, *Peyton Place*, she of the shortest little haircut ever seen on a female in the pages of *Photoplay*. The question on America's mind was this: Was Frankie on the verge of proposing to young Mia?

The Vineyard has been the setting for many a glitzy proposal (or proposal-manqué, such as in the case of the non-nuptials of Ben Affleck and Jennifer Lopez in the summer of 2003), so the press poured in by boat and by plane during that balmy weekend way back when. Their mission: to catch the Chairman of the Board pitching matrimony to the lovely and yet funny-looking ninety-five-pound actress.

To the local press, Vineyarders declared one and all that they truly "could not care less" about whether the visiting lovey-doveys intended to tie the knot. It was a different situation, however, with the camera-laden national press and the hoards of tourists, who simply could not confine themselves to island decorum, which has always flatly stated, Let Everyone, Big and Little, Famous and Unknown, Alone. Thus, all along the Edgartown harbor, our tiny police force fought a losing battle to keep the throngs of the curious at bay.

And what did they expect to observe on the decks of the *Southern Breeze*? Miss Farrow wearing a skimpy bikini over her little boy body, with Frank Sinatra on his knees before her, a velvet-clad jewelry box clutched in his hands?

To give the fans their due, they'd been fed by frantic rumors: Frank and Mia had visited the Edgartown courthouse and were now officially married. Or they weren't yet married, but a helicopter was due to plump down on the yacht and carry them off to Las Vegas where an Elvis impersonator would marry them. Newspapers and radios announced that the imminent engagement was the betrothal of the century.

And where did this certainty come from? Well, who could argue with this: It was generally known that a married Sinatra would frown on his wife in the work force. Now, out west on the set of *Peyton Place* word had leaked out that in the upcoming season Miss Farrow's character, Allison, was slated for a concussion caused by a fall, and that, alas, she would die from it. Was this not proof enough that she intended to give up her studio trailer in exchange for keys to her future husband's multiple domiciles?

Frank and Mia gave the crowds their money's worth when they strolled into town to buy ice cream cones, walked in and out of restaurants, always to the accompaniment of press bulbs flashing and onlookers madly cheering as if the romantic pair had recently won the Nobel Prize for Romance.

When the weekend ended, the *Southern Breeze* swanned out of the harbor, leaving in its wake news of absolutely nothing regarding the couple's future plans.

Now we know, of course, that Frank and Mia did indeed marry, not surprisingly, only to later divorce, still less surprisingly. That so many people cared so deeply is the only shocking part of the story.

The Jacqueline Bouvier Kennedy Onassis Teardown

NOW HERE'S A tantalizing tidbit, filled with Freudian undertones of family dysfunction.

You know the most famous summer home on American soil? The Vineyard vacation manse of Jackie O, only a couple of decades old, and built on the stunning waterfront plateau of nearly four hundred acres in the plushest, priciest part of Aquinnah? Postcards and tour guides are bedecked with aerial views of the sprawling estate. You've seen it, right? So you can picture it. Well, guess what? It's gone.

Mrs. Onassis died in '94, leaving her summer home to son, John F. Kennedy Jr., and her daughter, Caroline Kennedy Schlossberg. In July of '97, John Jr.'s life, and that of his wife, Carolyn Bessette Kennedy, and sister-in-law, Lauren Bessette, were tragically lost when his single-engine plane crashed into the sea only twelve and a half miles south of his late mother's estate.

That left sister Caroline in sole possession of the country home. In November 2002 she applied to the town of Aquinnah for a permit to demolish the existing structure. The permit was granted, and the house was razed. A brand new five-thousand-square foot dwelling went up on the original site. Also, if you'll recall, virtually all of Mrs. Onassis' goods were disposed of at auction conducted by Sotheby's: twenty-five-hundred dollars for a set of hair rollers, ten thousand for a broom and dustpan. Arguably nothing remains of Jackie O's at her eagle's nest perch in Aquinnah—except her ghost. She just might be miffed that this monument to her life has met the blade of an earthmover shovel.

Mrs. Onassis never had much to say: There will never be a coffee table book devoted to the Wit of Jackie. Her only known philanthropy was her help in saving Grand Central Station in New York. For that we are truly thankful, but . . . was there no other cause to which her time, her name, and her tens of millions of dollars might have been devoted?

But one thing we've always assumed about the lady is that she was in fact a loving mom and grandmom. And perhaps she was. Of course she was! But there may have been other dimensions to the family dynamic—shades of Aeschylus and even Tennessee Williams—kept hidden all these years. The razing of her mother's beloved country estate makes you wonder if Caroline didn't have an ax or two to grind with Mother Dearest. After all, for anyone who happens to adore his or her mother—even if she's sometimes irritating as hell—would be disinclined to annihilate mom's home.

We know that Caroline is set with money, but the choice she made in razing her mother's home was not, in the long view, a fiscal stroke of brilliance. Should the time come to sell the property, it will mean less to everyone that it belonged to Caroline Kennedy Schlossberg, than if the original post and beams from Jacqueline Kennedy Onassis's summer house had been retained. Oh well. It's still worth a little something.

Too Sexy for Their Shirts

IT WAS BOUND to happen. After John Jr.'s plane plunged into the waters off Martha's Vineyard, the rumor mill was agog with the "news" that the figure behind the other Most Famous Tragic Death, Princess Diana, had had a one-night fling with the dashing young man. The fact that they both had connections to the Vineyard only cemented the pure kismet of the two of them hooking up.

The story was leaked by one of the loopier members of the Princess of Wales's entourage, a woman named Simone Simmons, a mystic and "energy healer" (whatever that is; it's not

Literally Too Sexy for His Shirt

John F. Kennedy, Jr., disports in the Vineyard waters that later took his life.
KEVIN WISNIEWSKI

exactly listed in the Yellow Pages). Ms. Simmons squeezed two books out of her confidante service to Diana, the second entitled *Diana, the Last Word* containing the scoop about the Night of Love.

It happened—*if* it happened—in New York City in '92. Kennedy had tried to woo the princess for a profile for his political magazine, *George*. The shy—and, let's face it, somewhat vapid—royal shrank from the idea of providing fodder for an article. On the other hand, she and Kennedy had a lot to gab about, and as they stared at one another across the coffee table of the young man's hotel suite, they might have been cognizant of the fact that each was looking at his and her most perfectly mirrored mate, both of them being rich, gorgeous, in buff physical shape, and idolized more than is healthy for any one person in this modern age.

Moreover, both were semi-available. Diana was estranged from Prince Charles and living alone in her quarters in Buckingham Palace. John had just dumped Daryl Hannah, though he had also started to date his future bride, Carolyn Bessette.

So according to Ms. Simmons, the two beauties burned up the sheets. Back in London, Diana, in a burst of giggles, spilled out the story to her energy healer friend. Whether he said "I'll call you" and she murmured "I had a lovely time" will never be known. And in hindsight we're aware that, if it happened, the event required no rematch.

The story of this alleged tryst in turn led to a fine conspiracy theory: The possibility of a partnership between the British royal and the American royal was a threat to the stability of the western world (why that should be so is impossible to fathom), so covert steps had to be taken to assassinate both of them. (Realistically, once one of the lovers was "bumped off" in 1994, what need had the forces of darkness to eliminate the other two years later?)

Unless Carolyn Bessette had CIA connections and wished to dispose of any potential rival . . . ? Nah.

Bruce Willis Getting Frisky

BRUCE WILLIS COMES to the Vineyard a lot. Every summer, in fact. For the most part he maintains a low profile, but people have often caught him whooping it up, knocking back highballs and blowing strong into his harmonica, in the semiprivate setting of Balance, an Oak Bluffs restaurant owned by his friend Benjamin deForest.

(Balance closed its doors in the summer of 2005. Ben is hanging up his chef's hat to try his hand at an acting career out in Hollywood.

He'll be staying with—guess who?—Bruce Willis. It pays to let movie stars wail on their harmonicas in your restaurant.)

At his island hangout, Willis reportedly wasted no time romancing the lovely waitresses clad in tight-fitting black slacks, white shirts, and black bow ties. A young lady I know who waitressed at Balance for four years told me the movie star's score was as follows: Waitresses hit on: 137 (some of these were repeat efforts). Waitresses seduced: 0.

Larry David Unleashes His Enthusiasm

ANOTHER EX-HUSBAND story: Marty knew Larry David from his TV writing days when David was doing *Seinfeld* and Marty was working with Garry Marshall as an on-set writer for *Runaway Bride*. But still the lanky, stoop-shouldered David looked out of place when Marty ran into him a few years back at an opening at the Field Gallery in West Tisbury.

"Take a good look at me," said David. "You'll never see me again on Martha's Vineyard. I never visit a place more than once."

Several days later Marty ran into the man again at yet another exhibit. In the cranky voice Larry David has made famous on his show *Curb Your Enthusiasm*, his emotional range running from whiney to sour to argumentative, he told Marty, "My wife is out shopping with a real estate agent. She wants to buy a house here. What'll I do?"

Marty shrugged. "You'll have to write her a lot of postcards, since you won't be coming back."

Mike Wallace: Always the Interrogator, One Time the Interogatee

OVER THE YEARS we've seen him pulling no punches. The star of *60 Minutes* has asked the hard-hitting questions of heads of state, mafiosi, and corrupt CEOs. You wouldn't think that someone with so exacting a sense of decent deportment might in fact mis-deport himself. Yet it happened, and the perks of Mr. Wallace's celebrity insured that "L'Affair Hit and Run" was basically hushed up. It was, however, in the immediate aftermath, the talk of the island.

In the late afternoon of July 31, 1992, on Martha's Vineyard, a young waitress named Lisa White headed east in a compact car along the airport road when a Ford station wagon lumbered out from a dirt road and onto the highway directly in Ms. White's path. She swerved to avoid a collision and ended up slamming into a tree. She later described the incident to a reporter from the *National Enquirer*, and my retelling of her experience is taken from her account in that article.

The front end of Ms. White's car ended up wrapped around the trunk like a metallic tree-hugger. Shocked, dazed, with blood seeping down her face, she staggered from her vehicle as the other car rumbled on down the road away from the accident. Sobbing, she hailed a passing motorist in a pickup truck and shouted at him to go after the Ford wagon. The driver of the pickup gave chase.

Some ten minutes later the station wagon returned. Mike Wallace, longtime summer resident of Vineyard Haven, was at the wheel. Striding across the street with the determined look we've seen on his face so many times, he went on the offensive, demanding to know how fast Ms. White had been going. He was dismissive of another motorist who had witnessed the incident and pulled over, as good citizens are supposed to do.

When a patrol car eventually rolled to a stop behind the wrecked compact, Mr. Wallace took the policeman aside to confer in hushed tones. Then, with a nod from the cop, the newsman turned, glowered at the accident victim and the self-described witness, returned to his station wagon, and puttered away.

The maximum penalty for leaving the scene of an accident in Massachusetts is two years in prison and a one-thousand dollar fine. The following day, Roy Bruette, spokesman for *60 Minutes*, released an announcement to the press. He maintained that on the afternoon of the accident the weather had been too foggy to enable Mr. Wallace to safely turn around and go back to the young lady's car. A local journalist (now retired and wishing to remain un-named) told me that his survey of the area dis-closed multiple turn-off spots on the minimally trafficked two-lane road.

Thanks to home police scanners, no island mishap goes unremarked, so on that July night Mr. Wallace in his Ford station wagon was the number-one topic of conversation around barbecue grills. Some of the mainland media picked up the 30 Minutes of Misbehaving story, but our local papers remained noticeably unengaged. For one thing, we do protect our celebrities, especially the fabulous older brigade, and for another thing, the Vineyard press are fond of promoting the quainter side of island life. (I've always thought that a *Vine-yard Gazette* headline about World War III would read something like: "Neutron Bombs Explode on All Seven Continents; State of Affairs Will Not Interfere with Rhododendron Display at Garden Club on Saturday.")

The events of July 31, 1992, in my opinion, reveal a personal growth opportunity for Mr. Wallace that was clearly turned aside. It's not the end of the world that the newsman forgot to look both ways when he drove out onto the highway; we all experience driving boo-boos. And his mind may have been on matters so lofty—death squads in Bosnia? the November elections?—that he failed to realize he'd caused another driver to careen into a tree. Truly, we do all make mistakes. And that's the key—we make mistakes, even those of us who've built a career around exposing other peoples' errors. When we're in the mode of Doing The Right Thing, we apologize, we express concern, we follow up with the person we've harmed, and in whatever way we care to express it, we say something along the lines of "my bad."

In the end, we can only imagine how Mr. Wallace, relentless interviewer, might have raked Mr. Wallace, quavering interviewee, over the coals on prime-time television as he zeroed in on what happened on that fateful afternoon in July.

The D.L. on O.J.

IT WAS AUGUST of '95, and for weeks America had been glued to TV sets to watch the tele-vised trial of O.J. Simpson for the murder of his wife, Nicole, and a wrong-place-at-the-wrong-time young man named Ronald Gold-man. On the defense legal team, the famous attorney, Alan Dershowitz, who summers with his wife and daughter at their house in Chil-mark, was home for a weekend of R and R.

Enter my son Charlie, then a short, bespec-tacled cutie-pie in the fifth grade. Charlie's friend from Toronto, Aaron, was down for the summer in his family's house in Katama. Aaron's parents, Deenah and Fred Mollin, were friends of the Dershowitzes. Still with me? Okay, Aaron invited Charlie along to an after-noon party at the renowned lawyer's house.

Charlie was eager to go. He had it in his mind that somewhere during the course of the afternoon, if he sat close to Alan Dershowitz, the man would sling an arm around the young-ster and tell him the real story, along the lines of, "I'm swearing you to secrecy, son, but O.J.'s guilty as hell. He came to me right after the murder and smeared some of Nicole's blood over my tee shirt, the very one I'm wearing. See? If you lift it up you can detect stains the dry cleaner couldn't get rid of."

Hours later Charlie returned, his bubble burst. There was no way to cozy up to Dersho-witz. He seemed to make a concerted effort to stay away from the rollicking kids. "He was in the pool, but as soon as we jumped in, he got out and sat in the hot tub."

It was a sad ending to my boy's high hopes, but it illustrates the beauty of living a normal life surrounded by abnormally famous people: If we resided in, say, Framingham, Massachu-setts, there is little likelihood of Charlie meet-ing anyone attached to the Murder of the Cen-tury. But here on island, the usual six degrees of separation often factors down to two.

Acknowledgments

MY HEARTFELT GRATITUDE goes to my inestimable editor, Karin Womer, with whom I've now birthed three books (the first, *Haunted Island*, is in its eighth printing); to Eulalie Reagan, archivist at the *Vineyard Gazette*, for her envelopes of primo material; to Steve Durkee for his help with *Gazette* photographs; to Elizabeth Ilgen Fritz for a bang-up copy editing job; to Keith Gorman at the Martha's Vineyard Historical Society for hooking me up with some great vintage pictures, and to Jim Sollers for his hilarious cover art.

A thousand kisses go to the people who've supplied me with some of my best scoops—my beloved ex-husband, Marty Nadler, king of the great anecdote; the late Milton Jeffers, keeper of the stories; Edgartown police chief Paul Condlin for his hilarious crime log; animal control officer Sharon Rzemian for amazing critter tales; Claire Nickerson Hall for pointing me in the direction of the Nathaniel Hawthorne intrigue; the late Barbara Nevin for introducing me to people in the know, and to many others who are duly mentioned as their stories pop up in these pages.

Over the years so many people have come and sat on my porch and added to my grab bag of island lore. My gratitude to each and every one of you.

Big love to my son, Charlie, soon to graduate from Boston University; every Mother's Day I thank him for letting me be his mom (there's a New Age line of thinking that before we're born we pick our parents), and he always replies, "No problem." More love and a big hug to Charlie's smart and sassy (and of course beautiful) girlfriend, Olga Musatovova.

And much love to my nearest and dearest, who keep me laughing and thinking in almost equal measure: sister Cindy Mascott; brother Owen Mascott; sister-in-law Faith Russell; luminous friend Margaret Maes; and my best chum from high school days, M.I.A. (to me, not to herself!) for lo these thirty-seven (yikes!) years, Cynthia Gruber Renahan, who called just as I was wrapping up this book—the circle is complete.

Finally, a fond farewell to my cocker spaniel, Chopper, who died in September 2005, my boon companion through a cumulative hundreds of miles of East Chop rambles, my protector in our haunted bedroom in the yellow Civil War–era house across from Eastville Beach, and the Tonto to my Lone Ranger during that crazy February when we stayed at the Nashua House. It snowed in our room, and every time we ventured out for a walk, Chopper's paws would freeze up and I'd have to heft him back to the inn. He's buried in East Chop in the open field behind our original home, so his spirit romps by the shore—and for all we know, pees on the carpets inside our old cottage—just like old times.

H. N.

Further Reading

ANYONE ATTEMPTING to write, critique, or analyze anything about the Vineyard will need to jump in the deep end with the multi-kilo three-volume *History of Martha's Vineyard, Dukes County, Massachusetts*, by Charles Bank, M.D., George H. Dean publisher, 1911. Mr. Banks wrote in the stilted style of the Edwardian age, but he covers every last bit of information, from the arrival of the first white settlers in the 1600s to his own (now long-ago) era. The third book is strictly devoted to island genealogy, so if your surname doesn't happen to be Mayhew, Norton, West, or Daggett, you may find little to interest you there.

Another treasure trove of data is *The Dukes County Intelligencer*, the publishing arm of the Martha's Vineyard Historical Society (which until 1996 was known as the Dukes County Historical Society). Monthly journals have been rolling off the press since 1959, and are rife with the most scrupulous research. The same august group has just released a fresh new tome on island history, entitled, explicitly enough, *The History of Martha's Vineyard*, by Arthur R. Railton.

For more straight, roll-up-your-sleeves social studies, there's a slim paperbound volume first released in 1923 by the Pyne Printery and still available in local bookstores: *Martha's Vineyard: History—Legends—Stories*, by Henry Franklin Norton. The prose, like Charles Banks's, suffers from early-twentieth-century clunkiness, but the book sports some swell old photographs.

To plumb the seemingly bottomless well of Methodist Campground history, turn to the excellent *City in the Woods*, by Ellen Weiss, Oxford University Press, 1987, and *Martha's Vineyard Campmeeting Association 1835–1935*, by Sally W. Dagnall, Oxford University Press, 1984, and, finally, *A Centennial History of Cottage City*, by Chris Stoddard, Oak Bluffs Historical Committee in 1978.

Also writing about Oak Bluffs in the final quarter of the last century was novelist Dorothy West, some of whose town columns have been anthologized in *The Dorothy West Martha's Vineyard*, published by McFarland and Company, 2001.

The yeoman of island writing was Henry Beetle Hough, editor of the *Vineyard Gazette* from the 1930s clear through the 1970s, a gentleman who could not stop churning out wonderful linguistic portraits of his life and times here, as the following list shows:

Martha's Vineyard Summer Resort 1835–1935, Tuttle Publishing Company, 1936

Country Editor, Doubleday, Doran, and Company, 1940

Singing in the Morning and Other Essays about Martha's Vineyard, Simon & Schuster, 1951

The Vineyard Gazette Reader, Annals of Martha's Vineyard: 121 Years of Its Newspaper, edited by Mr. Hough, Harcourt, Brace, and World, 1967

Tuesdays Will Be Different, Dial Press, 1971

Mostly on Martha's Vineyard, Harcourt, Brace, Jovanovich, 1975

To the Harbor Light, Houghton Mifflin, 1976

All this, plus Hough penned a rash of novels inspired by island living—on top of issuing a weekly newspaper (biweekly in summer). This man wins the prize for being the most Vineyard-obsessed of all of us.

Several other island writers from the last century also produced nonfiction works full of island tableaus:

> *Tales and Trails of Martha's Vineyard,* by Joseph C. Allen, Little, Brown, 1947
>
> *An Island Summer,* by Walter Magnes Teller, Knopf, 1954
>
> *Time's Island: Portraits of the Vineyard,* by Nancy Stafford, M.I.T. Press, 1973 (includes scads of photos from pre-tourist days)
>
> *Martha's Vineyard, an Elegy,* by Everett S. Allen, Little, Brown, 1982 (re-issued in 2005 by Commonwealth Editions)

The African American experience is ably covered in two dandy books: *African Americans on Martha's Vineyard, A History of People, Places, and Events,* by Robert Hayden, Select Press, 2nd ed. 2005, and *Lighting the Trail,* by Elaine Cawley Weintraub, Massachusetts Foundation for the Humanities, new ed. 2005.

Another pair of books define island Native American studies: *Moshup's Footsteps: The Wampanoag Nation, Gay Head/Aquinnah,* by Helen Manning, Blue Cloud Across the Moon Publishing, 2001, and *Lifeways of the Wampanoag,* by Raymond Bial, Benchmark Books, 2004.

Island topography and geology are amply addressed by still another couplet of books: *Moraine to Marsh, a Field Guide to Martha's Vineyard,* by Anne Hale, Watership Gardens, 1988, and *Cape Cod, Martha's Vineyard, and Nantucket, the Geologic Story,* by Robert N. Oldale, On Cape Publications, 1992.

Two lighthouse compendiums can be found on local library shelves: *Famous Lighthouses of New England,* by Edward Rowe Snow, Boston Printing, 1945, and *Lighthouses of Cape Cod, Martha's Vineyard, and Nantucket, Their History and Lore,* by Admont G. Clark, Parnasus Imprints, 1992.

Milton Mazur's *People and Predicaments,* published by Harvard University Press in 1976, is a super psychological study of island character behaviors (and misbehaviors). It came out thirty years ago but could have been written yesterday; that's how deeply it's all "plus c'est la meme chose." Anyone planning on moving to the Vineyard year-round would do well to first read Dr. Mazur's book straight through, swallow a few aspirin, and take a little more time to think it over.

For background on the Kennedy/Kopechne fiasco, I turned to:

> *The Bridge at Chappaquiddick,* by Jack Olsen, Little, Brown and Company, 1970
>
> *Death at Chappaquiddick,* by Thomas L. Tedrow, Pelican Publishing, 1979
>
> *Senatorial Privilege: The Chappaquiddick Cover-Up,* by Leo Damone, 1984

Stories from New England's whaling days have been recorded for centuries, but two books with a particular focus on Vineyard whalers are *The Captain's Daughters of Martha's Vineyard,* Chatham Press, 1978, which contains recollections by the Eldridge Sisters—Nina, Mary, Ruth, and Gratia—as told to Eliot Eldridge Macy, and *Zeb, Celebrated Schooner Captain of Martha's Vineyard,* by Polly Burroughs, re-released by Insiders' Guide, 2005.

Of miscellaneous but no less fascinating interest are the following six offerings:

> *The* Jaws *Log,* by Carl Gottlieb, Newmarket Press, 2001
>
> *Noman's Land, Isle of Romance,* by Anne M. Wood, Reynolds Printing, 1931

Four Girls at Cottage City, by Emma D. Kelley-Hawkins, Schomburg Library of Nineteenth Century Black Women Writers / Oxford University Press, 1988 (fiction but highly evocative of setting and times)

Everyone Here Spoke Sign Language: Hereditary Deafness on Martha's Vineyard, by Nora Ellen Groce, Harvard University Press, recent edition 2005

Yankee Diva: Lillian Norton and the Golden Days of Opera, Ira Glackens, Coleridge Press, 1963

Three for a Nickel: Martha's Vineyard Postcards 1900–1925, by Patricia H. Rodgers, Acqua Press, 2002

Two of the islands greatest eccentrics have entire books dedicated to them and their exploits: *Consider Poor I: The Life and Works of Nancy Luce*, by Walter Magnes Teller, Dukes County Historical Society, 1984. and *Craig Kingsbury Talkin'*, by Kristen Kingsbury Henshaw, tereski presski, 2005.

The lion's share of these texts are out of print, but they're all fully available—albeit behind locked glass cabinet doors—at Vineyard libraries. A kind word to the librarian wins you a small brass key and hours of engrossing reading.

About the Author

HOLLY NADLER bought a home on Martha's Vineyard in 1981 and has since become one of the island's most knowledgeable residents when it comes to ghosts and gossip. In fact, she's known locally as the Ghost Lady because of her two previous books, *Haunted Island* and *Ghosts of Boston Town,* and the haunted house walking tours she leads during the summer.

"I love history, both global and local," she explains, "and I especially like stories with any kind of glamour, excitement, or mystery."

Holly has also written for television comedies and has seen her articles published in magazines such as *Cosmopolitan, Lear's, The Utne Reader, Woman's World, Cape Cod Life, Vineyard Style,* and *Martha's Vineyard Home & Gardens.* Like any good writer, she's also a reader, and—fulfilling every book lover's dream—she runs her own bookstore: Sunporch Books, in Oak Bluffs.

MARTY NADLER